State Constitutions for the Twenty-first Century

Vol. 1

SUNY series in American Constitutionalism
Robert J. Spitzer, editor

State Constitutions for the Twenty-first Century

Vol. 1

The Politics of State Constitutional Reform

Edited by

G. Alan Tarr
and
Robert F. Williams

State University of New York Press

Published by
State University of New York Press, Albany

Printed in the United States of America

For information, address State University of New York Press,
194 Washington Avenue, Suite 305, Albany, NY 12210-2384

Production by Michael Haggett
Marketing by Anne M. Valentine

Library of Congress Cataloging-in-Publication Data

The politics of state constitutional reform / edited by G. Alan Tarr and Robert F. Williams.
p. cm. — (State constitutions for the twenty-first century ; v. 1) (SUNY series in American constitutionalism)
Includes bibliographical references and index.
ISBN 0-7914-6613-2 (hardcover : alk. paper)
1. Constitutional law—United States—States. 2. Law reform—United States—States. I. Tarr, G. Alan (George Alan) II. Williams, Robert F. III. Series. IV. Series: SUNY series in American constitutionalism

KF4550.Z95P65 2005
342.73—dc22

2004030457

10 9 8 7 6 5 4 3 2 1

Contents

Introduction

G. Alan Tarr

If one compares American state constitutions with their federal counterpart, one is immediately struck by how differently the documents deal with constitutional change. Although the framers of the federal Constitution wanted to make constitutional change easier than it had been under the Articles of Confederation, they remained wary of an excessive "mutability of the laws," and they worried that too frequent constitutional change would undermine popular attachment to the fundamental law.[1] The Federal Constitution makes no express provision for its own replacement—any convention proposing a new national constitution would, like the Philadelphia Convention of 1787, be operating on the fringes of legality. It provides two mechanisms for proposing amendments (proposal by Congress or by constitutional convention), but it requires supermajorities in both instances: a two-thirds majority in each house of Congress to propose an amendment or petitions from two-thirds of the states to call for a convention. Finally, the Constitution requires an extraordinary, geographically dispersed majority (three-quarters of the states) to ratify proposed amendments.[2]

In contrast, from the outset most states made the amendment of their constitution, the replacement of their constitutions, or both relatively easy, and over time the general trend has been to facilitate state constitutional amendment and replacement.[3] Many states expressly authorize the revision of their constitutions, and altogether the states have adopted 145 constitutions, an average of almost three per state.[4] (Louisiana holds the dubious distinction of having adopted eleven constitutions in less than two centuries, prompting one wag to describe constitutional change in Louisiana as "sufficiently continuous to justify including it with Mardi Gras, football, and corruption as one of the premier components of state culture."[5]) The states have also developed an array of methods for proposing constitutional amendments—constitutional convention, proposal by the legislature, proposal by constitutional commission, and proposal by initiative—and many state constitutions authorize multiple methods for proposing amendments. Most states have also adopted a simple majoritarian system for ratifying amendments—a majority of those voting on the proposal, regardless of turnout or voter drop-off, suffices for ratification. The effect of these arrangements is seen in the frequency with which states amend their constitutions. Current state constitutions contain more than 5,000 amendments, and most have been amended more than 100 times, Alabama's 1901 constitution more than 740 times.[6] If anything, the pace of amendment appears to have quickened in recent years—from 1994 to 2001 the states adopted 689 constitutional amendments.[7]

Given the frequency of constitutional change, it might seem odd to devote a volume to the obstacles to state constitutional reform and how they might be overcome. Yet despite the proliferation of constitutional amendments—or perhaps to some extent because of it[8]—state constitutional reform has been relatively infrequent during the twentieth and early twenty-first centuries. This is reflected in the decline in constitutional conventions: whereas the states convened 144 from 1800 to 1900, they called only 64 since then, and none since 1984. And whereas the states adopted ninety-four constitutions during the nineteenth century, they have adopted only twenty-three since then and only one in the past quarter century.[9]

Of course, it is possible to introduce significant constitutional reform without calling a convention or adopting a new constitution—amendments proposed by constitutional commissions, by initiative, or by state legislatures may also produce constitutional reform. But in thinking about constitutional reform, it is important to distinguish it from the ordinary constitutional change that is so prevalent in the states. Any alteration of a state constitution, no matter how technical or minor, qualifies as constitutional change. In contrast, constitutional reform involves a more fundamental reconsideration of constitutional foundations. It introduces changes of considerable breadth and impact, changes that substantially affect the operation of state government or the public policy of the state.[10] The replacement of one constitution by another obviously qualifies as constitutional reform. So too may major constitutional amendments or interconnected sets of amendments. However, most constitutional change in the states does not qualify. Most amendments involve relatively minor adjustments, attempts to deal with specific problems without altering (or even considering) the broader constitutional foundations of the state. This is particularly true of those constitutional amendments that are proposed by state legislatures (and state legislatures are the most prolific source of amendments). This is hardly surprising. From firsthand experience state legislators understand the adjustments needed in the law of the state, many of which—given the level of detail in state constitutions—must be accomplished via amendment. In addition, state legislators benefit from the political status quo and therefore are usually reluctant to introduce amendments promoting fundamental reform, as such amendments could jeopardize their position.

It may perhaps advance our understanding of the distinction between ordinary constitutional change and constitutional reform to recall the analogous distinction drawn by state courts between constitutional amendment and constitutional revision. Most states that employ the constitutional initiative permit it to be used to propose constitutional amendments but not constitutional revisions, and opponents of far-reaching initiatives have challenged them in court, asserting that the changes they contemplate amount to a revision of the state constitution. In ruling on such challenges, state judges have had to identify criteria for distinguishing amendments from revisions. Thus, the California Supreme Court noted that "our revision/amendment analysis has a dual aspect, requiring us to examine both the quantitative and qualitative effects of the measure on our constitutional scheme. Substantial changes in either could amount to revision."[11] Similarly, the Florida Supreme Court asserted that an amendment "if approved would be complete within itself, relate to one subject and not substantially affect any other section or article of the Constitution or require further amendments to the Constitution to accomplish its purpose."[12]

The distinction introduced here between constitutional reform and ordinary constitutional change, like the distinction between constitutional amendment and constitutional revision, is admittedly not an exact one. There will doubtless be close cases, and the line between constitutional reform and ordinary constitutional change is hardly precise. Nonetheless, the distinction is important because it underlines why frequent change is not the same as fundamental change. It also highlights why constitutional reform remains a crucial issue in the states.

It may well be, as the Virginia Declaration of Rights asserts, "[t]hat no free government, or the blessings of liberty, can be preserved to any people but . . . by a frequent recurrence to fundamental principles."[13] But even if this is not the case, in the first decade of the twenty-first century, reconsideration of the foundations of state constitutions is particularly timely. For one thing, we are asking more of the states than we have in the past. No longer are the states merely called on to address their traditional responsibilities. The federal government has devolved new responsibilities for policy development and implementation to the states, both because of budgetary problems at the national level and because of a perception that some endemic problems might be more effectively addressed at the state level.[14] State citizens too have increased their demands and expectations. The states are therefore being expected to address new problems and to generate novel solutions for long-standing, intractable ones. Are the states up to the challenge? During the 1960s and 1970s, various commentators raised questions about state governmental capacity, about whether the states had the ability to manage and implement programs to deal with their pressing problems.[15] These concerns about state capacity led to several noteworthy innovations, ranging from strengthening the governors' appointment, personnel, and budgetary powers to professionalizing state legislatures and consolidating state bureaucracies.[16] Despite these steps, questions about state capacity persist today. Because the states' constitutional arrangements have a major impact on state governmental capacity, constitutional reform may be crucial in determining how effectively the states meet their new responsibilities.

In addition, many state constitutions are quite frankly in need of major overhaul or replacement. As noted, the frequency of amendments to state constitutions has tended to obscure the infrequency of fundamental change, particularly during the twentieth and early twenty-first centuries. More than two-thirds of the states now operate under constitutions that are more than a century old. Of course, there is nothing intrinsically wrong with "old" constitutions—the federal Constitution was drafted more than two centuries ago, and few would wish to see it replaced. Indeed, one might argue that for constitutions, durability is a virtue rather than a vice. Yet, unlike the federal Constitution, contemporary state constitutions do not continue in operation because of popular veneration for the document or for its drafters—indeed, according to one survey, only 52 percent of respondents even knew that their state had a constitution.[17] Moreover, there are several reasons why these older state constitutions may be ripe for reexamination.

First, most existing state constitutions, written in the latter half of the nineteenth century, were not designed for the long haul. Their drafters by and large shared the Jeffersonian belief in constitution-making as a progressive enterprise.[18] Instead of emphasizing constitutional continuity and deference to the wisdom of the past, they asserted that the practices and institutional arrangements embedded in state constitutions needed to be constantly readjusted in light of changes in circumstances and in political thought. They also maintained that the experience of self-government in America constantly expanded the fund of knowledge about constitutional design, so that later generations were better situated to frame constitutions than were their less experienced, and hence presumably less expert, predecessors. Whether or not they were correct, this affected how they did their work and what they expected future generations to do with it. As William Andrews Clark, the chairman of Montana's 1889 convention, put it: "As the generations come and go, developing rapidly successive changes and conditions, requiring new methods and additional powers and restraints, we may expect that the genius and wisdom of our successors will eliminate, supplement, and amend" the work of the 1889 convention.[19] Thus, the very drafters of existing state constitutions expected that their work would be subject to periodic reexamination and reform and welcomed that prospect.

Second, the very character of current state constitutions implies the need for periodic reform. In comparison with the federal Constitution, state constitutions tend to be far more detailed and far more willing to elevate policy pronouncements to constitutional status.[20] For example, whereas article III of the Federal Constitution uses only 377 words to establish the federal judiciary, article VI of the New York Constitution uses 15,310 words to establish the state judiciary.[21] This propensity to detail and to constitutional legislation is particularly common in constitutions that were drafted during the late nineteenth century (when twenty-six of today's state constitutions were written) or that incorporate the constitutional initiative (as do eighteen state constitutions). Yet it is apparent in most other state constitutions as well, reflected in the fact that half of state constitutions are more than 25,000 words long. My point here is not to open a debate on whether it is wise to include extensive detail in state constitutions or to constitutionalize policy matters. That topic has been extensively debated, and there are respectable arguments on both sides of that issue.[22] Rather, my point is that the decision on constitutional detail, whichever way one goes, has foreseeable consequences. For the American states, which have by and large repudiated constitutional minimalism and embraced constitutional detail, the effects of that choice are highlighted in Chief Justice John Marshall's famous opinion in

McCulloch v. Maryland (1819). As Marshall observed, in order for a constitution to "endure for ages to come," it could not "partake of the prolixity of a legal code," but would rather have to confine itself to marking "great outlines" and "important objects," lest it lose the capacity to respond to new situations.[23] Detail is the enemy of flexibility, and flexibility is the key to durability. In opting for constitutional maximalism the states recognized that, as changes in circumstances and attitudes occurred, their constitutions would become outdated and in need of reform. It is not surprising, therefore, that there has been little reverence for the founders of state constitutions and even less reluctance to tinker with their handiwork. The states have made it easy to introduce needed changes, and most state constitutions have been amended more than once for every year they have been in operation.

If a constitutional amendment indicates a defect in a constitution, then one could conclude from this proliferation of amendments that the older state constitutions—and the younger ones too, for that matter—have not survived because they have successfully solved the problems besetting the states. Yet it is also possible to view the frequent constitutional amendment in the states positively, treating it as an alternative mechanism for constitutional reform, the twentieth century's analogue to the nineteenth's reliance on constitutional conventions and constitutional revision. This seems far too sanguine an assessment. Although in some instances states have pursued fundamental reforms via amendment, usually amendment is not an adequate substitute for more comprehensive reform. Indeed, constitutional amendments typically correct specific problems in documents that were designed to meet the problems of another era, without consideration of the broader constitutional design.[24] Moreover, in many states the proliferation of piecemeal amendments, adopted at various times by majorities with quite different political agendas, has destroyed the coherence of state constitutions as plans of government.

Third, in assessing the need for state constitutional reform, one must acknowledge the distrust and dissatisfaction felt by citizens in many states with the governments created by their constitutions. This is not to say, of course, that state constitutions are to blame for all the deficiencies of state governments. Yet neither are they blameless—state constitutions do make a difference. This dissatisfaction is reflected in low voter turnout for state elections and in poll data on public attitudes toward state government.[25] These certainly belie any notion that the state constitutions have survived because of popular satisfaction with the governments they have created.

The dissatisfaction is indirectly reflected in the increasing resort to direct democracy for policy making in the states, which indicates a perception that state institutions are not appropriately responsive to citizen concerns.[26] Popular distrust is reflected as well in the adoption of constitutional amendments designed to chasten or thwart the institutions of state government by limiting the tenure of officials, reducing their powers, and transferring their policy-making responsibilities to the people. These reforms range from term limits for state legislators to constitutional restrictions on increases in the rate of state spending to the demand for referenda on all new taxes.[27]

Interestingly, whereas ordinary politics under state constitutions often produces popular distrust and disinterest, constitutional reform can sometimes have the opposite effect. In the past, campaigns for constitutional reform have had a transforming effect on many of those involved in them. For example, although many delegates to state constitutional conventions have been political novices, their experience as delegates has propelled many to pursue careers in public service. The delegates often cite the convention experience as among the most important in their lives, a chance to be statesmen rather than politicians. Ordinary citizens who have become involved in campaigning for constitutional initiatives also testify about how much they learned from the experience and how committed they became to staying involved in the political life of the state as a result.[28] For voters, too, constitutional reform can have an energizing effect. Data in several states that use the constitutional initiative indicate that it increases voter interest and turnout on election day.[29]

Finally, constitutional reform—particularly the adoption of a new constitution—can be a source of pride and a unifying force. Looking beyond the borders of the United States, one sees this in South Africa, where the postapartheid constitution has become a potent symbol of self-government and of national unity.[30] This is likewise true in several of the countries that emerged from communist rule in the late twentieth century. Within the United States, similar experiences are found in states such as New Jersey and Montana that adopted constitutions in the last sixty years.[31]

The chapters in this volume survey recent efforts to introduce constitutional reform, analyzing the factors that contributed to the success or failure of those efforts. These case studies have scholarly interest, as far too little is known about the politics of state constitutional reform and about how that political activity fits into the broader scheme of state politics. The studies also have practical import for constitutional reformers, because their authors draw from the case studies broader lessons that might inform reform efforts in other states. Let me highlight key elements in each of these studies.

The Florida Constitution of 1968 provides for a unique system of constitutional reform, mandating the periodic establishment of a revision commission that has the authority to take its proposals directly to the voters, without legislative approval or review. In her chapter Rebecca Mae Salokar assesses Florida's experience with this innovative mechanism. She notes that in 1978, the first time the commission proposed amendments, none of its proposals were ratified. In 1998, in contrast, voters endorsed eight of the commission's nine proposals. In part, of course, differences in the substance of what was proposed explain the divergent outcomes. In part, too, factors outside the control of the commission may have influenced the results—in 1978, an initiative legalizing casino gambling was also on the ballot, prompting in response a major "vote no" campaign that affected the prospects of all ballot propositions. Yet in part differences in process help account for the commission's greater success in 1998. The 1998 commission better reflected the state politically and demographically, so there were no groups that opposed the commission's recommendations because they felt excluded from the process. The 1998 commission made a major effort to consult the public prior to developing its proposals, which gave them a greater legitimacy. And the 1998 commission had sufficient funding to publicize and explain its proposals prior to ratification, thus ensuring an informed decision. Salokar concludes that the learning experience from 1978 to 1998 bodes well for the continued success of the revision commission in the future.

In the mid-1990s the California Constitutional Revision Commission proposed a set of major constitutional amendments to the California Legislature, but the Legislature rejected all its proposals. The defeat of the Commission's proposed amendments stands in marked contrast to the virtually continuous amendment of the California Constitution via the constitutional initiative (as well as by amendments proposed by the Legislature). In his chapter Bruce Cain concludes that the disparity reflects the difficult set of veto points that proposals for constitutional revision must navigate, in contrast with the relatively straightforward path for constitutional initiatives. Once initiative proponents gather sufficient signatures, an initiative goes directly on the ballot, bypassing the legislature, and merely needs to secure popular approval. In contrast, constitutional revision requires that a proposal secure the approval of the commission, of the legislature, and of the electorate, and at each point affected groups can block adoption. In theory the commission seems to offer a better approach to constitutional reform, with extended deliberation and an array of proposals closely tied to a set of articulated values, in contrast with the piecemeal and disjointed change produced by the initiative process. But in practice, Cain concludes, for commissions to be effective, they may need to tailor their proposals to suit those in a position to prevent adoption of the proposals, rather than submitting what they might view as simply the "best" recommendations.

Virginia in 1970 adopted a new constitution that was drafted by an eleven-member commission and revised by the Virginia General Assembly before submission to the electorate for ratification. The success of Virginia's campaign stands in sharp contrast to the contemporaneous failure of reform efforts in New York, Rhode Island, Maryland, New Mexico, Oregon, Arkansas, and Idaho. In his chapter, A. E. Dick Howard analyzes why the constitutional reformers in Virginia succeeded and considers how political changes have altered the prospects for reform in the early twenty-first century. Howard credits the political realism of the drafters of the Virginia Constitution, who at times sacrificed theoretical elegance in order to avoid making unnecessary enemies and avoided altogether some issues that might have antagonized important blocks of voters. He also emphasizes the crucial role played by Virginians for the Constitution, a privately funded organization that led the campaign for ratification. This group created a grassroots network throughout Virginia, bringing information about the constitution to voters and countering the claims of opponents. The group also created a climate for approval by demonstrating the nonpartisan character of the constitution through endorsements from political leaders of all ideological stripes and from diverse community groups. Howard concludes that given the increased partisanship of contemporary politics, with powerful single-issue groups and pervasive popular distrust of government, the task of constitutional reform would be far more difficult today than it was in the past.

Alabama's 1901 Constitution is the nation's most amended, with more than 700 amendments as of 2003. Yet despite its manifest deficiencies, the numerous efforts in Alabama to promote constitutional reform, which began as early as 1915, have faltered. In his chapter Bailey Thomson examines the factors that frustrated reformers in the past and considers why the current campaign, mounted by Alabama Citizens for Constitutional Reform (ACCR), has greater prospects for success. Whereas previous reform efforts were championed by political leaders who either failed to spend the necessary political capital for reform or fell victim to political intrigues, ACCR's campaign involves an independent citizens' group that has adopted a two-pronged approach. ACCR has mounted an effective grassroots strategy, making use of newspaper coverage and public events to inform and mobilize the state's population. It has also enlisted business leaders, representatives of other groups, and former officials from both political parties to demonstrate a broad consensus in favor of reform. These efforts have succeeded in placing constitutional reform on the political agenda, with both the incumbent Democrat and his Republican challenger endorsing reform in the 2002 gubernatorial election. When Republican Bob Riley was elected, one of his first acts was to appoint a commission to develop proposals on five constitutional reform issues, with the expectation that the commission over time would address other issues as well. While the ultimate outcome remains unknown at this writing, the Alabama experience demonstrates the possibilities of bottom-up constitutional reform.

Like Alabama, New York has experienced major problems attributable, at least in part, to constitutional deficiencies. Unlike in Alabama, however, the legislature is not an obstacle to constitutional reform, because New York is one of fourteen states in which the question of whether or not to call a constitutional convention is automatically placed on the ballot periodically. In his chapter Gerald Benjamin examines why, despite the problems with the government of New York, voters in 1997 overwhelmingly rejected calling a constitutional convention. Uncertainty about what a convention might propose was a major factor. The New York Constitution prescribes that the subject matter of the prospective convention cannot be limited in advance, and both legislators and powerful groups within the state were concerned more about how an unlimited convention might jeopardize their interests than about how constitutional reform might solve the problems plaguing government in New York. The failure to mount an effective campaign in support of a convention also was crucial. Governor Mario Cuomo had championed the idea of a convention, but after his defeat by Governor George Pataki, the main advocate of the convention no longer held political office, and Pataki's support for the convention was lukewarm. This lack of leadership, combined with limited funds and lack of organization, frustrated efforts to inform and mobilize potential supporters. In contrast, groups against the convention united in opposition and, with the backing of organized labor, mounted a media blitz and worked the phone banks just before the election, claiming that the convention would be dominated by career politicians. Because voters typically do not have deep-seated convictions about whether or not a convention should be called, this opposition tactic proved effective: more than 60 percent of those voting on the question rejected a convention, and large numbers of voters failed to vote on the issue altogether.

Advocates of constitutional reform often assert that constitutional commissions and constitutional conventions are superior mechanisms of constitutional change, because they encourage due deliberation and a comprehensive consideration of the state constitution. However, as Anne Campbell's chapter demonstrates, the constitutional initiative can also be the vehicle for well-considered reform. Her case study of the adoption of a constitutional initiative on campaign finance reform in 2002 shows that use of the constitutional initiative to pursue one's goals is often a last resort, when reform through other political institutions is blocked by entrenched interests, either because the reform will alienate key constituencies or because it threatens the self-interest of politicians. In the case of campaign finance, sponsoring groups employed the constitutional initiative only after their proposals were twice blocked by gubernatorial vetoes and their successful statutory initiative was gutted by subsequent legislation. The constitutional initiative's long gestation during legislative consideration provided ample opportunity for full deliberation on its contents. Moreover, the prospect of defeat at the polls after a long and expensive effort to get on the ballot served to discipline the advocates of campaign finance reform, ensuring that they crafted a proposal that would win voter support. In this sense then initiative advocates find themselves in the same predicament faced by constitutional commission members, as described by Bruce Cain. Constitutional reformers must espouse not what they view as the best policy simply but rather good policy that seems likely to prevail at the polls. This, of course, is not necessarily a bad thing—the requirement of popular support for fundamental reforms is basic to our system of government.

Several conclusions emerge from these case studies. First, constitutional reform can be pursued through a variety of avenues, not just through constitutional conventions. This is important, given the apparent loss of interest in conventions—Virginia changed its constitution via commission, Alabama chose a commission over a convention despite the preference of reformers, and New York overwhelmingly rejected a convention call. Second, good ideas are not enough to secure constitutional reform. Reformers need to inform and interest the public in reform, which means showing how it benefits them personally. However, if they succeed in this task, popular support for reform can be used as it was in Alabama to persuade politicians to take up the cause. Third, constitutional reform efforts must be pursued in a political context not of the reformers' making. In particular, reformers must deal with officials suspicious of how reform may affect their positions and their power and with established groups intent on protecting their interests. Reformers must avoid antagonizing potential opponents unnecessarily and may have to compromise in order to accommodate them. The failure of reform in New York is traceable to the reformers' inability to reassure powerful groups in the state that a convention would not propose changes detrimental to their interests. Fourth, despite the obstacles to reform identified by the authors, the conclusion is that reform can succeed. The reformers won in Virginia and Colorado, they largely won in Florida, and they may succeed in Alabama. They failed in California and New York, but even in those states the failure may be less than complete. In Florida, after the first commission's proposals were rejected, several were resubmitted and adopted as piecemeal amendments, and it may be that studies and proposals in California and New York will reemerge, as political developments underscore the need for constitutional reform. This in turn underlines a final point, made most eloquently by Governor George Busbee in 1983 during the successful campaign to revise the Georgia Constitution: "Constitutional revision is not for the faint of heart. It is not a Sunday drive in the mountains. It is an incredibly difficult, sometimes tedious, sometimes exhilarating, always challenging undertaking requiring the cooperation of all."[32]

The Ford Foundation has provided generous support for *State Constitutions for the Twenty-first Century*, and I gratefully acknowledge its crucial role in this project. Julius Ihonvbere, my program officer at The Ford Foundation, was an enthusiastic convert to the importance of state constitutional reform in the United States and recognized that constitution-makers in other federal systems could benefit a great deal from the state constitutional experience. The educational leadership at Rutgers University (Camden) has created a vibrant intellectual atmosphere that encourages scholarly endeavors. Provost Roger Dennis underwrote the creation of the Center for State Constitutional Studies and has been among its strongest supporters ever since. Margaret Marsh, Dean of Arts and Sciences, and Rayman Solomon, Dean of the Law School, have provided steady encouragement for the Center's work on this project. Their support is most appreciated.

Robert Williams, Associate Director of the Center for State Constitutional Studies, has worked tirelessly on the project, and I have benefited immeasurably from his friendship, his wise counsel, and his good judgment. Sylvia Somers, the Center's invaluable Administrative Assistant, has helped to keep the project on course with her usual blend of efficiency, dedication, and good humor. I shall not attempt to thank individually the many scholars, officials, judges, and others who have contributed their insights and advice on this project—the list would be too long, and I would worry about leaving out important contributors. They will, I hope, find in *State Constitutions for the Twenty-first Century* ample evidence of how valuable their insights were.

A final note: Bailey Thomson, who authored the chapter on constitutional reform in Alabama, died shortly after completing the manuscript. All who knew him will miss his gentle demeanor, his professionalism, and his dedication to improving government in his home state.

Notes

1. See, for example, Federalist #10 and #49. For an exploration of leading founders' views on constitutional change, see Stephen Holmes, "Precommitment and the Paradox of Democracy," in Jon Elster and Rune Slagstad, eds., *Constitutionalism and Democracy* (New York: Cambridge University Press, 1988).

On the difficulty of formally amending the Federal Constitution, in comparison with other national constitutions, see Donald S. Lutz, "Toward a Theory of Constitutional Amendment," *American Political Science Review* 88 (June 1994): 355–70. Lutz emphasizes that this does not mean that the Federal Constitution is rarely changed, merely that it is rarely changed through the formal amendment process. Constitutional change can also be introduced through less formal channels—for example, through judicial interpretation. See also Sanford Levinson, ed., *Responding to Imperfection: The Theory and Practice of Constitutional Amendment* (Princeton: Princeton University Press, 1995).

2. The Federal Constitution requires that amendments be approved by three quarters of the states, expressed via vote in the state legislature or in a specially convened constitutional convention. This requirement ensures that no single section of the country can foist an amendment on another unwilling section. The emphasis on ratification of amendments by component units is typical of federal systems. See Daniel J. Elazar, *Exploring*

Federalism (Tuscaloosa, Ala.: University of Alabama Press, 1987), and Ronald L. Watts, *Comparing Federal Systems* (2d ed., Montreal and Kingston: McGill-Queen's University Press, 1999).

3. For an overview to the early twentieth century, see Walter F. Dodd, *The Revision and Amendment of State Constitutions* (Baltimore: Johns Hopkins University Press, 1910). For a perceptive review of the debates in state conventions about constitutional reform, see John Dinan, " 'The Earth Belongs Always to the Living Generation': The Development of State Constitutional Amendment and Revision Procedures," *Review of Politics* 62 (Fall 2000): 645–74.

4. *Book of the States 2001–2002* (Lexington, Ky.: Council of State Governments, 2002): 14, table 1.1.

5. Mark T. Carleton, "Elitism Sustained: The Louisiana Constitution of 1974," *Tulane Law Review* 54 (April 1980): 560.

6. *Book of the States,* p. 5, table B. These figures substantially underestimate the frequency of constitutional amendments in the states, because they do not include amendments to prior state constitutions.

7. *Book of States,* p. 5, table B.

8. In some instances, popular willingness to ratify amendments may encourage piecemeal change, whereas the electorate's rejection of proposed amendments may produce more comprehensive reform. For example, in Louisiana the legislature called the convention of 1972 only after voters rejected all fifty-three proposed amendments in 1970 and thirty-six of forty-two proposed amendments in 1972. See Lee Hargrave, *The Louisiana State Constitution: A Reference Guide* (Westport, Conn.: Greenwood Press, 1991), p. 16.

9. *Book of the States,* p. 14. For discussion of the change and its causes, see Albert L. Sturm, *Thirty Years of State Constitution-Making: 1938–1968* (New York: National Municipal League, 1970), and G. Alan Tarr, *Understanding State Constitutions* (Princeton, N.J.: Princeton University Press, 1998), chapter 5.

10. To avoid dispute about whether particular changes are positive or negative, the distinction between reform and ordinary change is drawn in terms of breadth of the changes, not in terms of whether the changes move the state in a progressive or regressive direction. For example, under this definition, the shift to a whites-only electorate in the South during the late nineteenth century qualifies as constitutional reform.

11. *Raven v. Deukmejian,* 801 P. 2d 1077, p. 1085 (Cal. 1990).

12. *Adams v. Gunter,* 238 So. 2d 824, p. 825 (Fla. 1970).

13. Virginia Declaration of Rights, sec. 15.

14. See, for example, Pamela Winston, *Welfare Policymaking in the States: The Devil in Devolution* (Washington, D.C.: Georgetown University Press, 2002); John Holahan, Joshua Wiener, and Susan Wallin, *Health Policy for the Low Income Population: Major Findings for the Assessing the New Federalism Case Studies* (Washington, D.C.: Urban Institute, 1998); and Timothy J. Conlan, *From New Federalism to Devolution: Twenty-five Years of Intergovernmental Reform* (Washington, D.C.: Brookings, 1998).

15. See, for example, the report of the Kestenbaum Commission, Commission on Intergovernmental Relations, *A Report to the President for Transmittal to the Congress* (Washington, DC, June 1955), Commission for Economic Development, *Modernizing State Government* (1967); and U.S. Advisory Commission on Intergovernmental Relations, *The Question of State Government Capability* (Washington, D.C.: Advisory Commission on Intergovernmental Relations, 1983).

16. These reforms are summarized in Jon C. Teaford, *The Rise of the States: Evolution of American State Government* (Baltimore: Johns Hopkins University Press, 2002), chapter 8.

17. Advisory Commission on Intergovernmental Relations, *Changing Public Attitudes on Governments and Taxes, 1991* (Washington, D.C.: Advisory Commission on Intergovernmental Relations, 1991), 14.

18. Christian G. Fritz, "Alternative Visions of American Constitutionalism: Popular Sovereignty and the Early American Constitutional Debate," *Hastings Constitutional Law Quarterly* 24 (winter 1997): 287–357, and Christian G. Fritz, "The American Constitutional Tradition Revisited: Preliminary Observations on State Constitution-Making in the Nineteenth-Century West," *Rutgers Law Journal* 25 (summer 1995): 945–98.

19. Quoted in James J. Lopach. *We the People of Montana: The Workings of a Popular Government* (Missoula: Mountain Press, 1983), p. 7. For an overview that places the Montana constitutional experience in broader perspective, see G. Alan Tarr, "The Montana Constitution: A National Perspective," *Montana Law Review* 64 (Winter 2003): 1–21.

20. Constitutionalizing policy matters may be seen as a particular instance of constitutional detail. In elevating a policy to constitutional status, a state constitution is choosing to elaborate the policy rather than merely authorizing the legislature to act or providing broad guidelines for such action.

21. Christopher W. Hammons, "State Constitutional Reform: Is It Necessary?" *Albany Law Review* 64 (2001): 1330.

22. See Tarr, *Understanding State Constitutions*, chapters 4–5.

23. *McCulloch v. Maryland*, 17 U.S. (4 Wheat.) 316, p. 406 (1819). For a contrary view on the relation between detail and durability, see Hammons, "State Constitutional Reform," pp. 1335–41. Hammons' conclusion that longer constitutions last longer is subject to two caveats. First, his conclusion may rest not on the length of the constitutions but on styles of state constitutional change—the long constitutions of the late nineteenth century have survived in part because the approach to constitutional change has shifted. Whereas nineteenth-century reformers emphasized wholesale constitutional revisions, twentieth-century advocates of change have opted more for constitutional amendment. Second, the durability of which Hammons speaks is not lack of change—longer constitutions are more frequently amended than short constitutions. Durability entails nonreplacement, not the absence of constitutional change.

24. A perfect example is found in Alabama, where more than 700 amendments have made the 1901 Constitution unwieldy but have not introduced much reform, prompting continuing calls for its replacement. See Bailey Thomson, ed., *A Century of Controversy: Constitutional Reform in Alabama* (Tuscaloosa: University of Alabama Press, 2002).

25. See, for example, the poll data reported by the Council for Excellence in Government, found at: www.excelgov.org/display/Content.asp?keyword=ppp070199.

26. Data on proliferation of initiatives are found in Richard J. Ellis, *Democratic Delusions: The Initiative Process in America* (Lawrence: University Press of Kansas, 2002), Appendix.

27. For term limits, see for example Oklahoma Constitution, art. V, sec. 9a and 10a, and Oregon Constitution, art. IV, sec. 4. For constitutional restrictions on state spending, see for example California Constitution, art. XIII B, and Colorado Constitution, art. 10, sec. 20. For limitations on state taxing power and the requirement of referenda or extraordinary majorities for new taxes, see for example California Constitution, art. XIII A, and Colorado Constitution, art. 10, sec. 20

28. See Ellis, *Democratic Delusions*, pp. 116–23. Ellis emphasizes that such ordinary citizens are a small proportion of those proposing initiatives.

29. See Caroline J. Tolbert, Johan A. Grummel, and Daniel A. Smith, "The Effects of Ballot Initiatives on Voter Turnout in the American States," *American Politics Research* 29 (November 2001): 625–48.

30. On the South African Constitution and its place in the postapartheid polity, see Heinz Klug, *Constituting Democracy: Law, Globalization, and South Africa's Political Reconstruction* (Cambridge: Cambridge University Press, 2000), and George E. Devenish, *A Commentary on the South African Constitution* (Durban: Butterworths, 1998).

31. In both Montana and New Jersey, hour-long television documentaries—*For This and Future Generations* (Montana) and *The Opportunity of a Century* (New Jersey)—were produced by PBS marking the anniversary of the states' constitutions, and in each officials and citizens alike testified to their pride in the state constitution.

32. George D. Busbee, "An Overview of the New Georgia Constitution," *Mercer Law Review* 35 (Fall 1983): 1.

Part I

Constitutional Commissions and Constitutional Reform

1

Constitutional Revision in Florida

Planning, Politics, Policy, and Publicity

Rebecca Mae Salokar

Contemporary state constitutions are not static documents and nowhere is this more true than in Florida where citizens have adopted a variety of methods for modifying their basic law. The Florida constitution contains five types of reform mechanisms: constitution revision commission, legislative proposal, citizen initiative, convention, and a commission for taxation and budget reform. While many states utilize citizen initiatives, legislative amendments and conventions to change their constitutions, Florida is the only state that provides for a regular review of its constitution by a revision commission, a body that is empowered to take its proposals directly to the people without legislative review.

Article XI of the Florida constitution provides for the regular review of the state's basic law by mandating that a constitution revision commission (CRC) meet to "examine the constitution of the state, hold public hearings, and file . . . its proposal, if any, of a revision of this constitution or any part of it" (sec. 2). Proposed revisions are then submitted to the electorate for approval at the next general election (sec. 5). Adopted in 1968, Article XI called for the first review to take place ten years after its adoption and every twenty years hence. Florida has since witnessed two iterations of the revision commission process, in 1977–78 and 1997–98, and the outcomes of each were quite different. The first commission failed to get public approval on any of its proposed revisions while the latter commission saw eight of its nine proposals adopted by the electorate.

What accounts for the differing experiences of the two CRCs in Florida is the focus of this chapter. A comparative analysis of the two commissions provides an opportunity to identify factors that likely contribute to the success of this unique reform process. Using commission documents and state records as well as observations from key members of each commission, my research suggests that planning, politics and procedures, policy and publicity are critical elements in the successful reform of state constitutions by autonomous commissions. The experiences in Florida also teach us that measuring the success of these commissions only in terms of electoral support for revision proposals fails to recognize the value of the revision process to the body politic on a much broader level. Constitution revision commissions play an important role in formalizing a policy agenda outside the traditional political arena, and their deliberative processes are inherently valuable to the public's knowledge and perceptions of state constitutions, and to public discourse.

The first section of this chapter examines the historical background of the constitution revision process and its inclusion in the 1968 Florida Constitution followed by a sketch of the general procedural framework employed by the Florida commissions. The balance of the chapter is organized into four sections that focus on planning, politics and procedures, policy, and publicity, factors that contributed significantly to the variance in outcomes between the 1977–78 CRC and the 1997–98 CRC. Examining the histories of each commission with the lens of these variables allows us to see distinct differences that undoubtedly contributed to the electoral success or failure of Florida's autonomous constitution revision process.

THE CONSTITUTION REVISION COMMISSION IN FLORIDA

Floridians have had an active history of constitution writing and reform, witnessing six constitutions since 1839. Like many states, Florida regularly tinkered with its basic law. The Constitution of 1885, for example, was amended 147 times between 1885 and 1968.[2] Florida had also seen a legislatively appointed revision commission, an experience that may have laid the groundwork for the autonomous constitution revision commission that exists today. The current constitution was adopted in 1968, but has its roots in the mid-1940s when the state bar association made revision a priority, publishing two draft proposals for a new constitution. However, the first serious effort to revise the 1885 constitution took place in 1955 when the death of Governor Dan McCarty not only highlighted ambiguities in the constitutional order of succession, but opened the door to an "enlightened conservative" governor, Leroy Collins, who led the charge for reform.[3] At the urging of Collins, the Florida Constitution Advisory Commission was established by the legislature in 1955. While proposals were generated by the Commission and subsequently adopted by the legislature, the state's high court nullified them on technical grounds.[4]

It was several more years before reform actually took place. Talbot D'Alemberte, a leading scholar of constitutional legal history in Florida and key player in constitutional reform in the 1970s, suggests that the revision of the Florida constitution in the 1960s was rooted in both the national push for reapportionment of state legislatures that gained viability with the "one man, one vote" mandate in the 1962 U.S. Supreme Court case of *Baker v. Carr* and in the broader-based reform efforts of other states.[5] In 1964, Florida voters approved a constitutional amendment offered by a more demographically representative legislature "that allowed revision of the constitution without a constitutional convention."[6] In amending Article XVII of the 1885 constitution, Floridians agreed that

> either branch of the legislature, at any regular session, or at any special or extraordinary session called for the purpose, may propose by joint resolution a revision of the entire constitution or a revision or amendment of any portion or portions thereof and may direct and provide for an election thereon.[7]

With this amendment, the citizenry of Florida transformed their history of constitutional conventions and legislative amendments into a new era of revision commissions.[8]

Backed by public support, the legislative will for constitutional reform came in the form of a statutory revision commission (SRC) that met during 1965–66. In late 1966, it submitted its proposals for significant constitutional change to the legislature. The legislature adopted most of the SRC's suggestions, included its own revisions, and put the revised version of the constitution before the voters. On November 5, 1968, Floridians adopted their current constitution and led the country in crafting one of the most liberal endorsements for future constitutional reform.

What was new to Florida in the 1968 constitution was the addition of two reform processes, the citizen initiative and the revision commission, to the traditional menu of constitutional change by convention and legislative amendment. The citizen initiative process permits the electorate to place single-subject amendments directly on the ballot after securing a constitutionally defined number of signatures from fellow citizens. It is the most restrictive of the reform mechanisms and was used sparingly during the first twenty years of the new constitution. More recently, however, initiatives in Florida have become a frequent tool of narrow, special interests that employ the process as a way to end-run a legislative or executive branch that has refused their demands.[9]

The 1968 constitution also made Florida the first state to institute a unique, deliberative process of reform. It called for the establishment of an autonomous revision commission that would take its proposals directly to the electorate without legislative approval or review.[10] The constitution mandated that the commission be assembled at future established times, thus, institutionalizing a wholesale review of the state's basic document.

> Within thirty days after the adjournment of the regular session of the legislature convened in the tenth year following that in which this constitution is adopted, and each twentieth year thereafter, there shall be established a constitution revision commission.[11]

Made up of the Attorney General and thirty-six other members appointed by each of the branches (fifteen by the governor, nine each by the house speaker and the senate president, and three by the chief justice of the supreme court), the commission is constitutionally charged to "adopt its rules of procedure, examine the constitution of the state, hold public hearings, and, not later than one hundred eighty days prior to the next general election, file with the secretary of state its proposal, if any, of a revision of this constitution or any part of it."[12] Those proposals are then put on the ballot at the next general election and require a simply majority for adoption.

Since the ratification of the 1968 constitution, two revision commissions have proposed changes to the state's constitution. The first commission, organized in the tenth year after the adoption of the 1968 constitution, failed to persuade the electorate to support a single proposal it put on the 1978 general election ballot. Yet two years later when the state legislature proposed abolishing the revision commission process, voters were unwilling to dismantle the process and rejected the legislature's constitutional amendment that would have done so. Subsequently, the legislature proposed yet another mechanism of constitutional reform—a topical revision commission to address only tax and budget reform, which resembles in form the constitution revision commission. Citizens supported the institution of a Taxation and Budget Reform Commission in 1988, and it became the fifth tool for constitutional revision in Florida. The three proposals that were placed on the ballot by this specialized commission were adopted by the electorate in 1992.[13]

In 1997, Florida's second constitution revision commission got underway. The electoral failures experienced by the commissioners and staff of the first commission were certainly warnings to government leaders as they began thinking about appointing commissioners to examine Florida's constitution a second time. But the success of the Taxation and Budget Reform Commission in 1992 was a good omen. Ultimately, the 1997–98 CRC saw eight of its nine revisions adopted by the Florida electorate.

The history of Florida suggests that this state typically embraces constitutional change. Chesterfield Smith, the chair of the 1965–66 SRC, who is recognized as the master craftsman of the 1968 constitution that included these multiple paths for reform has said, "It is my own personal judgment that above all other matters, the new provisions in the 1968 Constitution authorizing means for further constitutional changes are the most important things in the new constitution."[14] Floridians have now learned how to make good use of these tools for change; it simply took a little practice. The development and practice of the constitution revision process in Florida, and the differences between the two commissions are the focus of the balance of this chapter.

The Commission Process

Florida's 1968 Constitution includes several clear mandates regarding the constitution revision process. It defined who would select members of the commission and how many appointments they would each have, when the commission would meet, what the commission would do (review the constitution, hold public hearings, draft revisions, if any), and by when it must complete its work. Beyond these parameters, it has been through practice that a logical process of reform has developed.

The commissions have used the State Capitol in Tallahassee as their home base and meet in the senate chambers. With the space in the Senate has also come the resources of that body in terms of the active participation of the Secretary of the Senate (who served as Secretary of the CRC), electronic voting devices, recording equipment, court reporters, and any other logistical or institutional needs the commission may require. The commission also has easy access to government documents available at the state archives as well as research sources at Florida State University.

The commission process formally starts on the date of the first meeting of the constitution revision commission as determined by the appointed chair in accordance with the constitutional parameters of "within 30 days of the end of the legislative session" (July 6, 1977; June 16, 1997). It officially expires on the date of the general election where its proposed revisions are scheduled to appear, which will always be in November of the year following the commission's initial meeting. The entire formal process from start to finish takes about sixteen months. In practice, however, the commission's final meeting is dictated by when it must submit its revision proposals to the custodian of the state's records, which has typically been in early May of the election year (May 11, 1978 and May 5, 1998). Thus, the 1997–98 CRC met for nearly eleven months, about two weeks longer than the 1977–78 CRC.

Generally, the first meetings of the commission in June and July are organizational meetings. Introductions are made, speeches and admonitions by the state's political leaders and former commission members are given, committee assignments are divvied up, and the commission is oriented to its work. The second commission also adopted its rules at this early stage and in both instances, schedules were fleshed out for the coming months.

The second phase of the commission's work begins in July and August and may continue into September. This is when the commission holds

TABLE 1.1
Constitutional Revision Commission Timetable

June	*July*	*Aug.*	*Sept.*	*Oct.*	*Nov.*	*Dec.*	*Jan.*	*Feb.*	*Mar.*	*Apr.*	*May*
Organizational meetings				Committee meetings and referrals to full commission					Adoption of revision ballot measures		
							Adoption of draft proposals				
	Public hearings to solicit proposals							Public hearings on draft proposals			

*Revisions must be submitted to the Secretary of State no later than 180 days before the general election.

public hearings in locations across the state to solicit input from citizens on issues they perceive as important in revising the constitution. The first CRC held ten public hearings in the state's largest cities, traveling from Pensacola in the northwest to Jacksonville in the northeast to Miami in the south between August 18 and September 26, 1977. The 1997–98 CRC expanded that schedule slightly by holding hearings in twelve cities over a nine-week period starting in July and running through mid-September.

The proposals raised by citizens and interest groups at these hearings are recorded, fashioned into general statements by commission staff and considered by the full commission at meetings in Tallahassee that take place between September and December. Public proposals must be moved by a commissioner and receive ten votes in order to be sent to committee for further consideration. The first commission moved 232 issues culled from the public hearings to its priority list; the 1997–98 CRC sent 186 proposals to committee.[15] Additionally, proposals offered by individual commissioners were considered by the commission and some advanced to committee under the same rule.

Most of the committee work takes place between September and December. Generally, committees are able to amend and combine proposals, but are obligated to return the proposals to the full commission with recommendations in support or opposition. Committees are not permitted to eliminate proposals from consideration. Strict timetables may be set for the committee's review; the 1997–98 CRC required the committee's report on proposals within three commission workdays but waived the rule on a number of occasions. As the proposals return to the full commission, each is given careful consideration and put to a vote sometime between mid-November through February. The work of the Style and Drafting Committee becomes important around this time as it reviews each adopted proposal for clarity and legal sufficiency, and begins to develop recommendations on the forthcoming difficult balloting decisions.

The commission takes to the road again in late February or early March to share its proposals with the public and solicit citizen comment. Each commission held only three public meetings during this phase (1977–78: Jacksonville, Tampa, and Miami; 1997–98: Ft. Lauderdale, Tallahassee, and St. Petersburg). When it returns to Tallahassee to finalize its work, which is due in early May, the commission begins the most arduous part of the process.

The final month of meetings, generally held in March and April, are when the working relations between commissioners are tested. In this final phase the commission reviews all of the proposed changes, finalizes the language of the amendments, assembles them into revision measures, and reaches agreement on ballot language (a summary of the revision that is constitutionally limited to seventy-five words). Personal agendas that may have been suppressed throughout the process are most likely to come to the forefront of debate during these late days. But every member perceives that how the revisions are packaged (whether they are grouped, how they are grouped or whether they stand alone), the ballot language that appears before the voters (sometimes the only information that uninformed voters may have in casting their vote), and the sequence or order in which those revisions appear on the ballot are essential factors to the ultimate success of the constitution revision process.

The products of these final meetings are the revisions that will be placed on the November general election ballot. By constitutional fiat, the commission must report its revisions to the Secretary of State at least 180 days prior to the general election. The 1977–78 CRC submitted eight proposed amendments to the constitution, which included more than eighty-seven changes: forty-seven substantive and forty procedural.[16] None of the revisions were supported by the popular vote in November 1978. The 1997–98 CRC ultimately proposed for the public's consideration nine revisions, which contained thirty-three distinct amendments.[17] Of these, eight revision measures were successfully adopted by the voters and incorporated into the Constitution of 1968. The success of the latter commission is due in large part to the experiences of the first commission, and one of the most significant lesson learned involved good planning.

PLANNING: ESSENTIAL FOR SUCCESS

Any administrator with a mere month of experience knows that planning is an essential tool for any operation—be it public or private, nonprofit or commercial, military or educational. Planning and preparation are lubricants in a well-oiled machine and are critical to efficient and effective operations. Political leaders in Florida knew that in the tenth year after the adoption of the 1968 constitution the state would see its first revision commission under Article XI, Section 2. Governor Reubin Askew was the first governor to serve his entire tenure under the new constitution (1971–1979) and he appointed the first chair and the fourteen other commissioners to the CRC. He was also a member of the 1965–66

SRC that produced the 1968 constitution. But Askew and his advisers encountered some confusion in the language of the article addressing the timing of the first CRC.

Article XI, section 2a of the 1968 constitution called for the commission to convene "within thirty days after the adjournment of the regular session of the legislature convened in the tenth year following that in which this constitution is adopted." Given the legislative timetable already established, that would have meant that the commission could assemble as early as June 3, 1978, but not later than July 3, 1978. Two other provisions, however, muddied the constitutional waters. First, the constitution mandated that citizens must vote on any revisions or amendments promulgated under the constitution at "the next general election held more than ninety days after the [amendments or report of revision] is filed with the secretary of state."[18] That meant that the revisions would appear on the November 7, 1978 ballot, and therefore must be submitted to the Secretary of State no later than August 5, 1978. This would give the commission not more than two months to do its work. But the section specifically addressing the commission process further required the commission to file any revisions with the Secretary of State at least 180 days prior to the next general election, which would have meant on or before May 11, 1978. It was a logistical impossibility if the earliest the commission could meet was June 3 of the same year.

Recognizing the constitutional quagmire, Governor Askew sought an advisory opinion from the Florida Supreme Court in November 1976. In his request he outlined the dilemma and asked the court to rule on whether he had the authority to appoint members to the commission not later than thirty days after the adjournment of the 1977 (rather than the 1978) legislative session with the view that the revisions would appear on the 1978 general election ballot. Alternatively, if advancing the process was not an option, the governor asked the Court to provide him guidance as to when he should appoint commissioners and when revision proposals must be filed.[19] Options were suggested that included appointing the commission following the 1978 legislative session and balloting any revisions in 1980. The governor also suggested that perhaps he could appoint the commissioners in advance of the 1978 legislative session, but recognized the implications for individual commissioners who might also be legislators.

In a decision that would unsettle judicial conservatives, the Florida Supreme Court recognized that they were "being asked to rewrite one or more of the provisions in order to make the document work."[20] Acknowledging that the difficulty stemmed from the original timing of the 1968 revision process itself (it had been anticipated by the drafters that the electorate would vote on the revision in 1967), the court determined that there was

> absolutely no way to reconcile without judicial gloss the disharmonious provisions which appear in that section. Under these circumstances, we must abandon as fruitless any notion that we can "interpret" or "construe" particular language within the Constitution to achieve a result which is not only workable but reasonably consistent with the intent of the people.[21]

A majority of the justices (5–2) agreed that it would be better to allow the electorate to vote on constitutional revisions earlier rather than waiting until the 1980 general election. In addition to holding as close to the intent of the drafters as possible in meeting the ten-year review, the justices also recognized that an intervening election of state legislators and key executive offices would cloud a later revision process. "Elective political activity is antithetical to this constitutional review process, unlike the other two reserved in Article XI."[22]

The final order of the court issued on February 15, 1977, directed the governor to appoint his commissioners within thirty days of the 1977 legislative session's adjournment and direct that they submit their revisions to the Secretary of State not later than May 11, 1978, for appearance on the November 1978 ballot. The Court went further by establishing a standard timetable for future commissions. The second commission would assemble after the completion of the 1997 legislative session with its revisions, if any, appearing on the 1998 ballot.[23]

The court order cleared the constitutional confusion and provided a reasonable timetable for the commission's work to be conducted, but it left little time for planning. State officials tasked with appointing members had about four months to solicit volunteers to serve and the governor had to identify a chair to manage a process that had virtually no form other than the sketchy constitutional mandate "to adopt rules, review the constitution, hold public hearings and submit revisions, if any." There were no provisions for a staff (paid or unpaid), no budget or method to request one although public funds would clearly be needed in order to provide travel to the public hearings and the resources necessary to manage meetings of thirty-seven commissioners, and no way to determine where these meetings would be held. Add to this lack of framework the fact that between the issuance of the court's order and the appointment of commissioners, the 1977 legislative session was preparing to meet. Attention—by politicians, the media and the public—was focused on the annual legislative session and not on constitutional reform.

The 1977 legislative session managed to direct some attention to the forthcoming exercise in constitutional revision, but not all of it was positive. One unsuccessful measure initiated in the House was a joint resolution to amend the Florida constitution such that the upcoming CRC would be required to submit its proposals to the legislature for review before taking them to the voters.[24] On the other hand, the session did provide an opportunity to lay some groundwork for the upcoming commission. Legislators authorized the chair of the commission to "employ personnel and to incur expenses related to the official operation of the commission or its committees, to sign vouchers, and to otherwise expend funds appropriated to the commission for carrying out its official duties."[25] The forthcoming commission also received a special appropriation of about $300,000 in operating funds with which to do its work.[26] With these authorizations, the chair of the commission could hire an executive director who would begin the organizational work necessary to support a 37-member commission.

At the two state university law schools, Florida State University and University of Florida, grants were issued to prepare research material and develop background analyses on the constitution that would be useful to the incoming commission.[27] Robert Shevin, the Attorney General who by nature of his office was the only constitutionally named member of the 1977–78 CRC, also had his staff prepare a report on issues that merited the CRC's attention.[28] These meager efforts at advance work saw little use, however, given the hectic pace at which the commission was forced to work.[29]

Late in June 1977, Governor Askew announced his appointments to the commission followed shortly by the announcements of the other appointing authorities. Because this was the state's first experience in naming commissioners to the CRC and in light of the timetable imposed by the court's decision, there was little, if any, coordination between the chief justice, governor, senate president, and house speaker in selecting the citizens who would serve on this historic commission. While potential commissioners were being identified by the appointing authorities, the legislative session consumed most of the state's attention. Conversations between the executive and legislative branches were likely to be about lawmaking and each political leader probably viewed their selection of commissioners to be an autonomous decision made without consultation or consideration of the other branches' selections. On July 6, 1977, this lack of coordination in appointments was visible. The thirty-seven commissioners who arrived in Tallahassee to review the state's constitution were predominately white, mostly male and very connected to "old" Florida both in terms of the historical bias toward rural and northern interests as well as their connections to ebbing dynasties of power. It was not a good omen for a state that was experiencing rapid social change and grappling with issues like women's rights, gay rights, crime and violence in its growing urban areas, increasing environmental concerns, and a burgeoning influx of immigrants from the Caribbean and Latin America.

Governor Askew, a Democrat from North Florida, named Talbot D'Alemberte as the chair. D'Alemberte brought to the commission the invaluable experience of having directed the 1972 legislatively produced revision of article V, the state's judicial article. He was a seasoned politician (Fl. House, 1966–72), well connected to the state's bar, and an attorney who had earned a reputation as one of the state's foremost constitutional scholars. D'Alemberte was from South Florida (Dade County) and his appointment may have been an effort to visibly minimize the regional differences that regularly injected themselves into Florida state politics in those days.

As chair, D'Alemberte selected attorney Steven J. Uhlfelder, a 1971 graduate of the University of Florida's College of Law, to serve as executive director. Uhlfelder had not more than a month to lay the groundwork necessary to manage a thirty-seven-member commission that was constitutionally mandated to hold public hearings as part of its review process and to submit its product just ten months after its first meeting. To his credit, it was Uhlfelder's willingness to share his experiences and observations on the 1977–78 CRC that subsequently guided the second commission in its preparatory work.[30] And the lessons learned from those path-breaking days of 1977 paid off handsomely for the 1997–98 CRC in its planning stages.

The 1997–98 CRC process got a jumpstart on planning that its predecessor never enjoyed. In June 1996, nearly a full year before the second revision commission would meet for the first time, Governor Lawton Chiles signed an executive order establishing the "Governor's Constitution

Revision Steering Committee," a committee created with the support of the legislative leadership.[31] The idea for a steering committee seems to have started in the legislature, which had passed a bill calling for a similar committee. It was vetoed by Governor Chiles who was unhappy with the legislative bias of the proposed committee's membership.[32] The governor established instead an advance team for the constitution revision process that brought together all of the key players of state government. He appointed his General Counsel, W. Dexter Douglass, as his designee to the committee and the order called for Douglass to serve as chair of the steering committee. Douglass, Attorney General Bob Butterworth, Senate President Jim Scott, Speaker Peter Wallace, and Judge Thomas Barkdull (designated by the Chief Justice) first assembled on August 20, 1996, to begin planning the 1997–98 CRC that would first meet in June of the following year. They had a full ten months to lay the necessary groundwork for Florida's second experiment with a constitution revision commission.

The steering committee was formally charged by the executive order to carry out a range of tasks that indicated careful reflection on the 1977–78 CRC experience. That reflection was not surprising in that General Counsel Douglass had served on the 1977–78 CRC and knew well the trials of a process that evolved as it occurred. But two more recent experiences also contributed to the identification of planning issues. First, the issue-specific Taxation and Budget Reform Commission had met in 1990, and successfully placed three measures before the voters in 1992. Second, the 1994 legislature had commissioned a 23-member Article V Task Force to examine and make recommendations regarding the judicial article of the Florida constitution. Both of these experiences contributed to a corpus of knowledge that, when combined with the events of the 1977–78 CRC, provided valuable planning information on everything from logistics to policy substance.

The governor's order also called for the employment of an executive director who would be housed in the Office of the Governor. Chairperson Douglass looked to the most recent exercise in constitutional examination, the Article V Task Force, which just completed its work. With the steering committee's unanimous support, he appointed the task force's executive director, Billy Buzzett, as the 1997–98 CRC's executive director. Buzzett previously served as attorney to the State House of Representatives and had built a reputation for efficient budget management and effective staff organization. Buzzett had also recognized the importance of his work on the Article V Task Force in anticipating the upcoming CRC, calling the task force a "mini-constitutional revision commission" that could proffer policies for the CRC's consideration and "test the electorate's appetite for comprehensive change to the Constitution."[33]

Although the steering committee was advisory in nature, it was specifically directed to address organizational needs like budget proposals, develop drafts of meeting schedules and timetables for commission work, flesh out an organizational structure (committees), plan and launch a public information campaign, and identify potential research needs and issues for the commission. The committee was also charged with developing draft rules and procedures that could quickly be considered and adopted by the commission as one of its first orders of business. As Judge Barkdull noted at the first meeting of the committee, "the 1978 revision commission spent its first three months organizing."[34]

The steering committee benefited from the presence of Judge Barkdull who had served on both the 1965–66 SRC and the 1977–78 CRC, having been the chair of the rules committee at the earlier commission and a member of the rules committee at the latter. Given these experiences, Barkdull was tasked with developing a working document that would facilitate the early adoption of the commission rules in the following year when the commission convened. He would once again establish himself as the expert on procedural matters and was consulted repeatedly during commission meetings.

Having the Senate President and the House Speaker at the same table facilitated the budgeting process for the upcoming commission. During the 1996 legislative session, an early budget appropriation of $100,000 was committed to the work of the steering committee through an unusual category called "administered funds."[35] In the following year, a special appropriation was secured in April for an additional $200,000. It was earmarked for staff, equipment, per diem and travel expenses and designed to be used immediately (Florida's fiscal year begins on July 1).[36]

The 1997 legislature, which met before the commission convened, also allocated $1.6 million of its general appropriation for the commission's work and allowed the balance of the funds to be carried over into 1998 rather than reverting to the general fund, as typical public practice requires.[37] Since 1997 would be the year in which the commission undertook its numerous public hearings across the state, significant spending was expected. The commission's operating costs were supplemented in 1998 with an additional appropriation of $200,000.[38] These appropriations did not include the costs of fulfilling the constitution's requirement that all proposed amendments (not just the commission's) be published in one newspaper in each county of the state prior to the general election; those funds were a separate line item in the state budget. Even considering inflation, the fiscal resources enjoyed by the 1997–98 CRC far surpassed the shoestring budget that Executive Director Uhlfelder managed twenty years earlier. As Douglass noted in his review of the 1997–98 CRC, "This was unprecedented and laid the foundation for the Commission to begin its work immediately."[39]

The Steering Committee was authorized to exist until the day the constitution revision commission first met. While it was strictly advisory in nature, its work was critical to the efficient operation of the commission and it relieved the commissioners from distractions not essential to their substantive work. As I discuss later, the planning process also formulated issue agendas for the commissioners that facilitated their work. Of all of the factors that I examined, the difference between the two commissions with respect to planning was the most glaring distinction. But even the best laid plans may fail, and this first steering committee knew well that it would take more than planning to guarantee a positive constitutional reform experience in Florida.

Politics and Procedures

Nowhere in the Florida constitution is it suggested that the revision commission should be divorced from politics. In fact, that its commissioners are chosen by the state's governmental leaders to examine a document that allocates political power virtually guarantees that issues of politics will be the subtext to all discussion. From the selection of commissioners to the adoption of the rules to the substance of the revisions, politics is the heart and soul of constitutional reform. In this section I examine some of the key differences between the two revision commissions, differences that stem from issues of political power and procedures.

When the 1977–78 CRC was assembled, all of its members were appointed by officials in the Democratic party save the judicial appointments (and even they necessarily fell at that end of the political spectrum). Many of the commissioners who served on the 1977–78 CRC were either sitting politicians, former politicians, or attorneys. While several commissioners came from fields like medicine or education, they were typically activists or scholars who knew well the political arena because of their careers and their connections. All of them were able to take time away from their careers and to serve uncompensated. With no coordination between the political leaders making the appointments, the commission was a fairly homogeneous group that did not reflect the increasing diversity of the state.

Much would change in the political climate of Florida over the intervening twenty years. In 1996, Florida was living under divided government. Both bodies of the state legislature were in Republican hands, the governor and the elected attorney general were Democrats, and the Supreme Court may have been the most liberal (by Florida standards) of the three branches. The implementation of a steering committee that brought the appointing authorities together early to discuss and plan the upcoming commission combined with the political realities of state government guaranteed that the 1997–98 commission would be more diverse, a fact anticipated by Uhlfelder and Buzzett in an article written in advance of the 1997–98 appointments.[40] Chairman Douglass acknowledged that the appointing authorities were "cautioned . . . to be sensitive to the needs of all Floridians and to create a commission that was inclusive and representative of the state's diverse population."[41] And they did.

The membership of the 1997–98 CRC had more women and reflected the racial and ethnic diversity of the state more so than its predecessor. Every region was represented and the membership brought to the table the full range of political perspectives from the very conservative Kenneth Connor of Tallahassee (appointed by the speaker) to the feminist attorney Ellen Freidin of Miami (appointed by the governor). Because of this diversity, the 1997–98 CRC was necessarily more tempered in its directions and deliberations. Consensus had to be reached in order for this body to be successful; as a result, moderation prevailed on matters of both substance and form.

Conventional wisdom tells us that the rules employed when governing bodies make decisions are important to the outcomes. Revision commissions in Florida were given constitutional authority to adopt their own rules and procedures and are required only to hold public hearings and to submit proposals, if any, within a certain time frame. Thus, CRCs are subject to no other state laws beyond the dictates of the constitution unless they choose to hold themselves to other standards. This autonomy was established early by the Supreme Court's 1977 advisory opinion to the governor.[42] It was reinforced in an opinion issued by the Attorney General in response to an inquiry from Chair D'Alemberte as to whether the state's Administrative Procedure Act applies to the CRC proceedings. The Attorney General ruled that it did not.

> The commission . . . has been granted the constitutional authority to establish its own rules of procedure . . . in order to ensure that the commission be independent and free from interference from any branch of government. . . . To permit one branch of government to impose rules of procedure upon another coordinate constitutional branch or entity would destroy the constitutional independence of such branch or entity.[43]

Therefore one of the first acts of the commission must be to adopt the rules and procedures that will govern its work.

The 1977–78 commission modeled its rules on three sources: the rules used by the 1965–66 SRC, Roberts' Rules of Order and the procedures governing Florida's legislative bodies. When the Florida legislature drafts amendments to the state constitution, it must do so by joint resolution with the support of two-thirds of the members in each house. This supermajority requirement was imbedded in the draft rules provided to the 1977–78 CRC. It sparked "vigorous debate" and a discussion that touched on philosophical considerations of political power, the influence of majorities and minorities, and acknowledgments of Florida's propensity to amend its constitution regularly[44]. Ultimately, the first commission settled on requiring only a simple majority (19 votes) to adopt revision proposals. But as the 1977–78 CRC tried to finish its work in April 1978, it realized that the rule was problematic and subsequently amended it. The new rule required a two-thirds majority for amendments to the proposals that had already been adopted and for final adoption of each revision.[45]

The experience of the 1977–78 CRC and the repeated advice of its executive director combined with the political diversity of the 1997–98 CRC meant that the adoption of something more than a simple majority voting rule was virtually a given in the subsequent commission. The key player in framing the rules for the second commission was Judge Barkdull who had more experience with constitutions and commissions than any of the members. As a senior statesman of sorts, he gently prodded and occasionally lectured his colleagues to see their roles as different than mere lawmakers. His philosophy of the commission process was expressed passionately during the critical stages of the decision-making process and is worthy of restatement here.

> We need to look to the Constitution's basic principles. We must give up personal preferences in exchange for the ability to offer to the people of Florida needed changes in our state's basic structure of government. We each should give our support for a proposal only if we truly believe it is needed to effect constitutional change, and not merely to satisfy a personal desire.
>
> As we have begun to take our definitive votes of this commission, I hope you will also [*sic*] examine [the proposals] to determine which you believe are truly needed for constitutional change, and leave to the Legislature the further consideration of those proposals that might be the subject of general law or merit additional constitutional review.[46]

It was this philosophy that eventually found its way into the rules of the 1997–98 CRC.

The commissioners required twenty-two votes in order to adopt a proposal for inclusion in the revision package. The majority-plus rule was also applied to the packaging of those revisions, a process critical to selling the revisions to the public. This meant that throughout the meaningful voting stages of their work commissioners had to work toward consensus. The legislatively appointed commissioners, for example, could not dominate the revision process without the support of at least four other members. The gubernatorial appointees needed to secure at least seven other votes, which meant that they had to reach beyond the court's commissioners and the attorney general. The decision rule encouraged early bargaining and compromise as proposals advanced to the ballot.

One of the problems faced by both commissions stemmed from the way in which the revisions were presented to the public. Rather than addressing only those articles that needed to be changed, the earlier commission saw as its task a total revision of the constitution. The 1997–98 CRC took a more conservative approach, offering revisions limited to particular sections of the constitution as deemed necessary. But the politics of logrolling—a ploy common to legislative activity—was employed by both revision commissions. Logrolling is essentially a strategy whereby one desirable policy is tied to a less desirable one in order to secure the passage of both. "The voter is left with the unappetizing position of weighing his or her aversion for one (or more) against his or her attraction to the others in the grouping."[47]

Commissioners know that how the ballot is ordered and the way in which revisions are packaged or bundled can make or break the proposal on election day. The 1997–98 CRC carefully placed several measures as "stand-alone" issues. Gun control, for example, has long been a divisive issue and the commission had adopted two proposals that affected gun sales and background checks. Rather than subject several proposals to the unpredictable vote on the gun measure, the commission opted to let the matter go to the voters as a single issue. Yet in what they called the "Ballot Access, Public Campaign Financing, and Election Process Revisions," there was a little something for every political perspective. The package protected third parties and independents from discriminatory practices; instituted campaign financing for those who agree to spending limits; opened the primary process to voters who lived in districts dominated by one party; and standardized school board election practices across the state by making them nonpartisan. It also contained a statement setting the voting age at eighteen in order to bring the Florida constitution in line with federal law.

While the bundling of proposals was far more excessive in the 1977–78 CRC, the 1997–98 CRC did not eliminate it entirely. But it does seem that their packaging decisions were made a bit more strategically and thoughtfully. With the exception of the "technical revision" (a catchall that included everything from literary changes to gender neutral language throughout the constitution to clarification of previous constitutional enactments that needed "adjustment"), the contents of each package ultimately contained elements that were, in fact, related to each other thematically.

A final observation on the political aspects of the two commissions comes from issues regarding lobbying and lobbyists. Former Executive Director Uhlfelder warned the steering committee in September 1996 that it needed to find a way to regulate lobbyists; he even suggested that the commission meet away from Tallahassee as a way to avoid the attention of those who, unsuccessful in plying the legislative waters, would seek out favors through the commission process.[48] In his end-of-commission review, which appeared in a special edition of the *Florida State University Law Review*, Uhlfelder specifically noted the colloquy of Commissioner Don Reed who called for the abolition of the CRC process. "I will guarantee you that there is a large portion of the membership of this Commission that does not decide the questions for themselves."[49] Perhaps in response to Uhlfelder's warning, the 1997 Legislature revised the statute regulating lobbyists to include those who would lobby constitution revision commissions.[50] CRC members were also subject to the state's ethics provisions that mandate reporting of gifts of $25 or more, bars gifts in excess of $100 from special interests and lobbyists, but permits commissioners to engage in social lobbying (wining and dining). However, the admonition by Uhlfelder and adherence to the "letter of the law" did not keep the 1997–98 commission out of trouble in their first months of work.

In July 1997, as commissioners headed across the state to listen to citizens comment on the constitution, the body made a major faux pas in accepting invitations to three parties sponsored by key lobbyists. One reception was hosted by an automobile dealership owned by a former state Democratic Party chairman and by BellSouth, the largest local telephone company in the state. The others were sponsored by state trial lawyers, major law firms, and a high-powered lawyer/lobbyist. While some other receptions were low-key events, these three merited the media's attention due to the glitz and glamour of the locations and the menus, which fed into the perception of blatant lobbying.[51]

When the story broke in late July 1997, Chairman Douglass was quoted as saying that "the parties are harmless events where members mingle with local leaders." In fact, the soirees were part of a publicity package put together by the commission leadership as a way of introducing the commissioners to the local elite of the state's major population centers. But in the face of mounting negative press, Douglass reconsidered his assessment and on August 1, issued a letter that ended receptions sponsored by special interests.[52] Within a week the commission had hired a public relations manager. However, Douglass attributed the hiring to a decision made weeks earlier based on his perception of declining media interest in the commission process.[53] His statement suggests that the public relations expert was already hard at work.

Politics and procedures are critical to the constitution revision process and while the ongoing struggles for power cannot be expunged from this forum, how those struggles are managed is important to the success of the reform process. One way to manage the political tug-of-wars is to adopt rules that are transparent and encourage bargaining, negotiation, and consensus. It may also behoove commissioners to recognize and act as though they are an ad hoc coordinate branch of government and expect to feel the pressures exerted by special interests, lobbyists, and the other branches. But commissioners are also expected by the public and the press to maintain the highest ethical standards and to appear unbeholden to special interests.

Policy: Substance Matters

The policy concerns buried in each of the revisions proposed by the two commissions were undoubtedly critical to the eventual adoption or rejection of the revision measures by the voters. Anticipating what the majority of the state's voting population would support in terms of substantive policy is necessarily a central concern of the commission's work. Members might wholeheartedly and even unanimously support a particular constitutional reform, but they must recognize that it is the public who must ultimately agree to the revision in the voting booth. Additionally, policy issues and events beyond the control of the CRC may impact the outcome of the commission's work. In short, substance matters.

The 1977–78 CRC met during a period of unsettled politics in Florida. While there is probably no ideal time to consider constitutional change, the late 1970s were probably the least desirable period to divine the direction of the state. Major social issues on the political scene cast an ominous shadow over the commission's work. Florida was grappling with women's rights and the ratification of the federal Equal Rights Amendment. Anita Bryant had just completed a successful referendum campaign against gay rights in Dade County. Racial tensions were still an undertone in a state where educational integration was slow to take hold and those tensions were further complicated by the growing ethnic diversity of South Florida. Crime was an issue across the state and many parts of Florida were trans-shipment points for illegal drugs. To make matters worse for the 1977–78 commissioners, a "citizen" initiative to allow casino gambling in parts of the state had garnered the requisite signatures and would be placed next to the commission's proposals on the November 1978 ballot.

The ultimate failure of the CRC proposals in 1978 has repeatedly been linked to the casino gambling initiative.[54] Consider that Governor Askew took a public stand against the initiative and focused the power and stature of his office on persuading the public to vote "no" on casinos.

With such a significant "vote no" message sent to the voters, some believe that the citizens of the state simply voted "no" on all of the constitutional measures, unable or unwilling to examine each proposal independently. The campaign in support of casino gambling was exceptionally well-funded and the issue simply dominated the entire election season.

Casinos were not the only problem. Askew, who earlier in the process seemed devoted to the commission's work, publicly criticized the commission in May when it finalized its proposals. He alleged that special interests influenced one of the ballot packaging decisions by tying tax breaks for business (pro-business) to increased homestead exemptions (pro-homeowner). A month later, Askew used his line item veto to eliminate a provision in the state budget for $750,000, monies necessary to advertise the CRC proposals.[55] Askew, incidentally, was a lame-duck governor and the gubernatorial race between Jack Eckerd (R) and Bob Graham (D) probably captured more of the citizens' attention than the revision proposals during the 1978 campaign.

The substance of the revisions also evoked opposition from expected and unexpected quarters. Revision 1, an omnibus proposal of over 50 changes to the constitution, included a personal right to privacy that generated support from gay rights groups despite explicit statements by commissioners that the proposal was not intended to protect sexual activity of this nature. Anita Bryant, a born-again Christian and nationally recognized entertainer known for her orange juice industry advertisements, was fresh from her success in "saving" Dade County by leading the campaign that overturned a gay rights ordinance (the Bryant campaign was titled "Save the Children"). Bryant focused her attention not on Revision 1 in 1978, but on Revision 2, which included the "little ERA," an attempt to ban sex discrimination. Bryant argued that the provision would open the door to gay marriages in the state. The League of Women Voters raised over $200,000 to support the revision, seeing it as a referendum on the future ratification of the federal ERA.

Even revisions that addressed structural changes to government organization and improvements in operations met resistance. The effort to revise the politicized nature of reapportionment process was contested by members of the legislature who had the most to lose by a "neutral" redistricting process. Florida's elected cabinet, historically cast as a device to keep the larger population areas from exerting too much control over the executive, was the focus of a revision designed to streamline the executive branch and eliminate some of the elected positions. The officeholders and their clientele groups mounted a vigorous campaign against the proposal, warning that it would place too much power in the hands of the governor. Chair D'Alemberte publicly accused groups of misrepresenting the substance and intended effects of the revisions to the public.[56]

In their retrospective analysis of the 1978 revisions, Uhlfelder and McNeely observe that while each of the CRC revisions were rejected by the voters at the ballot box, many were ultimately included in the state's constitution or adopted as statutes following the 1978 election. They suggest that the commission served as an important "blueprint for change" that "highlighted many significant public policy issues that had not been discussed or considered in Florida before."[57] One might liken the commission process to an incubator, where difficult policy issues are initially placed on the public agenda by the commission and despite a lack of support by the electorate, allowed to percolate until they are reintroduced later by either the state legislature, as a citizen initiative, or even by a subsequent revision commission. Thus, several of the public policy issues considered in 1978 remained on the state's agenda when the next constitution revision commission met twenty years later.

The 1997–98 CRC's substantive agenda was developed well in advance of its actual meetings. Unlike its predecessor, scholars, lawyers and people who had worked on the previous commission anticipated the second CRC and many offered ideas for revisions through articles, interviews, and discussions. The *Florida Bar Journal*, for example, ran a special edition in April 1997 that included an orientation to the revision process followed by ten articles that addressed potential topics for revision that ranged from funding the state court system to modifying the citizen initiative process.[58] The steering committee of the CRC, during its planning stages, gathered information and sought out research on issues that were ripe for revision. And articles appeared in law reviews across the state suggesting areas of the constitution in need of reform well in advance of the first commission meeting.[59]

The 1997–98 CRC ultimately grappled with some of the subjects that its predecessor (and even the 1965–66 SRC) had attempted to resolve. The establishment of a neutral reapportionment committee for redistricting in Florida was a personal favorite of Chair Douglass.[60] It had been considered by the two previous commissions, but the political implications of such a proposal prevented it from reaching the final stage of the commission's process despite surviving well into March 1998. State court funding was also on the agendas of the 1977–78 CRC and the Article V

Task Force. In 1998, this measure was included on the ballot as Revision 3 and adopted by the voters as part of a judicial reform package that provided a local option for selecting lower court judges using merit selection in lieu of elections. The judicial selection issue had also been one of the 1978 revisions rejected by the voters.

One other persistent reform measure that made the ballot in 1998 was the reorganization of the executive branch and the elimination of some of the elected cabinet officials. Revision 4 reduced the cabinet from six elected members (Commissioners of Education and Agriculture, Secretary of State, Attorney General, Comptroller, and Treasurer) to three (Chief Financial Officer, Attorney General, and Commissioner of Agriculture). Because Floridians had adopted term limits for its state officials in 1992 and in light of the precarious balance of power between the parties in the state, the 1997–98 CRC had a much easier time persuading the voters to support such a measure. More important, the governor and the affected cabinet officials offered no resistance and some even expressed open support for the reorganization. That the Secretary of Agriculture remained an elected cabinet official also meant, however, that the revision would not be challenged by the well-funded commercial farming and rural interests.

Related to the cabinet reorganization and the elimination of the Secretary of Education was a revision package on education that included a "feel good" measure that no rational citizen should have voted against. The ballot language of Revision 2 explained the proposal:

> Declares the education of children to be a fundamental value of the people of Florida; establishes adequate provision for education as a paramount duty of the state; and provides for the adequate provision for a uniform system of free public education as an efficient, safe, secure, and high quality system.

While most of the revision was aspirational, the standards and goals suggested by the revision have served as the underpinning of Governor Jeb Bush's revolutionary reorganization of public education in Florida in 2000–2001.

Two other measures worthy of mention are Revision 1 and Revision 5. Revision 1 proposed the merger of two state commissions, the Game and Fresh Water Fish Commission and the Marine Fisheries Commission, into a single organization—the Fish and Wildlife Conservation

Commission. It also removed some of the legislature's regulatory authority over marine resources and gave those powers to the proposed commission. The idea was not new. It had been conceived originally as a citizen's initiative petition, but was removed from the 1998 ballot by the Supreme Court when the justices determined that the proposed ballot language did not fulfill the statutory requirements for clarity and accuracy.[61] When the CRC included the reform as one of its proposals it also inherited the resources of the political action committee that had backed the original idea. The Fish and Wildlife Conservation Committee spent over $500,000 to secure the passage of the CRC's revision after the Supreme Court had removed their initiative measure from the ballot. While some of the commercial fishermen opposed the measure, there was little negative response to an exceptionally well-organized public information campaign. It is not surprising that Revision 1 received the highest level of voter support (72.3%) of the nine measures put forward by the 1997–98 CRC.[62]

Equality on the basis of sex once again found its way onto the ballot in 1998 in Revision 5. The proposal has resulted in probably one of the most awkward wordings of sexual equality found in any state constitution. With the commission's proposed changes in italics, article 1, section 2 of the Florida constitution now states, in relevant part:

> Basic Rights.—All natural persons, *female and male alike*, are equal before the law and have inalienable rights, among which are the right to enjoy and defend life and liberty, to pursue happiness, to be rewarded for industry, and to acquire, possess and protect property. . . . No person shall be deprived of any right because of race, religion, *national origin*, or physical *disability* [replacing "handicap"].

The particular phrasing, "female and male alike," was selected carefully to avoid even the most remote suggestion or implication that gay rights or gay marriages would be protected under the Florida's constitution. As discussed earlier, the political diversity of the membership of the 1997–98 CRC meant that conservative commissioners were wary of any attempt, intentional or not, to include homosexuals in the state's constitution. Including "sex" or "gender" in the nondiscrimination phrase of the basic rights provision would not have been acceptable due to the various judicial interpretations that have ensued in other states.

The issues that did not reach the voters may be as important as the ones that did in 1998. Briefly, proposals to modify or eliminate the citizen initiative process were introduced and discussed, but not adopted. Hot-button topics like abortion, sexual preference, religious freedom, equal opportunity, and medical marijuana use were referred to committee with the support of at least ten members, but failed to garner the majority-plus support of twenty-two commissioners on the floor. Some of these proposals were clearly controversial in their own right and they sparked divided support among the commissioners. However, I suspect that there were other measures that might well have had the personal support of more than twenty-two commissioners, but the failure to ballot them lies in understanding "the big picture of revision."

The 1997–98 CRC took its lessons on policy matters and substance from the election of 1978, and the debate on casino gambling. This latter commission knew that highly salient and controversial topics could send mixed messages to voters; those messages had the potential to spill over to the less controversial and more necessary revisions. And while the CRC cannot control substantive issues placed on the ballot by the legislature or the citizen initiative process, it could well ensure that its own revisions did not distract the voters from the serious work of reform. For the good of the entire revision process, commissioners approached their work strategically and found the necessarily middle road to successful reform.

PUBLICITY: MARKETING THE PROCESS AND THE PRODUCT

The final variable on which there was a vast difference between the 1977–78 and 1997–98 commissions is publicity. How each commission made the public aware of the revision process and "sold their bill of goods" to the voters varied so significantly that this difference probably shaped (or misshaped) the policy perceptions of the voters at the polls. Certainly, some of the distinctions between the two commissions on this issue are related to the well-considered planning process by the later 1997–98 CRC. However, differences can also be attributed to a philosophy of full disclosure and open debate that prevailed at the time of the first CRC and the simple absence of a role model for commissioners in marketing their product.

The 1977–78 CRC enjoyed little opportunity to plan its work and had only the experiences of the 1965–66 SRC as guidance in defining the process of constitutional revision. On matters like rules and procedures, looking to the SRC as a model was useful. But when it came to the phase of the constitutional revision process where proposals moved out of the commission and into the broader public arena for consideration, the 1977–78 CRC had no point of reference for what it should do and how it should do it. The SRC had pitched its proposals directly to the state legislature and not to the public. While a few of the SRC commissioners stumped for the revised constitution during the election of 1968, most were uninvolved in a public campaign that took its lead from legislators and a supporting governor. Thus, when the 1977–78 CRC concluded its scheduled meetings and submitted their revisions to the Secretary of State there was no precedent for mounting a public education campaign or pitching revisions to the voters. And as noted earlier, in 1978 the governor was consumed with the casino initiative, disenchanted with some of the commission's results, and had vetoed the funding of a publication that might have provided voters with some explanation of the CRC's revisions. Beyond the authorized and constitutionally mandated publication of the ballot language in newspapers across the state, little commission or government-sponsored information would reach the general voting public in Florida in 1978.

The 1977–78 CRC managed to get some coverage of its proposed revisions in several publications likely to be read by the state's lawyers. A special edition of the *Florida State Law Review* came out in the summer of 1978 with a series of articles on the major revisions, the commission's work generally,[63] and a summary and background analysis of each of the proposed revisions.[64] Unfortunately, the publication was neither physically available to the voting public nor intellectually accessible to the average citizen.

The other major discussion of the proposed revisions appeared in the *Florida Bar Journal*, which devoted its October issue to the constitutional revisions with an article by D'Alemberte on the revision process, followed by a series of articles that were juxtaposed in a Pro-Con format. In the comments of the Bar President that preceded the substantive articles, Robert Floyd explained the difficulty the Bar's Board of Governors was having in taking a position on the proposed revisions. The Board had decided not to examine most of the revisions, deciding to "consider only those areas which come within the ambit of the Preamble to Integration Rule and not try to be experts (as an official Board) in all areas."[65] This meant that only two proposals were looked at closely by the Bar in a formal way: the

Omnibus Proposal or Revision 1, which included 57 changes, and Revision 6, recommending the merit selection and retention method for judges on the state's trial courts. And Floyd specifically noted the difficulties with the Omnibus Proposal: "It covers so many different articles and such a wide variety of subject matter that it is going to pose a real problem for even those who have had time to digest it carefully to know whether to vote for or against."[66] The Constitution Committee of the Florida Bar voted 5–5 on the revision, a more favorable outcome than what the public rendered in November when it defeated the revision by over a 2-to-1 margin (71% opposed). The merit selection measure came the closest to being adopted of the eight revisions, rejected by just over half (50.8%) of the voters.

The pro-con format of the special issue of the *Florida Bar Journal* reflects the adversarial nature of the legal profession generally and may have been perceived to be a more open and fair way of presenting the commission's proposals. But it certainly did nothing to insure the passage of the revisions. What is more curious is that at least one of the "con" articles, written in opposition to the extension to the merit selection process, was prepared by a member of the 1977–78 CRC—and the future chair of the 1997–98 CRC—W. Dexter Douglass.[67] Twenty years later, the 1998 special issue of the *Florida Bar Journal* on constitutional revisions did not employ a Pro-Con approach to the CRC's proposals; Chairman Douglass wrote instead an article in support of the cabinet restructuring revision.

While efforts were made to keep the media and the public informed of the commission's work throughout the 1977–78 CRC, the coverage was limited primarily to the public hearing stages and the final days of decision making when the commission voted on its recommended proposals. There was little management of a public relations campaign after the commission disbanded in May and what press appeared about constitutional reform seemed to be sparked by the independent campaigns launched by opponents to the revisions (i.e., Anita Bryant) and the ever-persistent casino initiative. Three weeks before the election the state's largest newspaper, the *Miami Herald*, launched a series of nine articles that examined each revision proposed by the commission. Between November 1 and 3, the *Miami Herald* issued its editorial endorsements and supported all of the revisions save Revision 1 (the Omnibus Proposal) and Revision 7 (taxation and finance revision). But the *Miami Herald* was not a good gauge of Florida politics in the late 1970s.

As table 1.2 indicates, all of the commission's proposals were defeated and many by significant margins. The cabinet reorganization revision

TABLE 1.2
November 7, 1978 Election Results on Constitution Revision Commission Proposals

Revision	*% Approval*	*# Votes Cast*
Omnibus Proposal (56 changes)	29.2	2,135,809
Declaration of Rights (mini-ERA)	43.1	2,325,876
Legislative: Single-Member Districts and Reapportionment Commission	46.9	2,096,141
Executive/Cabinet Restructuring	25.1	2,155,609
Executive: Public Service Commission and Public Counsel	35.9	2,147,614
Judiciary: Merit selection of trial court judges	49.1	2,154,330
Finance and taxation	36.3	2,147,735
Education	36.3	2,125,268

Source: Florida Department of State, Division of Elections, November 7, 1978 General Election Official Results.

fared the worst followed by the "can of worms," as critics called the Omnibus Proposal. The revision to appoint a nonpartisan reapportionment commission and the judicial selection revisions fared the best, but still failed to secure enough votes to be adopted. In the governor's race (an open seat), 2.53 million citizens cast their vote. Some ballot roll-off is apparent on the constitution revision issues where the highest number of votes cast was on the mini-ERA provision (2.32 million). But over 430,000 voters apparently showed up to the polls and chose not to make a decision on the commission's proposed legislative revision.

The casino initiative that confounded the work of the 1977–78 CRC and consumed the governor's attention appeared after the CRC proposals on the ballot. Voters had to go through a minimum of thirteen other ballot questions to get to the casino question, but there is no doubt that they found it. The casino initiative failed to get even 30 percent of the vote (71.4% opposed), but over 2.4 million voters cast a vote on the issue. Only the governor's race received more attention on November 7, 1978.

That the 1997–98 CRC benefited from the lessons of the 1977–78 CRC when it came to marketing its proposed revisions to the voters would be an understatement of the way in which publicity was viewed by the most recent commission. Combined with its ability to engage in planning, the 1997–98 CRC developed a public relations strategy that went beyond simply selling the voters on revisions. Instead, the steering committee and the staff of the CRC dedicated themselves to educating all of the citizens about the Florida constitution, the processes of constitutional reform in the state, the work of the commission, its procedures and public hearings, and finally, its proposed revisions. By design, the 1997–98 CRC was perhaps one of the most open governmental processes ever seen in the State of Florida; the planners believed that if you could educate the citizens and provide them with clear options they too would recognize the value of meaningful reform.

Starting with the steering committee's work and ending with the November vote on the proposed revisions, an Internet site provided citizens with ongoing information about their constitution revision commission. A citizen's guide was developed by the Collins Center for Public Policy, a nonpartisan research center at Florida State University, entitled "You and Florida's Constitution Revision Commission." The guide was available online and distributed in print throughout the state. Staff members developed lesson plans and activities (puzzles, games, quizzes) for elementary and secondary school programs, and put out a "Kids Page" that was also available in print and online. When the commission was in session, transcripts of the proceedings were posted to the official web site usually within 24 hours and the commission's official journal was also available to the public on the web site. Between October 1996 and December 1997, the CRC web site had been visited over 12,000 times.

Traditional public relations strategies were also deployed. Staff and leadership were regular visitors to chamber of commerce meetings, civic groups, and classrooms around the state even before the commission began its work. For the broader public, the commission published a series of monthly newsletters, "Revision Watch," which included profiles of commissioners, factoids about Florida, and summaries of recent newspaper articles. As noted earlier, the commission also hired a public relations manager who worked with the commission in getting its news into the major media markets in the state.

In July 1998, the CRC leadership commissioned a statewide survey of 800 likely voters. For all of the public relations work that had been done during the previous thirteen months since the commission was sworn, the poll results were probably a bit disheartening to the staff. The survey showed that 88 percent of likely voters had not "seen, read, or heard" about any of the amendments and only 10 percent knew anything specific about the revisions despite the CRC's public campaign strategies.[68] But about 25 percent of those polled had heard about the constitution revision process. More optimistically, the results indicated healthy support for most of the revisions once voters were made aware of them. The most controversial issues of gun control and gender equality (which was once again the subject of a negative campaign despite the careful ballot language) had strong support among the public. The cabinet reorganization and the judicial selection revision proved to be the most likely to be opposed by potential voters, but they were also the items that elicited the highest "don't know" responses.[69]

The poll also generated some publicity of its own. The twenty-five-minute telephone survey cost $45,000 and elicited harsh Republican criticism over spending tax dollars in support of the revisions. The *St. Petersburg Times* reported the Republican Party's spokesman as saying, "The commission has done its job. We don't think they should be out there as spinners or advocates at that level."[70] Negative comments, however, could only generate more interest by the media and thus, more attention by the citizens. And if the poll was accurate, citizens simply needed to know what the revisions were in order to support them.

Commissioners from the 1997–98 CRC assumed various levels of responsibility in campaigning for (and in very few instances, against) the revisions. Commissioner Ellen Freidin was the sponsor and a visible proponent of the gender equality provision while Commissioner Ken Connor, who had negotiated the awkward language of the revision, persistently tried to scare the public into believing that the revision would open the door to gay rights and gay marriages.[71] Commissioner Katherine Fernandez-Rundle, the elected public prosecutor from Miami-Dade County, was a strong advocate for the gun control measure in the face of a well-funded campaign by the National Rifle Association. At the continued urging of Chair Douglass who worked actively for all of the revisions until election day, the 1997–98 CRC commissioners generally presented a united, bipartisan front even after they left Tallahassee in May.

The results of the long public education effort paid off for the constitution revision commission and the state of Florida on Election Day 1998. Curiously, the November 3 election resulted in the lowest voter turnout at a general election since 1962. Only 49 percent of the state's registered voters went to the polls in an election that sent U.S. Senator Bob Graham back to Washington, elected representatives to Congress, the state house, senate and six cabinet officials, and saw a relatively close race for the governor's mansion. Four amendments to the constitution appeared on the ballot above the nine CRC revisions.[72] Citizens seemed to be in an accepting mood adopting all but one of the constitution revisions proposed by the CRC by a margin greater than 55 percent (table 1.3). The education, conservation and gun control revisions mustered over 70 percent support.

TABLE 1.3
November 3, 1998 Election Results on Constitution Revision Commission Proposals

Revision	*% Approval*	*# Votes Cast*
Conservation and Creation of Fish and Wildlife Conservation Commission	72.3	3,638,579
Public Education	71.0	3,696,295
Judicial Selection and Funding of State Courts	56.9	3,564,688
Restructuring State Cabinet	55.5	3,512,545
Basic Rights (Gender Equality)	66.3	3,647,007
Local and Municipal Tax Exemptions/Citizen Access to Local Officials	49.8	3,521,237
Ballot Access, Public Campaign Financing and Election Process Revisions	64.1	3,492,757
Firearms Purchases: Local Option for Criminal History Records Check and Waiting Period	72.0	3,688,030
Miscellaneous Matters and Technical Revisions	55.0	3,399,994

Source: Florida Department of State, Division of Elections, November 3, 1998 General Election Official Results.

Rejected by the voters was a revision that had the *T* word in it—*tax*. In a state with a constitutional prohibition against an income tax and an increasing will to eliminate the intangibles tax, any proposal with the word *tax* in its title is likely to get a careful look. And if voters fail to understand the provision, it is likely to go down to defeat or barely pass muster. The only constitutional amendment that failed in 1998 was the CRC revision titled, "Local And Municipal Property Tax Exemptions and Citizen Access to Local Officials." Had voters understood the provision and its money-saving benefits to cities and towns, they probably would have supported it. In similar fashion, the first constitutional amendment on the ballot (proposed by legislative initiative) was a measure providing tax exemptions for historic properties. It squeaked through with 54.5 percent support.[73]

In sum, the ways in which each commission advertised its work to persuade the undereducated, largely inattentive and generally disinterested public to reform the state's constitution were very different. Experience, planning and technological advancements in information management gave the most recent commission a distinct advantage in capturing the general public's attention. That the CRC extended their publicity campaign beyond simply the revision "products" to matters of basic constitutional education contributed not only to the reform process, but to the development of more informed citizens in the state of Florida. The rewards of this educational effort may be seen when the next generation of Floridians goes to the polls to vote on the constitution revision commission proposals of 2018.

Conclusion

Florida's experiment with an autonomous revision commission has become a successful method of constitutional reform. While the differences between the 1977–78 and the 1997–98 processes are many, my examination of the two iterations suggests that the degree of planning, the nature of state politics and the craftsmanship of procedures, the policies impacted by proposed constitutional reforms, and an effective public relations campaign explain why one commission succeeded in gaining the voter's approval of its work while the other failed. The Florida experience also teaches us that revision commissions serve as agenda-setters whose influence can extend beyond their formal life span. Uhlfelder and McNeely's Monday-morning analysis of the 1977–78 CRC proposals points to the fact that over 40 percent of the significant revisions on the 1978 ballot were subsequently adopted either by the legislature as statutes or proposed as initiatives and put back before the voters as constitutional amendments that were successfully adopted. That percentage climbed even higher since the 1997–98 CRC successfully revived the gender equity issue, partially extended merit selection to trial judges, and managed to finally persuade the public to reduce the number of elected cabinet officials.

Revision commissions, whether autonomous constitutional bodies or statutorily constructed entities, might be considered by other states seeking an alternative to conventions and the traditional amendment process. Conventions typically involve significantly more participants than commissions, have the potential to be costly and time-consuming, and are perceived to be less predictable in terms of policy outcomes. While the election of delegates to conventions is certainly more democratic in form, appointed commissioners are able to represent both political elite and broader citizen interests. Due to their smaller size, commissions may also encourage deliberation and consensus-building that may not be as easily obtained through the convention process.

Revision commissions can also undertake reform on a broader scale than that available through the traditional legislative amendment process.

Legislative reform is generally piecemeal in nature; commissions are able to take a comprehensive view of the constitution, make changes where necessary, and promote internal consistency within the document. The commission process, with its public hearings, also provides for more citizen input than traditionally seen in the legislative amending process. Finally, most commissioners are not subject to the demands of electoral accountability faced by elected officials in the state and are therefore more free to take on politically sensitive topics and deliberate toward a consensual result that may be in the best interests of the state, as a whole.

States that consider invoking a revision commission process should pay heed to the lessons learned in Florida over the past three decades, but also recognize what we do not yet know about this method of reform. Further research needs to examine several aspects of the commission process in greater detail. How citizens get their information on revisions and the most effective means for delivery is directly related to the success of the reform process and merits scholarly examination. Research in this vein is also needed to improve our understanding of voting behavior on revisions, ballot roll-off, ballot ordering, and the language used to describe measures to the voters.[74] One might even go so far as to compare three sets of voters on a variety of measures: those who get messages of endorsement on legislative initiatives; those who vote on measures stemming from the legislative approval of a commission process; and Florida voters who, due to the autonomous nature of the revision process, must typically depend on the diligence of unelected and nonremunerated commissioners to mount a public information campaign in the absence of interest group activity.

Comparisons of the two types of revision commission processes, the autonomous and statutorily based, would also be valuable in order to determine whether the proposals of each vary as to substance or whether the willingness of commissioners to tackle highly salient or controversial issues varies. It may well be that a commission that must submit its proposals to a state legislature will act more constrained than an autonomous commission that might view itself as less constrained by the public. One way to detect such behavior would be through an analysis of the floor and committee deliberations of the statutorily based commission in search of language that anticipates legislative approval. Alternatively, the autonomous commission might also be constrained by the voting public and thus, visibly engage in anticipating voter reaction or interest group activity in its deliberations.

Constitutional reform is an important activity that keeps state government abreast of the changes in contemporary political society. Rooted in principles of republican democracy, Florida's autonomous revision commissions have shown that this regular and deliberative process can avoid the institutional politics of the legislature, the political agendas of the executive and the blatant pressures of special interest groups. As a result, the commission process provides the citizens of the state with a comprehensive examination of their basic law and offers the voters appropriate suggestions for reform.

Notes

1. W. Brooke Graves. "State Constitutional Law: a Twenty-Five Year Summary." *William and Mary Law Review* 8 (1966): 3.

2. While the 1885 document survived its first five years virtually untouched, at every general election from 1890 through 1968 voters were asked to consider one or more amendments, and in each decade of this time period at least ten amendments to the 1885 constitution were adopted, with an all-time high of 12 proposals offered and accepted at the election of 1966. Overall, Floridians adopted nearly 70 percent or 147 of the 211 proposed amendments. See Talbot D'Alemberte, *The Florida State Constitution: A Reference Guide* (Westport, Conn.: Greenwood Press. 1991), p. 9.

3. William C. Havard, "Notes on a Theory of State Constitutional Change: The Florida Experience." *The Journal of Politics* 21 (February 1959): 89–90.

4. *Rivera-Cruz v. Gray*, 104 So. 2d 501 (Fla. 1958).

5. D'Alemberte, *Florida State Constitution*, p. 10, and John Dinan, "'The Earth Belongs Always to the Living Generation': The Development of State Constitutional Amendment and Revision Procedures." *The Review of Politics* 62 (2000): 645–74.

6. D'Alemberte, *Florida State Constitution*, p. 11.

7. "Constitution Revision Commission (of 1998) Home Page." May-August 2001. http://www.law.fsu.edu/crc/.

8. Not unheard of in other states, the commission method was employed as early as 1872 in New York and Georgia. See Robert F. Williams, "Are State Constitutional Conventions Things of the Past? The Increasing Role of the Constitutional Commission in State Constitutional Change," *Hofstra Law and Policy Symposium* 1 (1996): 1–26.

9. Critics have warned that the narrow economic or social rights issues that are raised in the form of initiatives threaten to make the constitution "a state constitutional junkyard." See Daniel R. Gordon, "Protecting Against the State Constitutional Law Junkyard: Proposals to Limit Popular Constitutional Revision in Florida," *Nova Law Review* 20 (1995): 413–35.

10. Williams, "Constitutional Conventions," p. 15.

11. Florida Constitution, article XI, section 2a. In 1996 the Legislature proposed, and the citizens adopted an amendment to article XI, section 2, which required the establishment of the commission within thirty days after the adjournment of the 1997 legislature rather than, as expected, after the adjournment of the 1998 legislature. The change is discussed in detail later in this chapter.

12. Florida Constitution, article XI, section 2c. Because of the executive reorganization adopted by the 1998 revisions, the office of Secretary of State was eliminated in 2003. Thus one of the revisions proposed by the 1998 CRC transformed relevant constitutional language referring to this office as subsequently the "custodian of the records" on the effective date of reorganization.

13. The first Taxation and Budget Reform Commission (TBRC) originally placed four revision proposals on the 1992 ballot. One was removed by the Supreme Court because the ballot summary was not sufficiently clear—see *Smith v. American Airlines*, 606 So.2d 618 (Fla. 1992). This commission is scheduled to meet again in 2007, having had its schedule adjusted by a revision of the 1998 CRC. Under the original design of the TRBC, it was to meet every ten years starting in 1990. It will now meet every twenty years, between CRCs.

14. D'Alemberte, *Florida State Constitution*, p. 13.

15. Steven J. Uhlfelder, "The Machinery of Revision," *Florida State University Law Review* 6 (Summer 1978): 575–88, and W. Dexter Douglass, "The 1997–98 Constitution Revision Commission: Valuable Lessons from a Successful Commission." *Florida Law Review* 52 (2000): 275–83.

16. Steven J. Uhlfelder and Robert A. McNeely, "The 1978 Constitution Revision Commission: Florida's Blueprint for Change." *Nova Law Review* 18 (1994): 1491.

17. Douglass, "Constitution Revision Commission," p. 282.

18. Florida Constitution, article XI, section 5.

19. *In re: Advisory Opinion of the Governor Request of November 19, 1976 (Constitution Revision Commission)*, 343 So. 2d 17 (Fla. 1977), at 20–21.

20. Ibid., at 21–22.

21. Ibid., at 22.

22. Ibid., at 18.

23. Ibid., at 23–24.

24. Uhlfelder, "Machinery of Revision," p. 576. A similar effort was made in the 1978 legislative session and also failed. Additionally, a resolution that would have eliminated the constitution revision process was introduced that year, but was not approved.

25. Laws of Florida. "Constitution Revision Commission; powers of chair; assistance by state and local agencies." Chapter 77–201 and chapter 95–148, codified at 19 F.S. §286.035. 2000. 1997.

26. Telephone interview, Steven A. Uhlfelder, 23 July 2001.

27. Uhlfelder, "Machinery of Revision," p. 587.

28. Robert L. Shevin, "Report and Recommendations of Attorney General Robert L. Shevin to the 1978 Constitution Revision Commission." (June 1977). Tallahassee, Florida.

29. Uhlfelder, "Machinery of Revision," p. 587.

30. Uhlfelder, "Machinery of Revision; Steven J. Uhlfelder and Billy Buzzett, "Constitution Revision Commission: A Retrospective and Prospective Sketch." *The Florida Bar Journal* LXXI (April 1997): 22–29; Uhlfelder and McNeely, "The 1978 Constitution Revision Commission," and *Journal of the 1997–1998 Constitution Revision Commission*, pp. 19–20.

31. "Governor's Constitution Revision Steering Committee." Executive Order 96–194 (Fla.). 1996.

32. Douglass, "Constitution Revision Commission," p. 277.

33. Billy Buzzett, "The Article V Task Force: A Mini-Constitutional Revision Commission." *The Florida Bar Journal* (July/Aug 1995): 49.

34. "Minutes of the Constitution Revision Commission (of 1998) Steering Committee," August 20, 1996. 2001. http://www.aif.com/CRC/Minutes/CRC001.HTM through /CRC003.HTM).

35. Ibid.

36. Laws of Florida. "An act relating to the Constitution Revision Commission." chapter 97-7. 1997. This bill also directed the Joint Legislative Management Committee to provide support for the commission. W. Dexter Douglass reports that $100,000 was provided to the steering committee in 1996; $400,000 to the CRC in 1997; and $1.2 million in 1998—see Douglass, "Constitution Revision Commission," p. 277, footnote 12. I have scanned each bill and believe the data reported in my text are correct.

37. Laws of Florida. "Appropriations—General." Chapter 97–152 (see especially Item 1495A). 1997.

38. Laws of Florida. "Appropriations—General." Chapter 98–422 (see especially Items 1575, 2139, and section 13). 1998.

39. Douglass, "Constitution Revision Commission," p. 277.

40. Uhlfelder and Buzzett, "Constitution Revision Commission," p. 24.

41. W. Dexter Douglass, "The 1997–98 Constitution Revision Commission: A Progress Report," *The Florida Bar Journal* 72 (June 1998): 14.

42. *In re: Advisory Opinion of the Governor Request of November 19, 1976 (Constitution Revision Commission)*, 343 So. 2d 17 (Fla. 1977).

43. *Opinion of the Attorney General of the State of Florida: Constitution Revision Commission*, July 5, 1977, Op. Atty. Gen. Fla. 144 (1977), at 144.

44. Uhlfelder, "Machinery of Revision," pp. 582–83.

45. Ibid., at 584–85.

46. "Constitution Revision Commission (of 1998) Home Page." May-August 2001. http://www.law.fsu.edu/crc/: CRC Proceedings, 3/17/98, at 13–14.

47. Kelley H. Armitage, "Constitution Revision Commissions Avoid Logrolling, Don't They?" *The Florida Bar Journal* 72 (November 1998): 63.

48. "Minutes of the Constitution Revision Commission (of 1998) Steering Committee," August 20, 1996. 2001. http://www.aif.com/CRC/Minutes/CRC001.HTM through /CRC003.HTM).

49. Uhlfelder, "Machinery of Revision," p. 586.

50. Laws of Florida. "An act relating to regulation of lobbyists." Chapter 97-12, codified at 10 F.S. §112.3215. 2000. "Lobbyists before the executive branch or the Constitution Revision Commission." 1997.

51. Diane Rado and Peter Wallsten. "Constitution panel sought backers." *St. Petersburg Times.* 1 August 1997: 1B.

52. David Cox, "State Panel No Longer to Be Wined, Dined," *Tampa Tribune*, 2 August 1997: Fla./Metro 6.

53. Grady A. Epstein, "Constitution Panel Hires Image Help," *Tampa Tribune*, 7 August 1997: Fla/Metro 6.

54. Rebecca Mae Salokar, "Creating a State Constitutional Right to Privacy: Unlikely Alliances, Uncertain Results." *Constitutional Politics in the States.* Ed. G. Alan Tarr. Westport, CT: Greenwood Press, 1996. 73–97; Albert L. Strum, "The Development of American State Constitutions." *Publius* 12 (Winter 1982): 57–98; Uhlfelder and McNeely, "The 1978 Constitution Revision Commission," and Uhlfelder and Buzzett, "Constitution Revision Commission."

55. *Information Bank Abstracts: Miami Herald.* New York: The New York Times Company, 16 (24 June 1978).

56. *Information Bank Abstracts: Miami Herald.* New York: The New York Times Company, 27 (22 Oct. 1978).

57. Uhlfelder and McNeely, "The 1978 Constitution Revision Commission," p, 1507.

58. W. Dexter Douglass and Billy Buzzett. "Constitution Revision Commission: Planning the Process." *The Florida Bar Journal* 71 (April 1997): 16–21, and John F. Harkness, Jr., "The Florida Bar's Proper Role in the Constitution Revision Process." *Florida Bar Journal* 72 (October 1998): 10.

59. D'Alemberte, *Florida State Constitution*; Gordon, "Protecting Against State Constitutional Law Junkyard"; and Uhlfelder and McNeely, "The 1978 Constitution Revision Commission."

60. Following the completion of the CRC process, Douglass initiated a citizen initiative petition to create an independent nonpartisan commission that would reapportion both state legislative and congressional seats, stripping that power away from the legislature.

61. *Advisory Opinion to the Attorney General Re: Fish and Wildlife Conservation Commission: Unifies Marine Fisheries and Game and Fresh Water Fish Commissions*, 705 So. 2d 1351 (Fla. 1998).

62. The 1998 voting data beg for analysis on measures of turnout and ballot roll-off especially in light of the gubernatorial race, as well as comparative work on CRC proposals that appeared after four other constitutional amendments on the 1998 ballot.

63. Uhlfelder, "Machinery of Revision."

64. Alaine S. Williams, "A Summary and Background Analysis of the Proposed 1978 Constitutional Revisions." *Florida State University Law Review* 6 (1978): 1115–71.

65. Robert L. Floyd, "President's Page: Constitutional Revision." *The Florida Bar Journal* 52 (October 1978): 585.

66. Ibid.

67. W. Dexter Douglass, "Con: Merit Retention—Another Assault on the Elective Process," *The Florida Bar Journal* 52 (October 1978): 645–46.

68. Margaret Talev, "Constitution Revisions Do Well in Poll." *Tampa Tribune* 28 July 1998: Fla/Metro 6.

69. Peter Wallsten, "Poll Shows Voters Not Informed on Issues." *St. Petersburg Times* 29 July 1998: 1B.

70. Ibid.

71. David Cox, "Proposed Constitutional Amendment May Affect Suit." *Tampa Tribune*, 28 October 1998: Fla./Metro 1; and Curtis Krueger, "Voters Will Decide War of the Words." *St. Petersburg Times* 4 October 1997: 1B.

72. The four other amendments were all legislatively sponsored initiatives: Historic Property Tax Exemption and Assessment; Preservation of the Death Penalty, United States Supreme Court Interpretation of Cruel and Unusual Punishment; Additional Homestead Tax Exemption; and a measure permitting Recording of Instruments in Branch Offices.

73. "Florida Department of State, Division of Elections, November 3, 1998 General Election Official Results: Constitutional Amendment." 2001. http://election.dos.state.fl.us/elections/resultsarchive/Index.asp?ElectionDate=11/3/1998&DATAMODE=

74. Mark A. Smith, "The Contingent Effects of Ballot Initiatives and Candidate Races on Turnout." *American Journal of Political Science* 45 (July 2001): 700–06.

2

Constitutional Revision in California

The Triumph of Amendment over Revision

Bruce E. Cain

Constitutional revision has never been easy to achieve in California. Of the various alternative ways to reform a constitution, the most politically difficult path is by convention. Between 1879 (i.e., the date the current California constitution was adopted) and 1934, there were four failed attempts to convene new constitutional conventions. Prior to 1993, the experience with constitutional revision commissions had been somewhat more encouraging. Commissions were formed in 1929 and 1963, the latter leading to the highly important (but now controversial) proposal to create a professional, full-time legislature.

But if revision has been infrequent, constitutional amendment in California has been common. From 1879 to the mid-nineties, California ranked first in the nation in proposed amendments (812) and second in adopted ones (485), averaging 4.29 per year.[1] While there is in principle an important legal distinction between a revision and an amendment with respect to the quantity and quality of proposed changes, the reality is that the California courts have not been very concerned about enforcing the line between them. When, for instance, Proposition 140 imposed term limits on the state legislature and cut its budget by 40 percent, the state Supreme Court did not even seriously review the merits of the argument that this was a revision and not a mere amendment. And yet, there are many who would argue that term limits is the most significant change in postwar California government.

Hence, there is an odd puzzle in California. It is easy to amend, but almost impossible to revise the state constitution. Why is this the case? Does it matter? If major changes can be accomplished through the initiative process, then perhaps it is of no consequence that constitutional revisions are difficult to achieve. On the other hand, if a constitutional convention or a revision commission provides a more integrated perspective, then the shift away from revision and toward amendment may be misshaping California state structure in important and predictable ways.

In this chapter, I will consider the problems of constitutional revision in the light of the experiences of the 1993–96 California Constitutional Revision Commission.[2] This Commission undertook a comprehensive look at California governance and ultimately proposed some far-reaching and imaginative ideas. But in the end, these recommendations never got to a vote in the legislature, let alone a place on the ballot. While the prospects of constitutional revision in California in the immediate future are dim, new amendments continue to surface every two years. In the first section of the chapter, I contrast the obstacles Constitutional Revision faces as compared with those faced by Initiative Constitutional Amendments (ICAs) and Legislative Constitutional Amendments (LCAs). In the second section, I discuss the possible implications of sequential changes by amendment versus a more comprehensive revision.

THE VARYING PATHS OF REVISION AND AMENDMENT

California provides for several methods of constitutional change.[3] Revisions, intended as substantial changes in quantity or quality, can be proposed by a constitutional convention and then placed on the ballot directly. Another alternative is to form a constitutional revision commission whose recommendations are subsequently considered by the legislature and the voters. Constitutional amendments can be passed out of the legislature (LCAs) and placed on the ballot, or can go on the ballot directly in the form of a citizen's initiative (ICAs). As one might imagine, the politics of these procedures vary in important ways.

In the constitutional revision process, there are effectively three veto points. First, depending on the composition of the commission, proposals can be terminated inside the commission itself. For instance, the 1993 Commission was initially intrigued with the idea of a unicameral legislature. Given that the apportionment revolution had placed both the upper and lower houses on an equal population share basis, and that the requirement of deliberation by two houses often delayed the passage of bills significantly (and sometimes led to game playing and secret deals in conference committees), three prominent California state legislators strongly pushed for the adoption of either a parliamentary system (Senators Alquist and Keene) or at least a Nebraska-style unicameral legislature (Senator Lucy Killea). Others felt that there might be political value in linking what was likely to be the popular idea of unicameral reform (i.e., because it would save money) with the less popular idea of lengthening California's comparatively strict term limits to twelve years (which many legislators and insiders thought was far more important). Eventually, however, the idea died in the commission before it issued its final report. Enough of them feared that the idea was too controversial and would doom the rest of their proposals.[4]

A second veto point occurs when the legislature reviews the Commission's recommendation and decides whether and how to vote for them. In order for a revision commission's proposals to be placed on the ballot, they need the approval of two-thirds of the state legislature. The key interests at this stage are those of the legislators and the powerful interest groups that lobby and deal with the legislature regularly.

A good example of how legislator interests factored into the 1996 outcome was the Commission's proposal to reduce the number of statewide elected officials. While the conception of a plural executive was built into the original 1879 framework, the number of elected officials had expanded in recent years. Proposition 103 had made the office of Insurance Commissioner elected, and an earlier initiative, the so-called Big Green, had tried to create an elected Commissioner of the Environment.[5]

The allure of elected executive offices is that they enhance popular control, but many Commissioners and some scholars felt that they blurred the lines of accountability and opened the door to special interest influence. As evidence on this point, there was a subsequent insurance scandal in California, in which the elected Insurance Commissioner, Charles Quackenbush, created special political accounts for Insurance companies to contribute to in lieu of making larger settlement payments. The problem with elections as a form of control is that in order to get the funds necessary to win votes elected executives can end up being more beholden to special interests and less responsive to the needs of consumers than appointed officials. With this in mind, the Revision Commission recommended that three statewide elected officials be appointed (the insurance commissioner, the treasurer, and the superintendent of public instruction).

To be sure, the case for elected versus appointed officials can be argued either way on purely rational grounds, but the reality is that it was doomed from the start for crassly political reasons; namely, in a term limits era, state legislators did not want to close off options for running for a statewide office. Whatever this reform might do for clearing up lines of accountability and making decisions more efficient, it had the unfortunate political byproduct of leaving three fewer opportunities for those who wanted to continue their political careers.

Another example of legislative self-interest was the opposition to the unicameral legislature. Many in the State Senate were opposed to the Commission's unicameral idea, because they perceived that a single house would put them in a less prestigious position. Those in leadership positions could not be sure that they would retain them in a single house structure (e.g., would the leadership of the upper or the lower house control the new single house). Some did not like the idea of only being one of 120 members, representing significantly smaller districts. Still others thought that they would get less staff resources if they were part of a larger house.

Legislators, it should be said, did not oppose everything that the Commission came up with. Many of them were frustrated with the supermajority vote needed to pass the state budget and favored its abolition. They welcomed the recommendation for two-year budgets, the call for a four-year capital outlay plan, and the adoption of long-term budgetary goals and performance measures. And any loosening of the harsh term limitations would receive majority approval in the California legislature. Since initiatives were a constant source of problem for the legislature, they favored the Commission's mild reforms in this area as well. But the critical question was how much the legislature was willing to swallow to get what they wanted. In the end, the answer proved to be not as much as the Commission was asking for, especially given significant opposition from their key interest and constituency groups.

Interest groups of many different varieties figured prominently in the second stage of constitutional revision. Local government officials and teachers, for instance, were important players in the constitutional revision drama. Both liked the idea that they would get more opportunity to supplement revenue to local schools either through a two-thirds vote on property tax increases or a majority sales tax vote, but both objected strenuously to other aspects of the Commission's report. Special district officials feared that the Commission's Community Charter proposal would lead to widespread consolidations of their districts. Teachers feared that the elimination of the elected superintendent of schools would place too much power in the hands of the governor and his State Board of Education. In retrospect, this fear was highly colored by the fact that the sitting governor was a Republican who had crossed swords frequently with the teachers' unions while the Superintendent of Schools was a more sympathetic Democrat. This illustrates the predictable point that where people stand in the Constitutional Reform debate often depends upon where other people sit.

Also active in the revision discussions were the taxpayer groups. Elements of the Commission's proposals were clearly designed to court their support, for example, a requirement that the state's budget be balanced or that the state should maintain a 3 percent general fund reserve. But the taxpayer groups did not like the fact that the Commission tried to restore local control over local taxes under a simple majority vote or that it provided for supplemental school funding.

Clearly, all types of constitutional reform (i.e., revisions or amendments) will often have to overcome opposition by key interest and constituency groups. But, processes vary in terms of how and when interest group intervention occurs. A constitutional revision commission provides several opportunities: at the time commissioners are appointed, when the legislature takes up the commission's proposals, and then later in the electoral battle. At the point that the proposals reach the legislature, the most important power is negative; that is, the ability to block undesirable proposals by putting pressure on key legislators to kill the offending measures before they are placed on the ballot.

Finally, there is the electoral stage. Assuming the whole package, or at least some part of it, emerges from the legislature, it must be sold to the voters. Here again, elected officials and interest groups have some influence over the final outcome since they help run and finance the campaign for the proposition. They can also work against a measure, or allow it to die by not giving it the support it needs to win.

By comparison, constitutional change by amendment has fewer hurdles and veto points. A group of citizens can hire a consultant to help draft the changes they want. With the help of a professional signature gathering firm and a little financial support, the measure can gain enough signatures to go on the ballot with legislative approval. The key to success is winning the public's approval.

Opinion is divided as to whether the popular initiative process has been captured by special interests or not. Journalists like Peter Schrag and

David Broder believe that there are enough examples of interest groups getting what they want from the initiative process, but political scientist Elizabeth Gerber's research suggests that interest groups are more successful in stopping what they do not like than passing what they like.[6] Assuming that the latter is true at least, it has the same implication for constitutional revision and amendments: in the final stage of public approval, the opposition of key interest groups can seriously undermine the prospects of constitutional change.

In sum, the fact that there are greater obstacles facing revisions than amendments goes a long way towards explaining why California amends constantly and revises sparingly. But does it matter?

The Significance of Revision Versus Amendment

In theory, constitutional revision should be more comprehensive and qualitatively more significant than a constitutional amendment.[7] But what if revision occurs increasingly through amendment: What is gained and what is lost? The most important advantage should lie in the ability of a Revision Commission to consider how all the pieces fit together. Where the amendment process is piecemeal and sequential, the revision process affords the opportunity to logically relate proposals to goals, and to make the entire package of proposal coherent.

This is illustrated by the California Commission's early discussions. Formed at a time of an acute fiscal crisis amid the California recession in the early nineties, the Revision Commission was given a mandate to solve policy problems by fixing governmental structure. In all of its publications, the Revision Commission was careful to spell out its goals and to explain the connection between those goals and specific recommendations. In general, the five goals it focused on were: improving the accountability and responsiveness of state and local governments, eliminating barriers to efficiency, increasing flexibility, and enhancing fiscal integrity.

Most of the recommendations relating to the state's executive branch focused on the absence of accountability and responsiveness. In the words of the final report, "The current organization of the state's executive branch does not promote responsiveness or efficiency in the execution of state policy. The executive branch is divided among a dozen elected public officials with few direct lines of accountability. This dispersion of power creates inflexibility and fragmentation and reduces responsiveness and efficiency."[8] To this end, they proposed that the governor and lieutenant governor run on the same ticket, that there should be a reduction in the number of statewide elected officials, and that the Board of Equalization should be abolished.

By comparison, on the subject of the California legislature, the Commission was more concerned about its stability and effectiveness. It worried that the term limitations were too short to allow legislators to become knowledgeable: "Rapid turnover has resulted in large numbers of freshmen legislators who are not knowledgeable about the complexities of the legislative process. This lack of experience often results in an inability to deal with complex and difficult policy issues that involve some amount of history."[9] Its solution was to lengthen terms so that each member could serve three four-year terms in each house and that the limits should be staggered so that one-half of each house would be elected every two years.

Whether or not one agreed with the specific proposals, it is apparent that the Commission made a valiant attempt to link its recommendations tightly to a small set of specified goals. In its final report, the Commission very carefully spelled out the rationale behind each of its proposals. The Commission structure in this case permitted a deliberative methodology that attempted to make coherent proposals based on logic, testimony, and evidence. The meetings were open, and the actions of the body well documented by the press. By comparison, ICAs are composed in private and offer little documentation of how the proposals came into being.[10] From a democratic theory point of view, the revision process seems vastly superior in this regard.

However, there is more to contemporary constitution reform than rational logic and deliberation. A successful constitutional change must succeed in terms of political and popular logic as well. And because these last two screens are so important, it may be that the usefulness and practicality of deliberative constitutional revision is much diminished in the modern era. A closer inspection of the California's experience reveals that while the Commission made concessions to political logic and public opinion, they did not go far enough. That resulted in the quick demise of the Commission's final report. As a result, the most likely prospect of significant constitutional change in California is through the sequential passage of separately formulated ICAs and LCAs.

THE DOMINANCE OF POLITICAL LOGIC AND PUBLIC OPINION

In an ideal world, constitution making is a logical and analytical exercise. Decision makers define general goals that help link solutions to well specified problem in clear and coherent ways. In reality, modern constitutional revision is formed as much by political and electoral logic as by rational deliberation. Political logic refers to the appeal that changes have to key groups and constituencies in a society. As with policy, the political prospects of a constitutional change depend upon three considerations: first, the distributive consequences of given proposals; second, the relative power of winners and losers; and third, the ability of proponents to win over a sufficient number of swing groups to form a minimum wining coalition.

With respect to the first point, the distributive consequences, constitutional changes usually have material or power/influence consequences for various groups in the political system. Returning to the example of the 1993 Commission, the proposals to have the lieutenant governor run on the same ticket as the governor, or the suggestion that the elected superintendent of schools be made an appointed position, clearly would have strengthened the governor's hand. At the time it was proposed, it would have also fortified the position of Republicans relative to Democrats since the governor was a Republican and the lieutenant governor and the superintendent of schools were Democrats. In effect, the Revision Commission's proposals distributed power and influence in two dimensions: institutionally (in favor of the executive branch) and by party.

Political actors should probably discount the short-term partisan consequences if they believe that their party might eventually control the governorship. But that did not happen in the California case for two reasons: first, because the political stakes at the moment seemed so high, and second, because there had only been three Democratic governors prior to 1998 since the turn of the century. Far from assuming the Rawlsian veil of ignorance, players in the California constitutional battle scrutinized each proposal with a view toward how it affected them.[11] Predictably, the winners under the status quo resisted proposals that made them weaker, and vice versa, the losers under the status quo favored proposals that made them stronger.

The second consideration with respect to the prospects of constitutional reform is how powerful and/or numerous the winners (i.e., as defined above) are as compared to the losers. It is almost a certainty that any important constitutional change will affect important interests. The 1993 Commission could have taken a safer political route by not alienating hard-to-defeat interests, but this would have eliminated any proposals that affected taxes (because taxpayers groups are quite powerful in California and politicians do not want to be labeled as pro-tax), institutional structure (because politicians control the second stage of the revision process), and initiative reform (because the initiative industry can mobilize significant opposition in an election).

Alternatively, the Commission could have picked a dominant coalition of interests and made sure that all of its proposals favored them. Instead, it chose to give and take a little from everyone. The idea was that if everyone got something and felt that structural change was important (i.e., because there was a fiscal crisis), they would be willing to compromise and lose something as well. As the recession receded and the sense of crisis abated, the perceived pressure to do something dropped between the time of the Commission's appointment in 1993 and its final report in 1996. At some point in that period, the perspective of each affected constituency changed: instead of choosing between different reforms, the prospect of sticking with the status quo was now on the table.

From the Republican perspective, the Commission's recommendations gave them a balanced budget and enhanced gubernatorial power, but at the cost of losing supermajority taxing rules at the local level. Sticking with the status quo in 1996 looked more attractive. Conversely, Democrats liked the more flexible taxing authority the Revision Commission's proposals offered, but not the budget and executive branch changes. The status quo looked better to them as well. If there was a constitutional moment, it had surely passed by 1996. The better moment was in 1993 when the status quo did not seem viable.

The absence of swing groups was also a problem for the Revision Commission. Again, this was partly a matter of tactics. Many of the problems that the Revision Commission took on were important and highly polarized, and had been referred to them precisely because offsetting powerful interests or the fear of public retaliation had stalemated the normal political processes. For instance, since the passage of Proposition 13, property tax reform had become the third rail of California politics—untouchable for politicians who wanted to be reelected, because it impacted property owners in such a critical way. Or to take another example, even though many experts believed that initiatives had created a disjointed and highly constrained budgetary process, no elected official dared to propose amending direct democracy. The unstated premise of the 1993 Commission was that it could make hard political choices that the legislature and governor could not or would not make, but in the end, the Commission's proposals had to be vetted by the legislature and the voters anyway. The legislature would be vulnerable for the vote it took on the recommendations, and the public had the ultimate say without the benefit of participating in the Revision Commission's deliberations. The hope that the forces that stalemated the governor and legislature would not stalemate the Revision Commission was ultimately ephemeral.

THE VOICE OF THE PEOPLE

The ultimate determinant of the success or failure of modern constitutional revision is public opinion. The eighteenth-century federal model of a convention—respected notables whose proposals are ratified by state legislatures—is simply not relevant to modern state constitutions. All routes to revision and amendment in California lead ultimately to public opinion. The people ultimately determine what can and cannot be accomplished in terms of constitutional reform.

The public opinion aspect of constitutional revision consists of two parts: what the public will understand and what will appeal to them. The question of the public's comprehension is important, because there are many technical issues that voters will not readily understand nor have the patience to master. The recommendations of the California Constitution Revision Commission included several worthwhile proposals that unfortunately would have been hard to explain to the public if they had ever reached the ballot. For instance, the Commission's report calls for the "legislature to be authorized to include in a single implementation bill any statutory changes needed to implement the budget bill."[12]

Put simply, California currently limits all legislation to a single subject, preventing the legislature from combining all budget-related changes into one bill and forcing them to consider twenty to thirty different bills. If any of the implementing bills fails, it can throw the entire budget out of balance. Allowing the legislature to pass a single budget implementation bill would avoid this problem. However important to everyday legislative operations, it would be difficult to explain this clearly to voters and to convince them that this was worthy of their attention.

Normally, measures that appeal to voters are easy to understand and expressive of the public's general mistrust of government and politicians. A good example is the Commission's recommendation that the governor and legislators forfeit their salaries if the state budget is not passed by June 30 would likely pass overwhelmingly. The problem is that the simple solution is not necessarily the best one. California's budgetary problems required a systematic overhaul of the property tax system and the legislative approval process. Simply forcing legislators to make timely decisions does not address the underlying problems. But it would likely win, because it expresses the voters' frustrations with government.

There has been a decade-long debate in political science about how much voters understand about technical initiatives and whether they can finds ways to make good decisions without being informed.[13] Pessimists argue that voters make little effort to understand complicated measures, although they often have the sense to vote no when in doubt. Optimists believe that voters can choose as if they are informed (even when they are not) by paying attention to key interest groups and individuals who become informed for them. Because there is scholarly disagreement, it is hard to draw a firm conclusion about the voters' competence to judge constitutional issues. It is at least a potential problem for constitutional measures, because many of them are technical in nature.

Beyond the question of what voters understand, there is the matter of which voters control the outcome. In both the revision and amendment processes, the state's median voter controls the final outcome of any proposed change. Hence, successful constitutional reform in the contemporary era will have a majoritarian bias no matter whether it originates as an amendment or revision. Consider the question of initiative reform. Many in California believe that the initiative process has been used excessively and too often by special interests. But in order to change the initiative process, one would have to ask the voters whom the process has served well to give up their control over policy outcomes. This is unlikely to happen. If the majority retains control through direct democracy mechanisms, they are unlikely to surrender that control willingly. So in the end, the eighteenth-century concept of a constitution that balances the rights of the minority against those of the majority simply makes no sense at the state level. Measures that would protect or favor a minority against the majority's will cannot make it through the constitutional approval process.

Thus, the strategic issue a modern Constitutional Revision Commission faces is whether to make their "best" recommendations or to go forward with only those that meet the essential political and electoral requirements. The problem with the pure strategy is that while it might be bold and innovative, it will likely be unsuccessful unless the polity is in the grips of an extremely severe crisis. Unless the point of the revision effort is simply to make a high-minded statement about what should be done, it is not likely to be an effective strategy, if effective means something that results in actual change.

The alternative strategy is to work back from what is politically and electorally feasible to what is desirable. Identify the proposals that are likely to have a chance first, and then concentrate efforts there. Moreover, revision efforts have to become more sophisticated about public opinion just as the experts who run the campaigns for constitutional amendments have. Revision commissions should test their ideas immediately with polls and focus groups. While some might recoil in horror at a less deliberative and more political approach, the alternative is to surrender all constitutional change to the amendment process. As we have pointed out before, revision, even in a political form, offers a better hope of some coherence and logical connection between proposed changes. If the revision process is to succeed in the future, it cannot operate as if it is in an eighteenth-century political environment.

NOTES

1. Bruce E. Cain, Sara Ferejohn, Margarita Najar, and Mary Walther, "Constitutional Change: Is It Too Easy to Amend Our State Constitution?," in Bruce E. Cain and Roger G. Noll, eds., *Constitutional Reform in California* (Berkeley: IGS Press, 1995).

2. California Constitution Revision Commission, Final Report and Recommendations to the Governor and the Legislature, 1996.

3. See discussion in Bruce E. Cain and Roger G. Noll, "Principles of State Constitutional Design," in Cain and Noll, *Constitutional Reform in California.*

4. "Sacramento--State Panel Won't Push One-House Legislature," *San Francisco Chronicle,* February 7, 1996. http://www.sfgate.com/cgi-bin/article.cgi?file=/chronicle/archive/1996/02/07MNE38697.DTL.

5. Noll, Roger, "Executive Organization: Responsiveness v. Expertise and Flexibility," in Cain and Noll, *Constitutional Reform in California.*

6. Peter Schrag, *Paradise Lost: California's Experience, America's Future* (New York: New Press, 1998; David Broder, *Democracy Derailed: Initiative Campaigns and the Power of Money* (New York: Harcourt, 2000); and Elizabeth R. Gerber, *The Populist Paradox* (Princeton: Princeton University Press, 1999).

7. Lowenstein, Daniel Hays and Richard L. Hasen, *Election Law: Cases and Materials*, 2nd ed. (Durham: Carolina Academic Press, 2001), chapter 6.

8. California Constitution Revision Commission Report (1996), p. 15.

9. California Constitution Revision Commission Report (1996), p. 24.

10. Bruce E. Cain and Kenneth Miller, "The Populist Legacy: Initiatives and the Undermining of Representative Government," in Larry Sabato, Howard Ernst and Bruce Larson, eds., *Dangerous Democracy* (Lanham, Md.: Roman & Littlefield, 2001).

11. John Rawls, *A Theory of Justice* (Cambridge: Belknap Press of Harvard University Press, 1971).

12. California Constitution Revision Report (1996), p. 44.

13. Arthur Lupia, "Busy Voters, Agenda Control and the Power of Information," *American Political Science Review* 86 (1992): 390–404; Arthur Lupia, "Shortcuts Versus Encyclopedias: Information and Voting Behavior in California Insurance Reform Elections," *American Political Science Review* 88 (1994): 63–76; Thomas E. Cronin, *Direct Democracy: The Politics of Initiative, Referendum and Recall* (Cambridge: Harvard University Press, 1989); Arthur Lupia and Matthew McCubbins, *The Democratic Dilemma: Can Citizens Learn What They Need to Know?* (New York: Cambridge University Press, 1998); and David B. Magleby, *Direct Legislation: Voting on Ballot Propositions in the United States* (Baltimore: Johns Hopkins Press, 1984).

3

Adopting a New Constitution

Lessons from Virginia

A. E. Dick Howard

"The earth belongs always to the living generation."[1] So said Thomas Jefferson in developing a constitutional theory that included the belief that Virginia's Constitution should be revised at regular intervals "so that it may be handed on, with periodical repairs, from generation to generation. . . ."[2]

Despite such advice, some generations of Americans have shown more interest than others in revising their state constitutions. For about a quarter of a century—from the 1920s into the 1940s—no American state adopted a new constitution. By midcentury, however, interest in revising these fundamental laws had burgeoned. So widespread was the movement for constitutional revision that by 1970, a leading student of the subject commented that there was at that time "more official effort directed toward revising and rewriting state constitutions than at any time in the nation's history with the possible exception of the Civil War and Reconstruction era."[3]

Some of these revision efforts were notably successful, for example, the rewriting of the Hawaii Constitution, which was approved by the people of the state in November 1968. Other revisions ended in failure, perhaps the most conspicuous instances being those of New York in 1967 and Maryland in 1968. Indeed, in modern times, many states have found it more difficult to secure popular approval of a revised constitution. When Virginians went to the polls in November 1970 to vote on a new constitution for the Commonwealth, those who hoped the result would be favorable had before them the unfortunate experience of a number of sister states. Although some states had succeeded in at least partial revision, since 1967 the voters

---

This article originally appeared as "Constitutional Revision: Virginia and the Nation," 9 *U. Rich. L. Review.* 1–48 (1974). Reprinted with the permission of the *University of Richmond Law Review.*

of New York, Rhode Island, Maryland, New Mexico, Oregon, Arkansas, and Idaho had rejected proposed new charters for their states. Yet when Virginia voted on four questions comprising a revised Constitution, each one passed, and by percentages ranging from a low of 63 percent to a high (on the main body of the Constitution) of 72 percent.

Why some states have been successful in updating their constitutions and others have failed turns on a complex range of factors. The reasons for success and failure lie partly in circumstances peculiar to a given state and partly in patterns that tend to emerge whenever constitutions are revised. The account relates Virginia's experience to that of several other states which undertook to rewrite their constitutions during the years immediately before and after Virginia's action.

REVISING THE CONSTITUTION OF VIRGINIA

When Virginia undertook the constitutional revision which had its successful climax in the voting of November 1970, it had been forty years since the Virginia Constitution had been the subject of any thorough study. Even that previous revision, which took place in 1928, was a limited one, concerned largely with housekeeping changes. In fact, the document, as of 1968, was largely the product of the Constitutional Convention of 1901–02.[4] The Constitution that that body wrote was heavily influenced by late nineteenth-century attitudes tending to produce documents more nearly resembling detailed statutes than constitutions. As a result, by the late 1960s there was a rising realization that the Virginia Constitution was long overdue for updating.

The initiative for revision in 1968 came from Governor Mills E. Godwin, Jr. Realizing the need to bring Virginia's fundamental law into line with the Commonwealth's needs and aspirations, Governor Godwin, in his welcoming address to the General Assembly in January 1968, called attention to the effect of the "inexorable passage of time" on the Virginia Constitution. He therefore proposed that the Assembly authorize him to create a commission to recommend revision.[5]

By joint resolution the Assembly authorized the Governor to create an eleven-member Commission on Constitutional Revision.[6] Governor Godwin forthwith named eleven distinguished Virginians to the Commission, which was chaired by former Governor Albertis S. Harrison, Jr., a Justice of the Supreme Court of Virginia, and which was in every sense a "blue-ribbon" body.[7]

Moving promptly to their task, the commissioners appointed a University of Virginia law professor, A. E. Dick Howard, as executive director, who, in turn, organized the Commission's staff. The Commission was divided into five subcommittees corresponding roughly, but not precisely, to major areas of the Constitution. Each subcommittee was assigned legal counsel, drawn either from the practicing bar or from one of the law faculties in Virginia. Further to support the work of the Commission and its subcommittees, various individuals, mostly law students, were engaged to work during the summer of 1968 and produced about 150 research memoranda.

The Commission actively solicited the views of Virginia citizens. In April 1968 a letter signed by the chairman was distributed widely to individuals and organizations, inviting their ideas on any aspect of the constitution. Announcements of this invitation were given via newspapers, radio stations, and television stations throughout Virginia. Moreover, in June and July a series of five public hearings were held at different locations in the Commonwealth.

Most of the subcommittee work was done during the summer of 1968. The full Commission met with increasing frequency to deliberate proposals coming from the subcommittees, and by late fall a tentative draft for a revised constitution had taken shape. In addition to approving the text of the revisions, the Commission sifted and approved detailed commentaries to explain its proposals to the governor, the General Assembly, and the public at large. On January 1, 1969, the Commission concluded its work by delivering to the Governor and Assembly a 542-page report.[8]

Among the Commission's more notable proposals were those that would commit the Commonwealth to quality education for its youth and would include education among the fundamentals recognized by the Bill of Rights. To finance needed capital improvements, the Commission recommended allowing some state borrowing, the ceiling to be tied to the Commonwealth's general fund revenues. For the first time in Virginia's history, a clause forbidding discrimination on the basis of race, color, or national origin would be added to the Bill of Rights. The period of residence required for voting in Virginia would be reduced. Apportionment of seats in Congress and in the General Assembly would be based on population, and districts would be contiguous and compact. To remedy a gap in the old Constitution the Commission proposed a provision (modeled after the Twenty-fifth Amendment to the Federal Constitution) dealing with problems of a disabled governor. All cities and those counties over 25,000 population would be able to adopt and amend their own charters and to exercise all powers not denied them by the Constitution, their charters, or statutes enacted by the General Assembly. In keeping with rising concern about environmental quality, the Commission proposed a new conservation article.

In addition to these and other specific recommendations, the Commission overhauled the Constitution in general. Obsolete sections, such as those dealing with dueling and with the poll tax, were deleted. Applying the principle that a constitution embodies fundamental law and that unnecessary detail ought to be left to the statute books, the Commission proposed excising vast amounts of such statutory matter, especially in the lengthy and cumbersome corporations article. The revised Constitution also represented a general reorganization, so that closely related subjects would be dealt with together. Overall, the result was a crisper, more coherent document half the length of the existing Constitution (which was about 35,000 words).

Called into special session in March 1969, the General Assembly approved, with some significant changes, the bulk of the Commission's proposals. In some ways the Assembly was more cautious than the Commission, in other ways bolder. While the legislators agreed that the Commonwealth's capacity to issue general obligation bonds for capital projects should be expanded, they scrapped the Commission's notion that at least part of such a debt might be incurred without popular referendum. Sensitive to legislative prerogatives, the Assembly rejected a Commission recommendation that the governor have the authority to initiate administrative reorganization of the executive branch, subject to legislative veto. The legislature dropped the Commission's approach to greater autonomy for local government.

In other respects the General Assembly went further than had the Commission. Preserving the concept of a commitment to quality education, the legislators put teeth in the education article by way of a mandate of the localities to come up with their share of the cost of supporting public schools. The Assembly recognized that the time had come for annual legislative sessions, a step that the Commission had been unwilling to take. The legislators rewrote and strengthened the new conservation article, took a first step toward limiting the traditional appointing powers of judges, and enhanced the Assembly's control over the sometimes controversial State Corporation Commission.

There were those who had held their breath at the idea of a legislature writing a constitution. Many observers associated the legislative process with lobbying, horse-trading, and the representation of special interest. Some people would have preferred the calling of a constitutional convention, elected for the express purpose of rewriting the Constitution. But when the General Assembly had finished its work, much of the skepticism heard before the session had vanished. The *Washington Post*, for example, which confessed its doubts about the job the Assembly might do, had to admit that the revision, while hardly perfect, was a good one, perhaps even better than the draft that the Commission had submitted. "The General Assembly," concluded the *Post*, "has risen above itself. It has produced a document that, with all its shortcoming, would have been inconceivable in Virginia a decade or even five years ago."[9]

The revisions took the form of amendments to the existing Constitution. To become effective, an amendment must be approved by two sessions of the General Assembly, separated by an election of delegates, and then agreed to by the people in a referendum. Therefore the amendments that passed the 1969 special session were acted on a second time at the regular legislative session in 1970. At the 1969 session, steps had been taken to separate questions thought to be more sensitive or controversial into distinct items which could be voted on individually on the referendum ballot. The 1970 session, therefore, had before it the main body of the Constitution, which encompassed the bulk of the revisions, and five separate questions—two involving state borrowing, one that would repeal the constitutional prohibition on lotteries, one that would allow state aid to handicapped children in private schools whether church-related or not, and one that would allow the General Assembly, by special act, to change the boundaries of the Capital City.

The main body of the revisions was readily approved at the 1970 session, as were the questions touching lotteries and, despite some lingering "pay-as-you-go" sentiment, the provisions liberalizing state borrowing. The other two questions—those regarding aid to children in private schools and the Capital City's boundaries—were defeated. Thus four questions would go on the ballot in November 1970.

At the time it approved the Virginia revisions, the General Assembly was aware of recent experience in other states, notably Maryland, where new or revised constitutions had been soundly defeated at the polls.[10] One lesson learned from some of those referenda was the danger of presenting the voters with a take-it-or-leave-it package in which they were obliged to approve or disapprove all the constitutional changes in a single question.[11] The Virginia legislature deemed it wise to have questions thought to be more controversial, especially those regarding state debt, voted on separately. Thus the Virginia voter, in November 1970, would be entitled to vote "yes" or "no" on any or all of the four questions in any combination he or she saw fit.

The ballot was designed to be simple and straightforward. Each of the four questions had not only a number (as is customary) but also a brief title—"Main Body of the Constitution," "Lotteries," "General Obligation Bonds," and "Revenue Bonds—making it easier for the press and the public to talk about the propositions individually. The questions on the ballot were drafted so as to avoid legalese and to use instead ordinary English perfectly comprehensible to the layman. The ballot questions were brief and to the point and simply asked the voter to vote "yes" or "no" on each proposition.

In the spring of 1970, the first steps were taken toward the creation of a committee to inform the people of Virginia about the revisions on which they would vote in November. The committee was designed to be an entirely private effort, funded by private contributions. Governor Linwood Holton asked A. E. Dick Howard, who had been executive director of the Commission on Constitutional Revision and had served as counsel to the 1969 and 1970 sessions of the General Assembly, to create such a committee. He in turn assembled a staff for what came to be known as "Virginians for the Constitution." Since no state money was involved, a fund-raising effort was necessary, and James C. Wheat, a Richmond stockbroker, agreed to chair a finance committee to solicit private contributions.

In the campaign for ratification of the new Constitution, several objects were conceived. First was the task of informing and educating the public about the revisions, making fair and factual information available through pamphlets, the press and media, and whatever other channels might be available. Thus, those who wanted to study the amendments in detail would have full opportunity and encouragement to do so. In addition, on the assumption that many voters would not delve into the specifics of the revisions, admittedly a complex matter, it was thought important to foster a general climate of acceptance. The proponents hoped that a voter not completely informed on the details of the revisions, but seeing the state and local leaders with whom he or she identified supporting the new Constitution, would have less reason to mistrust the idea of accepting the proposed changes. Finally, it was thought that the campaign should work within the political process. Lest the campaign be too removed from grassroots sentiment, the active support and cooperation of political parties and leaders—Democratic, Republican, and independent—was sought at state and local levels alike.

A statewide steering committee for Virginians for the Constitution was assembled. Symbolizing the broad consensus of support which the revisions enjoyed, former Governor Godwin (then also active in the reelection campaign of independent U.S. Senator Harry F. Byrd, Jr.) would be honorary chairman, and his Republican successor, Linwood Holton, would be the campaign's chairman. The committee itself was remarkable for the diversity of the people it drew together. Named to the steering committee were all three men who had sought the nomination for governor in the 1969 Democratic primary—William C. Battle, Henry E. Howell, Jr., and Fred Pollard—men thus representing the full sweep of factions in that party. (The Republican candidate, the winner in 1969, was, of course, already represented, as the referendum committee's chairman.) Also named to the steering committee were the Republican and Democratic candidates for lieutenant governor and attorney general in the 1969 general election. Represented also were Democratic and Republican leaders from both houses of the General Assembly.

Joining the politicians were leaders from other walks of life—labor, business, education, youth, blacks, civic groups, agriculture, and local government. Named to the committee, for example, were the presidents of such major groups as the Virginia State AFL-CIO, the Virginia Congress of Parents and Teachers, the Virginia Municipal League, the Virginia Association of Counties, the Virginia Education Association, and the Virginia Federation of Women's Clubs.

The state steering committee came into being essentially to demonstrate the consensus for approval of the new Constitution, a spectrum of support cutting across party and faction lines. The work of day-to-day campaigning, however, had to be done at the local level, and could not be accomplished from Richmond. Hence an early step in organizing the effort of Virginians for the Constitution was the creation of campaign committees in the cities and counties of Virginia.

Just as the state steering committee was meant to reflect the major political and interest groups among Virginia's citizens, so were the local committees intended to mirror the character of the particular locality.

The executive director of Virginians for the Constitution or one of the several area coordinators contacted local political and other leaders to initiate a local effort. Special efforts were made to emphasize the nonpartisan character of the pro-constitution campaign. To the fullest extent possible, well-known Republicans, Democrats, and—because of the independent candidacy of Senator Byrd—supporters of Byrd were prominent in each local committee. In addition, the committee reflected the demography of that area, including as appropriate, farmers, businessmen, ethnic leaders, educators, and other representative persons. Typically state legislators and locally elected officials, such as councilmen, supervisors, and constitutional officers, were either formally on the local committee or publicly associated with it.

Normally a local committee had a chairman or cochairman who, selected for his or her stature in the community, might not necessarily do the day-to-day work of organizing the local campaign. Often a young lawyer, Jaycee, or some other young person was asked to serve as executive director of the local campaign. It was with the local executive director that the state office of Virginians for the Constitution and the area coordinator worked, and to him or her they looked for the marshaling of local resources.

Some things were best done at the state level, some in the localities. Virginians for the Constitution took the lead in creating themes for the campaign, printing information brochures, producing such paraphernalia as lapel buttons and bumper stickers, securing billboard space, buying television advertising time, and otherwise supplying most of the basic materials of a campaign. The state office looked to the local committees for the more personal effort best undertaken at the grass roots, including working with local civic groups, canvassing voters, arranging local press coverage of events, handling local newspaper and radio advertising, and manning the polls on election day.

To assist the local committees, Virginians for the Constitution created a manual giving ideas on local organizing. The manual suggested the creation of committees to be responsible for liaison with local organizations (such as service clubs, women's clubs, trade groups, etc.), for voter contact both before election day (as by mass mailings and door-to-door canvassing) and on election day (as by manning the polls and handing out sample ballots), for furnishing speakers to local groups, for handling local publicity and advertising, and for raising money to cover local campaign expenses. With the manual were included sample spots for radio advertisements, sample news releases, and other guides for local publicity.

At the state level, Virginians for the Constitution set out to reach the voters in a variety of ways. One of the first steps was to establish contact with major statewide organizations, such as the Jaycees, the AFL-CIO, the Retail Merchants, the Virginia Education Association, the Crusade for Voters, the League of Women Voters, the Virginia State Bar Association, and many others. Virtually every major group that was asked for a formal endorsement of the revised Constitution gave such backing, the chief exceptions being those service clubs (such as the Rotarians and Kiwanians) whose policies preclude stands on issues which, even if nonpartisan, are political.

In addition to giving endorsements, many of the statewide organizations took an active part in the campaign to inform the voters, by using their newsletters and other means to get information about the new Constitution to their own membership. Active support of the revised Constitution often came after action by an executive committee authorized to take such action, by vote of a statewide convention, or occasionally by a referendum within the organization statewide. An instance of such a poll was the vote taken by Jaycee chapters in Virginia; more than 92 percent of the Jaycees voting endorsed the main body of the Constitution, while slightly lower percentages endorsed the three separate questions.

The role of the press and media in informing the public was obvious. During the summer of 1970 the executive director of Virginians for the Constitution traveled throughout the state, visiting the editors and staff members of Virginia newspapers. At sessions sometimes lasting half a day, information was conveyed and questions answered, so that local papers could help voters evaluate the revised Constitution. Near the end of the campaign, in October, at the request of the *Richmond News Leader*, the executive director prepared a series of ten signed articles for publication in that newspaper; they appeared as well in papers in several other Virginia cities.

Virginians for the Constitution created a speaker's bureau. Any local group, such as a service club, which wanted a speaker on the Constitution could contact the Virginians' Richmond Office, and a speaker would be supplied. The roster of speakers included legislators, lawyers, college presidents, and many others. Approximately a thousand speaking engagements were filled in response to requests received at the Richmond office. Countless other talks were given by speakers arranged for by local campaign committees. To assist the speakers, Virginians for the Constitution prepared a package of speakers' notes, supplemented by fact sheets on specific questions that tended to arise in question-and-answer periods.

Yet another vehicle for reaching and informing the public was brochures that were distributed in large quantities to local committees to be mailed out, left at doorsteps, and used at public meetings. Virginians for the Constitution produced an attractive red-white-and-blue brochure that explained how the four questions would appear on the ballot and summed up the highlights of the proposed changes. Probably 500,000 of these brochures were printed and distributed. For those people who might want a more detailed analysis of the revisions, several publications were available: the full text of the Constitution, an article-by-article summary of the revised Constitution, and a factual question-and-answer sheet published by the Extension Service at Virginia Polytechnic Institute and State University.

In addition to conveying specific information about the Constitution, the proponents deemed it essential to create a general climate of awareness that there was in fact a revision underway and that the people would be asked to vote on it in November. The greatest misfortune would be for large numbers of voters to arrive at the polls in November and, on being handed a ballot, for the first time discover that constitutional amendments were being voted on. Since constitutional revision lacks the popular impact of a candidate's race, Virginians for the Constitution undertook to use a variety of means to stimulate general awareness so that voters would be in a position to make informed judgments at the polls. The animating spirit of the campaign was that apathy and indifference would likely be more formidable problems than would hostility and opposition.

A positive theme had to be evolved that people would identify with the new Constitution. Working with a Richmond advertising agency, Virginians for the Constitution evolved a "yes" theme—a red-white-and-blue "yes" with stars and stripes suggesting a Fourth of July spirit. This "yes" logo was used throughout the campaign—on brochures, lapel buttons, bumper stickers, billboards, window cards, and wherever visual identification was important. (Some young women who wore the "yes" button reported that not everyone who saw the button realized that it was limited to constitutional revision.)

In reaching particular groups of voters, special committees were created. A fifty-three-member group known as Rural Virginians for the Constitution was formed from distinguished citizens well known in rural areas, such as past presidents of Ruritan International and of the Future Farmers of America in Virginia. On the theory that many voters regularly read the sports page, whatever else they may read, there was formed Sportsmen for the Constitution, including tennis star Arthur Ashe, football pro Ken Willard, golfer Vinnie Giles, stock car driver "Runt" Harris, and all of the players on both the Virginia Squires basketball team and the Richmond Braves baseball team.

The campaign was scheduled for early summer through election day. The summer was spent largely laying the groundwork by creating a staff, establishing contact with statewide organizations, preparing copy for brochures, and making initial contact with people who might carry forward with the creation of local committees. Public campaigning before Labor Day, such as speech-making and advertising, would have been wasted effort, being simply too far ahead of the actual election date. It was agreed that the major effort at reaching and informing voters should take place during September and October, so that the campaign, like any other campaign, would not "peak" too early and thus be dissipated by election day.

Throughout there was emphasis on the nonpartisan nature of the revision effort. Governors Godwin and Holton, for example, appeared together in early October at a luncheon session arranged by the Virginia Council on Legislation. The climate of consensus for the new Constitution was heightened by the frequent appearances of well-known political leaders of every ideological hue—all in accord on the merit of the revisions. An especially poignant moment in the campaign came when the popular Lieutenant Governor J. Sergeant Reynolds, who had been hospitalized for treatment of a brain tumor, used his first public appearance to urge Virginians to vote in favor of the revisions.

As the campaign progressed, themes began to emerge. At first, Virginians for the Constitution had been using the rather bland appeal. "For a better Constitution, vote 'yes.'" As the Virginians' executive director and others began to go on the hustings to speak to local audiences, they frequently encountered a spirit of disenchantment with government at all levels—local and state as well as federal—engendered by the feeling that governmental decisions were increasingly being taken out of the hands of the people. Because the new Constitution would in a number of ways enhance popular government, the proponents of the Constitution fashioned a new theme: "Bring government closer to the people; vote 'yes.'" This theme was picked up widely, in speeches, on editorial pages, and elsewhere. It came as close as any one statement that emerged in the campaign to capturing the spirit of the new Constitution.

Organized opposition to the new Constitution was most vocal in Northern Virginia and in the Richmond suburbs, but resistance to constitutional change probably ran deeper in Southside Virginia. There the two debt proposals ran into long-held views about the virtues of a "pay-as-you-go" approach to state services. While most of the changes embraced in Proposal No. 1 (the main body of the Constitution) provoked no general opposition, the greater focus on the state's role (vis-à-vis the localities) in public education did stir resentment and apprehension. *The Farmville Herald*, for example, said that, whatever the merit of the other changes, it thought that under the Constitution the state could "prescribe the curriculum, the textbooks, the teachers, the schools, and take complete control of the schools and your child." Hence the *Herald* editorial writer intended to vote "no" on Proposal No. 1.[12]

Much of the Southside opposition was attributable to traditional conservatism. In the suburban areas of Richmond and Northern Virginia, however, there appeared a small but vocal band of opponents rather like those who have taken arms in constitutional referenda in Maryland and other states. These opponents entertained what may be called the "conspiracy" theory of government—that the new Constitution was a socialist plot designed to strip the people of Virginia of their rights. As one opposition pamphlet put it: "Why are these ruthless exploiters disguising more debt, more taxes, big bureaucracy, and approaching serfdom on individuals as needed constitutional change?" Over and over, opposition literature hammered away at the "conspiracy" theme—that the Constitution had been changed through "stealth and trickery," that the process of revision had been unconstitutional and a "transparent fraud," that the revisions were being sold through a campaign of "deception and misrepresentation." These opponents labeled it a "mail-order" constitution, drafted (depending on which opponent was speaking) in Chicago by the Council of State Governments, in Washington by the Department of Health, Education, and Welfare, or in New York by the United Nations.

To counter opposition arguments, Virginians for the Constitution prepared "fact sheets" which, in parallel columns, set out the opposition charges and the pro-ratification rebuttals. In a more general fashion, the proponents were able to appeal to conservative opinion by having at the fore of the campaign, state and local, unimpeachable conservatives, many of them active at the same time in the Byrd campaign. An amusing moment came when the chairman of the "Save our State Committee" of Northern Virginia, an opposition group, challenged the revision proponents to a debate. The challenge was accepted, and, when the debate took place, the affirmative case for the so-called socialist constitution was put by no less prominent a conservative than James J. Kilpatrick, the nationally syndicated columnist.

By the close of the campaign, endorsement for the new Constitution was overwhelming. Prominent political leaders of both major parties had lent their support. Almost all important statewide organizations backed its ratification, and while a few newspapers had voiced doubts about or opposition to the revisions, editorial support on a statewide basis was resounding. The *Richmond Times-Dispatch,* for example, declared that "Virginians who want to provide their state with a strong governmental framework on which to build for progress in the latter third of the 20th century will vote 'Yes' in the constitutional referendum next Tuesday."[13] The *Roanoke Times* called passage of the new Constitution "absolutely essential."[14] The *Washington Evening Star* urged its readers across the river to "[r]ally to this cause in the coming week, lest a priceless opportunity for advancement be lost."[15]

On November 3, the new Constitution was overwhelmingly adopted. All four propositions were approved. The largest margin of approval went to Proposal No. 1, the main body of the Constitution, which received the assent of 72% of those who voted.[16] Support for the Constitution was especially strong in Northern Virginia and in Tidewater. In Alexandria, for example, Proposal No. 1 carried by 84 percent of the vote, in Fairfax County, by 82 percent. In Tidewater the picture was similar; in Norfolk 82 percent of the voters approved Proposal No. 1. Such a strong showing at the two ends of Virginia's urban corridor was not surprising. What was perhaps more unexpected was the high margins in the traditionally more conservative Valley of Virginia, where Proposal No. 1 garnered 85 percent of the vote in Harrisonburg and a remarkable 91 percent in Lexington.

The areas of greatest weaknesses were some of the largely rural areas of Southside Virginia. Lunenburg County, for example, buried Proposal No. 1 with an almost two-to-one "no" vote, and the two debt questions fared even worse. Statewide, only nine counties and one city (Danville) rejected Proposal No. 1. The full measure of the success of the campaign for ratification is underscored when one tallies the results by congressional districts. With four questions on the ballot in ten congressional districts—a total of forty possible vote combinations—only one question lost in only one district (Proposal No. 4 lost in the Fifth Congressional District, a Southside district).

SUCCESSES AND FAILURES AMONG THE STATES: THE COMPARATIVE EXPERIENCE IN THE ERA OF VIRGINIA'S REVISION

That Virginia's voters would approve a new constitution was not a foregone conclusion. Defeats of new constitutions in other states—perhaps the most publicized being that in Maryland in 1968—would make one cautious about predicting the success of any constitutional revision. That major political and civic leaders had endorsed Virginia's new Constitution was no guarantee; the backing of a "who's who" of such leaders in Maryland had not saved the proposed Maryland Constitution. The new Virginia charter was attacked on many of the same grounds, including regional government and governmental spending, which had been used in Maryland. One opposition pamphlet reminded its Virginia readers, "Marylanders have done it . . . Virginians can do it too." Moreover, if Maryland's proposed Constitution was hurt by extraneous events—notably the riots of April 1968 in Washington and Baltimore—Virginia's political climate in 1970 was hardly uneventful, especially when there was a U.S. Senate race without precedent, featuring Senator Byrd running as an independent against nominees of the two major political parties. And while enough private money was raised to run a respectable informational campaign, money was tight enough that some important items had to be cut—there was, for example, no television advertising in Northern Virginia.

Despite the problems, the final vote was overwhelmingly "yes." A number of factors played a part in producing the highly successful outcome, and Virginia's experience may usefully be compared with that of other states—especially those which sought to revise their constitutions around the time of the Virginia revision—to shed some light on reasons why constitutional revisions succeed or fail.[17]

To begin with, how the groundwork for revision is laid, and by whom, is a significant factor. Constitutional revision in Virginia was, from start to finish, a highly deliberative process. Having the groundwork laid by a blue-ribbon study commission meant that, when the General Assembly met, the issues which it would debate had already been sharply defined by the Commission's report and commentary. Conscientious preparation may seem a simple enough goal to achieve,[18] yet in New York and Rhode Island a lack of planning and issue-sharpening have been suggested as reasons for defeat of revised constitutions.[19] In addition, both conventions had an image of being dominated by politicians.[20] Those who comprised the Virginia commission, on the other hand, were widely recognized as among the most talented, respected, and nonpartisan figures in the Commonwealth. Their prestige helped to put the General Assembly in an affirmative and responsive frame of mind when the legislators received the Commission's report.

There are two major methods by which states typically revise a constitution—by constitutional convention or by the state legislature. Either vehicle is usually preceded by a study commission. Whichever means, convention or legislature, is used, a keynote of the revision process must be political realism. One of the lessons to be gleaned from a study of constitutional revision among the states is that a new constitution can be killed by an overdose of partisan politics—partisanship that divides the revisors and voters alike. But a new constitution can also be killed by too little politics—a process which, through an excess of idealism or naïveté, is insulated from political reality.

One of the simplest lessons the Virginia revisors learned was that it was dangerous to make unnecessary enemies. A proposed change should be weighed to be sure that the benefits to be derived sufficiently outweigh the cost in terms of alienation of those who may oppose the change. A change of largely theoretical value may not be worth the electoral price paid for making it. For example, many state constitutions contain unenforceable, hortatory language in their bills of rights.[21] Reformers often scoff at such language and urge that it be removed.[22] The reformers who comprised the Maryland convention did excise the hortatory language of Maryland's Declaration of Rights. Having done so, they found themselves saddled with the opposition charge that the rights of Marylanders were being taken away.[23] It is hard to conclude that the change—of theoretical value at best (and even that can be argued)—was worth the cost.

Another rule often found in the textbooks is that only policy-making offices should be filled through popular election. Following this precept, the Maryland revisors stripped many of that state's constitutional officers, such as the clerks and the registrars of wills, of their constitutional status. The price of this decision was the spawning of a vigorous and vocal source of opposition to the new Maryland charter in every courthouse in Maryland.[24] Not only did the local officials oppose the Constitution, but many citizens, especially in rural areas, considered it important that such officers be elected rather than be appointed by other politicians.[25]

Another costly move by the Maryland convention was the decision not to require that a local referendum be held before legislative creation of regional governments.[26] There are valid policy reasons why regional government should not invariably be subject to local veto, but it is evident that the Maryland convention's decision badly hurt the revision effort in Baltimore County.[27] The regional government provision made it easy for opponents to appeal to racial fears in the area around Baltimore City, and the resulting negative vote in the county has been termed by one demographic analyst to be a principal cause of the statewide rejection.[28] Ordinarily these suburbanites could have been relied on to support the constitution, just as did those in the Washington suburban counties of Montgomery and Prince George's.[29]

In Virginia, by contrast, the revisors retained the philosophical language of the Bill of Rights, they avoided any direct assault on the constitutional status of local officers such as sheriffs and clerks (though making it possible through local referendum to abolish or alter such offices), and while recognizing the concept of regional government, they wrote in a requirement of referendum in the localities affected. As the *Washington Post* observed at the close of Virginia's 1969 legislative session, "The political realism so painfully missing in retrospect in Maryland a year ago and so prominent in Virginia's new effort gives the proposals a healthy chance of survival."[30]

How are the prospects for success in constitutional revision affected by the form the revision process takes? Specifically, are there reasons to prefer a convention on the one hand, or legislative revision on the other? Having a prestigious study commission prepare a draft and then having the legislature refine the document in the perspective of their own understanding of the political process was one of the greatest strength of the approach to revision in Virginia. But Virginia's experience may or may not be the best guide for other states.

Much could be said about the relative merits of having revisions undertaken by conventions or having legislatures tackle the job. Conventions are thought to be more representative of the people, are frequently composed of highly able, civic-minded citizens, are less political (because they are less highly structured than are legislatures),[31] are more focused on the task of constitutional revision (because they are called into being for that specific task), and are likely to be more willing to make fundamental changes.[32] On the other hand, they may be out of touch with political reality or may be dominated by ambitious politicians. Commissions, being smaller, may be able to work faster, and they may have more expert talent because they can be appointed from among the state's ablest citizens. Commissions are commonly more acceptable to legislatures than wide-open conventions because their proposals can be vetoed by the legislature if it wishes.[33] When the legislature, composed of politicians, has the final say, there is the risk, however, that the majority party will seek advantage for itself,[34] or at least that the legislators as a body will try to gain advantage over other branches of government.

Generalization about the relative merits of conventions or legislatures as revisors is difficult, because an examination of the behavior of conventions and legislatures in a number of states indicates that the circumstances of the particular state are crucial. In Maryland, to be sure, the convention operated in a political vacuum,[35] producing a document that took insufficient account of what the people or the interest groups would think of their work. Though they produced an excellent model constitution, they lacked that very closeness to the people which is considered one of the major advantages of using a convention.[36] The same tendency was present in the Connecticut convention, but more realistic delegates managed to curb the reformers and achieve a reasonable document which the voters accepted.[37]

In other states' conventions, there has been the danger of partisanship. In Michigan, though the convention began in a bipartisan spirit,[38] it ended with the Republicans, who formed a majority of convention delegates, agreeing among themselves on a constitution and producing a straight party line vote on the document.[39] Though that document was approved, partisan conventions in New York and Rhode Island found the people repelled by their behavior.[40] On the other hand, in such diverse states as Pennsylvania,[41] New Jersey,[42] and Hawaii[43] conventions met in a bipartisan spirit, recognized the need to compromise in order to achieve success, and produced documents that satisfied the major interests in those states. Indeed, in Pennsylvania, though the Republicans controlled the convention, the Republican president insisted on equal representation for Democrats on all convention committees.[44] Strong, conciliatory leadership has been suggested as one reason compromise was possible in some of these states;[45] conversely, weak leadership was a factor in producing a convention that bogged down in partisan wrongdoing.[46] The representativeness of the delegates, their responsiveness to the constituency, and their willingness to compromise their own wishes and those of their parties in order to win others over to the revisions were factors in successful revision efforts by conventions in Missouri,[47] Pennsylvania,[48] and Hawaii.[49] These revisions stand in contrast to the unrepresentative character and consequent unresponsiveness of the

Maryland convention and the partisanship displayed by New York and Rhode Island delegates.[50]

In Virginia the General Assembly proved that a legislature is not incapable of reform.[51] Its members did not fall prey to the evils of partisanship. They put their understanding of the citizenry into the effort, deciding, after much debate, to eliminate the potentially divisive handicapped children and Capital City boundary amendments, which could have provoked sectarian and racial feelings respectively. The legislators restrained themselves from using the Constitution to reflect the desires of the lawmakers' favorite interest groups. The members of the General Assembly approached their task with an understanding of the difference between constitution-making and ordinary legislating.

It seems, then, that, given favorable conditions, either a convention or a legislature can undertake a successful constitutional revision. Equally, given the wrong conditions, either can fail. As one observer has noted:

> With favorable prevailing winds and strong cooperative leadership, each structure appears capable of performing successfully in both the drafting and marketing stages. . . . Theoretical advantages, in brief, do not appear to have the political muscle that would make an extended comparative analysis of these structures very meaningful.[52]

The comparative lessons to be learned from other states' revisions seem to lie not so much in the particular method chosen (though this can be crucial in a particular state) as in factors of leadership, both within the body that shapes the revision and in the state at large when the proposals are laid before the people.

Political realism and a spirit of bipartisanship are important in creating an atmosphere of consensus. The absence of emotionally charged issues in Virginia made possible a consensus of political leadership backing the new Constitution. This spectrum of support was a key factor in the document's success at the polls. Not within memory have political leaders of such divergent views—indeed, often the bitterest of enemies in the political arena—combined so cordially and publicly in a common political undertaking. The symbolism of the liberal, moderate, and conservative factions of both major parties uniting behind the revised Constitution could not be lost on anyone with even a passing understanding of Virginia's political scene. As the *Roanoke Times* commented on the eve of election in 1970, "Surely if such arch political foes as Henry Howell and Mills Godwin can agree that constitutional changes are worthwhile, the rest of us can be certain that a yes vote is a vote for good government."[53]

Support by the political leadership of both major parties is not a guarantee of success. The leaders of the major parties supported the reform effort in Arkansas[54] and Maryland,[55] yet the effort failed for other reasons. Nor is a consensus of support absolutely essential to victory. In Michigan, for example, the state's Democrats strongly opposed the new Constitution for a number of reasons; for instance, because the Republican-dominated convention had apportioned the legislature so as to keep themselves in power.[56] The neutrality of the Republicans in Hawaii,[57] probably induced by such factors as provisions for collective bargaining by state employees,[58] did not lead to defeat of that Constitution or even of that provision. In Michigan, leadership in the ratification drive by the popular new governor, and convention vice-president, George Romney, may have overcome Democratic hostility. In Hawaii, the form of the ballot and the generally conciliatory nature of the convention may have offset any ill effects of the lack of general political consensus. Still, the lack of bipartisan support has undoubtedly influenced the vote in some states. For example, Republicans helped defeat the products of the Rhode Island[59] and New York conventions,[60] and the Democrats campaigned strongly against the ill-fated constitution drafted by the Republican-dominated legislature in New Jersey in 1944.[61]

Factors like bipartisan and grass roots political support, the endorsement of major newspapers of such disparate philosophy as the *Washington Post* and the *Richmond Times-Dispatch*, and the deletion of disruptive controversial issues indicate that the compromises made by the Virginia constitution-makers were widely accepted. Proposed constitutions in some states have been defeated because of the opposition of important blocs of voters whose interests were not protected. Experiences of other states have shown that offending one of the major parties can hurt, and that local officeholders can have an important impact as well. Conservation groups (New Mexico),[62] the Civil Liberties Union (New York),[63] and civic leaders and newspapers alienated by the self-interest shown by legislative draftsmen (Rhode Island)[64] have also been instrumental in the defeat of proposed constitutions. Of course, the political and economic interests of a state have much to do with who takes part in drafting a constitution, and the relative strengths of each no doubt have an effect on whether compromises are made.

The support of political leadership at the local level is an important consideration in seeking electoral approval of a revised constitution. In Virginia, all five associations of constitutional officers—the clerks, the sheriffs and sergeants, the Commonwealth's attorneys, the commissioners of revenue, and the treasurers—went on record in support of the new Constitution. Other local officials, such as councilmen, mayors, and supervisors, were often publicly active in support of the revisions. Added to these political voices were those of civic, business, labor, and other leaders, again not only at the state level but also in the counties and cities across the state. The result was a climate of support that tended to resolve, in favor of voting "yes," the voters' natural hesitations about constitutional revision.[65] The value of grassroots support in Virginia contrasts not only with the Maryland experience, but also with the unsuccessful revision efforts in Arkansas, Rhode Island, and New Mexico, which appear to have been damaged by the lack of support of civil groups, local government officials, and government workers.[66]

An aggressive campaign for ratification was another important factor in the result in Virginia. An observer of the Maryland experience has noted that the campaign there tended to be intellectual and sober,[67] not the sort of campaign likely to roll away the ennui with which most voters will regard a constitutional referendum.[68] The Virginia proponents set out, like those in Hawaii,[69] in the spirit that ignorance and apathy were likely in the end to be greater enemies than overt opposition. This was particularly a problem in Virginia because a commission and the legislature, rather than a more highly publicized convention, had drafted the document.[70] An early start,[71] organized along the lines of a statewide gubernatorial or senatorial campaign, and adequate (though by the standards of a statewide race for office, laughably modest) funding were components of the successful campaign in Virginia.

A catalyst of Virginia's referendum effort was the superb work of the local campaign committees. In some communities, one or more individuals were the spark plugs. In others, a local organization—oftentimes the League of Women Voters or the Jaycees—made the local campaign go. Some of the variation in votes from one community to another turned on predictable demographic characteristics, but in many cases a highly favorable vote in a community (especially in areas thought less receptive to innovation) was in good measure a function of an active local committee.

The Virginia campaign also succeeded in getting more usable information before the voters than is customary in a referendum effort. Not only was such a massive educational campaign probably without precedent in Virginia, a special effort was made throughout the campaign to translate the rather dry abstractions of constitutional revision into issues that touched the lives of individual citizens—education, environmental quality, consumer protection, and taxes. And there is reason to think that the central theme that evolved in the campaign—"Bring government closer to the people"—struck a responsive chord in citizens. In contrast, the Arkansas proponents never successfully translated the dry abstractions dealing with the structure of state and local government into terms the voters could understand. They never made the voters see that the new Constitution would mean something to them personally. Observers have assigned this as a major reason for the defeat in that state.[72]

Not only did the proponents in Virginia mount an effective campaign, but also the opponents of the revision never developed much popular support. In conservative Arkansas, the opposition was successful in confusing the voters with technical and insubstantial criticisms[73] and in convincing them that the increased flexibility of government would lead to increases in taxes.[74] Proponents committed the fatal error of responding defensively to the charges rather than explaining the benefits to be derived from the new document.[75]

Opponents in Virginia tried similar tactics, but they did not succeed. One reason is that the proponents were prepared to meet and rebut opposition attacks. Exposing half-truths requires, of course, an effective way to get the message to the people. In Maryland, the opponents could charge that rights had been eliminated when they had merely been rearranged,[76] or that the new Constitution would cost a lot of money[77] when realistic estimates showed it would cost just a fraction of what they claimed,[78] or that the new Constitution would enfranchise D.C. residents to vote in Maryland elections when an examination of the document would reveal the contrary.[79] They made effective use of such charges because of the inability of the proponents rapidly to respond.[80] In Virginia, by contrast, the proponents met opposition charges with fact sheets and other materials promptly put in the hands of local campaign committees, speakers, editors, and others, to rebut the attacks.

The Maryland opponents were also able to wrap themselves in a cloak of conservatism without fear of contradiction by conservative state leaders, since few Maryland leaders had unquestioned conservative credentials. In Arkansas, the conservative American Independent Party opposed the new document. This not only drained off support from the far right but also led many moderately conservative Democrats to tone down their support in order to avoid losing votes to AlP candidates.[81] In Virginia, on the other hand, "conservative" opponents of the "socialistic" Constitution were confronted by men like Mills Godwin and James J. Kilpatrick, men with whom conservative voters could readily identify.

Timing has been cited as an important factor in the success or failure of a number of recent revisions. Hostility over student uprisings at the University of Hawaii is thought to be one reason the eighteen-year old vote failed adoption in that state,[82] while the first collection of a newly imposed income tax[83] and riots in Washington and Baltimore following Martin Luther King's death have been considered important ingredients in the Maryland debacle[84] The proposed Arkansas Constitution faced a particularly fortuitous and lethal circumstance when labor campaigned heavily against repeal of a full-crew law that appeared on the ballot with the new Constitution. Labor voters were likely told to vote "no" on all the propositions of the complex ballot, with the result that not only the full-crew law but also an unopposed, widely supported franchise tax measure was defeated overwhelmingly.[85] By contrast, in Michigan, timing the campaign so that the popular new Governor Romney could rally voters to the new Constitution in the first months of his incumbency was undoubtedly an important factor in the success of the referendum in that state.

The length of time between completion of the document and the vote has sometimes been thought significant. One observer states that the two-month period in Pennsylvania meant that opponents had no time to organize, while the four-month period in Maryland enabled them to mount a more sophisticated effort.[86] Such conclusions ought to be regarded with caution. The opposition in Maryland was never well organized, though their arguments were effective.[87] The lapse of time between drafting a constitution and having the people vote on it can be to the advantage of either proponents or opponents, depending on who makes the best use of the time.

In Virginia, the proponents of the new Constitution were spared the impact of such unhappy events as urban riots, but they had reason to worry about the fact that in the fall elections there was a three-way Senate race, with Senator Byrd running as an independent, and that Byrd refused to take any public position on the proposed revisions. Having the Senator silent on a document that was at odds with his father's "pay-as-you-go" philosophy naturally made the proponents uneasy.

The backers of the new Virginia Constitution, however, were successful in enlisting prominent Byrd supporters to endorse it, both on the statewide level (where Byrd's campaign chairman, Mills Godwin, was also honorary chairman of the constitutional referendum campaign), and at the local level (where local constitutional campaign committees often had a Democrat, a Republican, and a Byrd supporter as cochairman). Thus the coincidence of the constitutional referendum with fortuitous external events had little harmful effect in Virginia. The other aspect of timing—the long lapse between legislative approval in the spring of 1970 (a *second* approval, for the legislature had given its first approval in the spring of 1969) and the vote in November—the proponents turned to their advantage by using the summer months to lay a careful groundwork and the weeks after Labor Day to campaign aggressively.

The form of the ballot was unquestionably a factor in the outcome in Virginia. There is general agreement that putting a revised constitution on the ballot as a single question was a central factor in the defeat of the proposed constitution in New York. Anthony Travia, president of the New York convention, insisted that aid to parochial schools be included and that the document be voted on as a single question on the ballot. He argued that the parochial school aid provision alone would capture 40 percent of the vote.[88] So controversial was the aid provision, however, that issue is generally acknowledged to have hurt more than any other.[89] The *New York Times* reflected what proved to be the prevailing view when, before that state's referendum on the revised charter, it carried an editorial entitled, "Take It or Leave It: We Leave It." The editorial explained:[90]

> As virtually its final act, the Constitutional Convention decided last night to offer New Yorkers the new Constitution on a take-it-or-leave-it basis. The voter must accept it or reject it in its entirety. To our regret, the considerable improvements this document does make in the existing constitution are insufficient in importance to offset a few features so highly objectionable that we can only recommend that the proposed constitution be rejected at the polls in November.

In Virginia, by contrast, the General Assembly sought to identify those questions that might be most controversial and to make it possible for the people to vote separately on them. Moreover, separating the questions on the ballot avoided the "take-it-or-leave-it" stigma and thus made it less likely that the voters would approach the revisions in general in a mood of distrust or apprehension.

Take-it-or-leave-it ballots have met with occasional success, as shown in Michigan, where voters approved a constitution submitted in that form in 1963. But the experience of New York, Maryland, and Rhode Island indicates that many citizens are likely to vote against an entire constitution when they dislike a particular provision rather than vote for it because of the things they like. Not only in Virginia but also in Florida, Hawaii, Pennsylvania, and Connecticut, submission of more than one question led to adoption of most or all of the revisions.[91]

The road to constitutional revision is rarely without its perils. To some extent the lessons learned in one state are of value in another, yet every state has its own unique political climate that calls for a tailored approach. Revisors will want to consider the form which the revision process will take (convention or legislature), which changes are really worth fighting for, how the revision will appear on the ballot, how the state's leadership and political forces can be enlisted in seeking ratification, how a campaign should be organized to reach the grassroots level, how to combat the twin evils of voter apathy and opposition distortions, and when all is said and done, how to ensure that a state's fundamental law is revised and presented in such a way that in reality it reflects the best aspirations of the state's citizenry.

Could It be Done Today?

If the decision were taken to rewrite a state constitution today, how would the situation differ from that confronting Virginia's constitution-makers in 1970? As a specific example, let me consider a hypothetical attempt to rewrite Virginia's constitution today. In many ways, Virginia is not the place it was in 1970. Its population has grown from about 4,650,000 in 1970 to about 7,3000,000 in 2002.[92] Republicans, a small minority in the General Assembly in 1970, now control both the houses of the legislature. Northern Virginia, the anchor of the state's Urban Corridor, has exploded in growth, partly because of the advent of the high-tech economy in the 1990s. No longer is it possible to speak of Virginia in the twenty-first century, as V. O. Key did in 1949, as a "political museum piece."[93]

Anyone who might seek to revise Virginia's Constitution today would face a landscape vastly changed from the one, daunting as it was, which confronted the revisors who carried the day in 1970. What are some of those challenges a generation later? What would constitutional reformers in Virginia's new century be obliged to consider as they set about their task, not only of drafting a constitution, but also of negotiating the shoals of legislative politics and of statewide referendum?

Partisanship

Party politics in 1970 were very much in flux. The Byrd Machine was breathing its last, the first Republican governor since the nineteenth century was in the statehouse, and U.S. Senator Harry F. Byrd, Jr., was running for reelection as an independent. By and large, during this transitional period, Virginia's politics had a moderate, indeed progressive, mode. A fair degree of consensus was possible in fashioning state policies on education, economic development, fiscal policies, and other essential issues of the day.

A generation later, partisanship is in the air. Consider, for example, the consequences of legislative redistricting. In Virginia, as in most states, the party that holds the majority of seats in the state legislature draws district lines to confer an advantage on that party. Virginia's redistricting in 2002 is a perfect case in point. By adroit districting, the Republican majority created as many "safe" seats as possible. Creating safely Republican districts required, of course, conceding other districts, fewer in number, to the Democrats. The result has been further to polarize politics in legislative elections and thus in the General Assembly itself. In districts where the general election no longer matters, the real contest, if any, is in the primaries. There the issues are likely to be fought out further from the mainstream of two-party politics. In the spring of 2003, several of the most senior and influential Republican legislators found themselves hard pressed by challengers on their party's right wing.[94]

In a state legislature, in which more and more seats are "safe," there tends to be a greater political and ideological gulf between Democratic and Republican members. Such polarization of politics, both in elections and in the legislative process, would surely weigh heavily on those who might contemplate a revision of Virginia's Constitution. The chances of finding common ground, hard enough in enacting legislation, would surely be all the harder in trying to shape the Commonwealth's fundamental law.

Special Interests and Single-issue Politics

Interest groups are as old as American politics—James Madison warned of the dangers of "faction"[95]—but recent years have seen their influence grow, both in state and national politics. The more complex the legislative process, and the higher the stakes, the more active special interests become. In Virginia, many interest groups are based in the business community (homebuilders, bankers, automobile dealers, etc.), but they include many other groups, such as teachers and public employees.

The adoption of the 1971 Constitution brought annual sessions of the General Assembly. One consequence is that lobbying takes place throughout the year, during legislative sessions and beyond.[96] Legislative staffs have grown, creating more occasions for interest groups to be involved in the making of policy. With more attention paid, more resources deployed, and more money at stake, what might formerly have been legislative detail becomes the deal-breaker of a delicate compromise.[97]

Their adversarial instincts whetted by legislative lobbying, interest groups could become a particular challenge for would-be constitutional revisors. Finding the kind of common ground that successful revision requires would likely be more difficult than in 1970.

The power of special interests is reinforced by the phenomenon of single-issue politics. Some voters and interest groups judge a candidate for office solely by the position he or she takes on the single issue about which that voter or group cares above all others. This phenomenon can be found on both the left and right wings of American politics. It can be those opposed to abortion or those defending a woman's right to choose; it can be those who want gun control or those who invoke the Second Amendment. Candidates know how difficult it is to persuade a single-interest voter to look past the one issue to the larger scene. Similarly, it is easy to imagine the drafting and referendum process in which a proposed constitution would, in the minds of some voters, be judged solely by whether it embraces their favored position. Single-interest groups would make every effort to have the draft constitution incorporate their views and, if it did not, then oppose it in referendum.

Money

No one would embark on a campaign to adopt a revised Constitution without thinking about money—lots of it. It was 1973 when a candidate for Governor of Virginia, Mills Godwin, first spent more than $1,000,000.[98] In

1981, the two parties spent between them $5.2 million in the governor's race. Twenty years later, in 2001, the two parties spent $31.4 million.[99] In June 2003, Governor Mark Warner, at a dinner in Northern Virginia, raised $1 million for his political action committee, setting a record for a single event hosted by a Virginia governor.[100]

Spending on legislative races has similarly soared. Senator John H. Chichester spent $33,000 for his first race for the state Senate in 1977; in 2003, he was projecting to spend $235,000.[101] A member of the House of Delegates from Albemarle County, Rob Bell, facing no opponent in the forthcoming November 2003 general election, had raised $111,161 by June and had major fund-raising events ahead of him.[102]

Much of the money flowing into American politics comes from political action committees (PACs). In Virginia, PACs are becoming increasingly important. Boutique PACs have come into being, their purpose being to help lawmakers of a particular political or ideological bent.[103] Former House of Delegates Speaker Vance Wilkins, Jr., helped foster the idea of leadership PACs; his Dominion Leadership Fund disbursed over $687,000 and helped the Republicans gain control of the General Assembly in 1999.[104]

The rise of PACs has undercut the role of the political parties as common ground for politicians. A lobbyist for the Virginia Automobile Dealers Association said that the politics of money had changed so much in his sixteen years of lobbying that he was foregoing contributions to the state parties and instead targeting donations.[105]

Constitutional reformers of the new century would need to ponder the lessons gleaned from spending on constitutional initiatives in other states. In California in one year (1998), $256 million was spent by groups on ballot question campaigns.[106] It is difficult to document the claim that the side that spends the most money necessarily prevails; passion and effort, including grassroots campaigning, count for something. But there are several studies showing that, in initiative campaigns involving high levels of spending (over $250,000 for each side), the side spending the most money is virtually guaranteed to succeed if that side *opposes* the initiative.[107] Such studies would be sobering to those considering a try at rewriting Virginia's Constitution.

Virginia's 2002 Sales Tax Referendum

In November 2002, citizens in Northern Virginia and in Hampton Roads were asked to vote on whether the sales tax in those regions should be increased by one-half and 1 percent, respectively. The revenues were to be used for transportation improvements. Governor Mark Warner, a Democrat, led the campaign, enlisting substantial bipartisan support, including Senator John Warner and Congressman Tom Davis.[108] Prominent members of the business community supported the tax, as did many major newspapers. A well-organized and -financed campaign spent $4 million in support of the referendum.[109]

An odd alliance opposed the tax proposal—environmentalists, who feared development and urban sprawl, and antitax conservatives. Altogether these groups spent less than $200,000.[110] But what they lacked in money, they made up for in an aggressive grassroots campaign depending on e-mail networks and energized volunteers. When the results were in, the proposals were defeated.[111]

How to explain the result? Environmentalism and antitax sentiment played an obvious role. But more appears to have been involved, namely a distrust of the politicians who supported the tax. A poll conducted shortly before the referendum reported that fully two-thirds of voters believed that the proponents would break their promise to use the tax proceeds solely for transportation.[112] Many voters, seeing developers among the biggest contributors to the campaign, decided that the tax would be little more than a subsidy for those developers. One commentator saw the vote as bespeaking a distrust of government itself:[113]

> There was no unifying message in the voters' discontent with business as usual. Except for this: there was an underlying frustration with elected leaders from top to bottom—an impatience, if you will, at representative governments that don't work smart anymore, especially on land development, taxes, commuting, and other big issues of the day.

The defeat of the sales tax proposal, despite ample funding for the campaign and the support of much of the state's political and business establishment, is an obvious note of caution to anyone who might wish to undertake constitutional revision in Virginia. One such defeat, however, should not be taken as making victory impossible under any and all circumstances. On the same day that the sales tax proposal died, Virginia voters readily approved over $1 billion in bonds for college construction and parks.[114] The voters also approved a state constitutional amendment involving the use of DNA evidence in criminal appeals.[115] Indeed, amendments to the Constitution of Virginia are routinely approved, partly because they usually are uncontroversial.[116]

Leadership

Ultimately, no factor is more critical to the success of a constitutional revision effort than leadership. Americans often realize how fortunate we are to have been blessed with the inspired and dedicated leaders who met at Philadelphia in 1787 to draft the nation's Constitution and who then led the successful campaign for its ratification by the states.

In the years since the founding, Virginia seems often to have been fighting a rearguard action—in the era of Reconstruction, for example, or more recently, in crafting "massive resistance" against school desegregation. However, Virginia in the 1960s and 1970s saw a genuinely remarkable cluster of leaders at its helm. These same leaders, seasoned in government, business, law, and the academy, played key roles in inspiring the idea of a new Virginia Constitution, in giving it content, and in carrying it to the people.

Governor Miles E. Godwin, Jr., called for the creation in 1968 of the Commission on Constitutional Revision. Of Godwin, it has been said, "Few political leaders have equaled Mills Godwin in comprehending the anatomy of Virginia politics or in translating into reality the aspirations of their constituents."[117] The only man twice elected by Virginia's voters to be their governor, he achieved a doubling of funding for public education, laid the basis for a statewide system of community colleges, and vastly expanded state support for higher education. His skill in leading the campaign for a major bond issue for higher education and mental health in 1968 anticipated the success, two years later, of the referendum on the new Constitution. As a biographer has concluded, "In many respects Godwin's first administration provided a textbook example of the art of leadership.[118]

When the Commission on Constitutional Revision assembled, around the table sat members who brought to their work a wealth of experience and insight. Colgate W. Darden, Jr., had been a farmer, a businessman, a lawyer, a state legislator, a member of Congress, Virginia's Governor, the President of the University of Virginia, and a delegate to the United Nations. Fond of quoting Thomas Jefferson, Darden, like Jefferson, believed in the link between education and self-government by a free people. An outspoken opponent of "massive resistance," Darden called education the "engine of civilization."[119] As President of the University of Virginia, he began the transformation of that venerable institution from a rather exclusive preserve of privilege to the dynamic capstone of education conceived by its founder, Jefferson. Within the 1968 commission, he led the way to establishing education as being among the Commonwealth's fundamental rights.[120]

Lewis F. Powell, Jr., also a member of the Commission on Constitutional Revision, was a nationally respected Richmond lawyer who had served as President of the American Bar Association. Soon after the adoption of the Virginia Constitution, Powell was appointed to the United States Supreme Court. Fellow justices have paid glowing tribute to the qualities of mind and character he brought to that tribunals's deliberations.[121] So central did Powell become to the work of the Court during his tenure that a civil liberties leader called him "the most powerful man in America."[122] Ever careful to listen to all perspectives, Powell was especially influential when the Court struggled with the "hard legal issues that lie at the center of moral and political debate."[123] In Powell, legal acumen and personal qualities came together in a way that made him such a respected jurist—and so important to the work of Virginia's commission.[124]

Another memorable figure who served on the Commission on Constitutional Revision was Hardy Cross Dillard. His life embraced more than one career. Steeped in the tradition of the humanities, Dillard was professor, then Dean, at the University of Virginia's Law School.[125] A West Point graduate, he directed the training of military government officers during World War II and later served as legal adviser to the High Commissioner of Germany. In 1970 he became a judge of the International Court of Justice at the Hague. Yale law professor Myres McDougal spoke for many when, of Dillard, he said, "He was teacher to all of us."[126]

Virginia's leading civil rights lawyer, Oliver W. Hill, served on the revision commission. In 1948, Hill was the first African American elected to Richmond's City Council. Active in the NAACP's long campaign against school segregation, Hill became the lead attorney in the Prince Edward County case, one of the five cases combined by the United States Supreme Court as *Brown v. Board of Education* in 1954. In 1999 President Clinton presented Hill, then ninety-two, with the nation's highest civilian honor, the Presidential Medal of Freedom.[127] Hill's presence on the constitutional revision commission symbolized the prospect that, in discarding the Commonwealth's 1902 Constitution (a classic post-Reconstruction document that institutionalized both the poll tax and school segregation), Virginia was on the verge of a new and more promising path. Still other commission members could be mentioned, but these several examples surely suggest that the revisors of Virginia's Constitution were no ordinary lot.

By the time the proposed new Constitution went to referendum in 1970, Virginia had elected its first Republican government since Reconstruction, Linwood Holton. Holton brought a special brand of decency to the Governor's Mansion. Declining to fight federal court school desegregation orders, Holton made front-page news throughout the nation when he escorted his thirteen-year-old daughter to a predominantly black Richmond high school. The repudiation of massive resistance could not have been more clear. J. Harvie Wilkinson III (later a federal court of appeals judge) summed up Holton's contributions: "a new air of openness in state government, two-party democracy in action, and, above all, racial understanding through personal tolerance and good will."[128] It is fitting that it was Holton who asked Professor Howard to organize the committee that campaigned successfully for the new Constitution's ratification.

The leaders who coalesced around the proposed Constitution of Virginia were not giants. Their era was not some kind of golden age. Those years saw more than enough political venality, petty politics, and social dislocations to go around. But that era did prove to be a propitious moment for constitutional change, and the Commonwealth's leaders seized that moment. Decades later, could Virginians do it again? Virginia does not lack for leadership, either in the public or private sector. But reviewing the special qualities that came to the fore during the 1969–70 constitutional revision effort, one can see that it would be no small challenge to bring together such a talented and dedicated team.

In sum, anyone who sets out today to revise Virginia's Constitution—or that of any other state—must ponder the considerable challenges. Those include partisanship, single-issue politics, the difficulty of finding common ground, the power of money, popular discontents and distrust, and the need for inspired leadership. The lesson of 1970 is that, given the right combination of circumstances, it can be done. The cautionary note sounded by the events of the years since 1970 is that it would not be easy.

NOTES

1. Jefferson to James Madison, September 6, 1789, *The Papers of Thomas Jefferson*, vol. 15, ed. Julian P. Boyd (Princeton: Princeton University Press, 1950), 395–96.

2. Jefferson to Samuel Kercheval, July 12, 1816, *The Writings of Thomas Jefferson*, vol. 10, ed. Paul Leicester Ford (New York: G. P. Putnam's Sons, 1892–1899), 43.

3. Albert L. Sturm, *Thirty Years of State Constitution-Making, 1938–1968* (New York: National Municipal League, 1970).

4. On the 1901–1902 Convention, see Ralph C. McDanel, *The Virginia Constitutional Convention of 1901–1902* (Baltimore: The Johns Hopkins University Press, 1928); Wythe W. Holt, Jr., "The Virginia Constitutional Convention of 1901–1902," *Virginia Magazine of History and Biography* 76 (1968): 67–102. Earlier revisions took place as a result of constitutional conventions in 1829–30, 1850–51, and 1867–68. For an account of the 1829–30 Convention, see A. E. Dick Howard, "'For the Common Benefit': Constitutional History in Virginia as a Casebook for the Modern Constitution-Maker," *Virginia Law Review* 54 (1968): 816–902.

5. Mills E. Godwin, Governor of Virginia, Address to the General Assembly, 10 January 1968, S. Doc. No. 1. 1968 Sess. For an evaluation of Governor Godwin's administration, see J. Harvie Wilkinson, "The Godwin Years," *The Commonwealth* (November 1969): 36.

6. H. J. Res. No. 3, 1968 Virginia Acts of Assembly, 1568.

7. The members of the Commission in addition to Governor Harrison, were Albert V. Bryan, Jr., George M. Cochran, Ted Dalton, Colgate W. Darden, Jr., Hardy Cross Dillard, Lewis F. Powell, Jr. These included two former governors of Virginia, a past president of the American Bar Association (later to be named to the Supreme Court of the United States), a law school dean (subsequently to become a Justice of the World Court at the Hague), and one of Virginia's leading civil rights lawyers.

8. For a more detailed discussion of the Commission's work and procedures, see Commission on Constitutional Revision, *The Constitution of Virginia: Report* (Richmond, 1969).

9. Editorial, *Washington Post*, 26 April 1969, sec. A, p. 10.

10. For a study of the Maryland experience, see John P. Wheeler, Jr., and Melissa Kinsey, *Magnificent Failure: The Maryland Constitutional Convention of 1967–1968* (New York: National Municipal League, 1970).

11. See notes 88–91 and accompanying text.

12. Editorial, *Farmville Herald*, 7 October 1970.

13. Editorial, *Richmond Times-Dispatch*, 28 October 1970, sec. A, p. 10.

14. Editorial, *Roanoke Times*, 18 October 1970, sec. A, p. 6.

15. Editorial, *Evening Star* (Washington), 27 October 1970, sec. A, p. 12.

16. Questions No. 3 and 4, the proposals dealing with general obligation bonds and revenue bonds respectively, were approved by 66 percent and 65 percent of the voters. Proposal No. 2, to delete the prohibition on lotteries, was affirmed by 63 percent of the voters.

17. For a superb example of a study from this era, see John P. Wheeler, Jr., and Melissa Kinsey of the rejection of a new Constitution for Maryland. J. Wheeler and M. Kinsey, *Magnificent Failure: The Maryland Constitutional Convention of 1967–68* (1970) [hereinafter cited as Wheeler]. Other studies include: R. Connors, *The Process of Constitutional Revision in New Jersey: 1940–1947* (1970) [hereinafter cited as Connors]; E. Cornwell and J. Goodman, *The Politics of the Rhode Island Constitutional Convention (1969)* [hereinafter cited as Cornwell], M. Faust, *Constitution Making in Missouri: The Convention of 1943–1944* (1971) [hereinafter cited as Faust]; N. Meller, *With an Understanding Heart: Constitution Making in Hawaii* (1971) [hereinafter cited as Meller]; W. Nunn and K. Collett, *Political Paradox: Constitutional Revision in Arkansas* (1973) [hereinafter cited as Nunn]; A. Sturm, *Constitution-Making in Michigan 1961–62* (1963) [hereinafter cited as Sturm, Michigan]; G. Wolfe, *Constitutional Revision in Pennsylvania* (1969) [hereinafter cited as Wolfe]; McKay, *Constitutional Revision in New York State: Disaster in 1967*, 19 *Syracuse Law Review* 207 (1968) [hereinafter cited as McKay].

18. See Sturm, *Thirty Years*, 98.

19. Ibid. at 103. Discussions of the New York experience include McKay, "Constitutional Revision in New York State: Disaster in 1967," 19 *Syracuse Law Review* 207 (1968); Fuld, *The Court of Appeals and the 1967 Constitutional Convention*, 38 NYSBJ 327 (1966); Kaden, *The People No! Some Observations on the 1967 New York Constitutional Convention*, 5 *Harvard Journal on Legislation*. 343 (1968); Nunez, *New York State Constitutional Reform—Past Political Battles in Constitutional Language*, 10 *William & Mary Law Review* 366 (1968); Sherry, *The New York Constitutional Convention: An Opportunity for Futher Court Structural and Constitutional Reform*, 18 *Syracuse Law Review* 542 (1967); Vanden Heuvel, *Reflections on Con-Con*, 40 NYSBJ 261 (1968).

20. Sturm, *Thirty Years*, 103; Cornwell, 80; McKay, 215–16, 220–21.

21. See Robert B. Dishman, *State Constitutions: The Shape of the Document* (New York: National Municipal League, 1968), 47–49. An example of such language is Article I of the Maryland Constitution: "That all government of right originates from the people, is founded in compact only, and instituted solely for the good of the whole, and they have at all times the inalienable right to alter, reform or abolish their form of government in such manner as they may deem expedient."

22. Ibid., 49.

23. Wheeler, 202.

24. Ibid., 5.

25. Ibid., 202–03.

26. Ibid.

27. Ibid., 231, 234.

28. Ibid., 5. Sturm, *Thirty Years,* 115. The Maryland Convention has captured the imagination of many writers. In addition to Wheeler, see, for example, Robert J. Martineau, "Maryland's 1967–68 Constitutional Convention: Some Lessons for Reformers," *Iowa Law Review* 55 (1970): 1196–1232; Thomas G. Pullen, Jr., "Why the Proposed Maryland Constitution Was Not Approved," *William and Mary Law Review* 10 (1968): 378–92.

29. Wheeler, 231.

30. Editorial, *Washington Post,* 26 April 1969, sec. A, p. 10.

31. Meller, 142.

32. Sturm, *Thirty Years,* 92.

33. Ibid., 92–93.

34. Connors, 88–89, 110–11.

35. Wheeler, 6, 51, 156–57. Wheeler cites the failure to compromise with political reality as a major reason for the defeat. Ibid., 214–15.

36. See Charles Thone, "A Constitutional Convention: The Best Step for Nebraska," *Nebraska Law Review* 40 (1961): 596, 602.

37. Sturm, *Thirty Years,* 94.

38. Sturm, *Michigan,* 54.

39. Ibid., 251. For discussions of the Michigan experience, see Melvin Nord, "The Michigan Constitution of 1963," *Wayne Law Review* 10 (1964): 309–67; "The Proposed Constitution: The Prose and Cons of It," *Michigan State Bar Journal* 42 (1963): 10–19.

40. Sturm, *Thirty Years,* 97–98.

41. Wolfe, 30, 56.

42. Connors, 193.

43. Meller, 79.

44. Wolfe, 30. For another discussion of the Pennsylvania Convention, see M. Nelson McGeary, "Pennsylvania's Constitutional Convention in Perspective," *Pennsylvania Bar Association Quarterly* 41 (1970): 175–88.

45. Connors, 200; Meller, 53–55; Wolfe, 38, 56.

46. McKay, 214.

47. Faust, 164–66.

48. Wolfe, 42, 55–56.

49. Meller, 143.

50. See text at notes 33–34, 38.

51. Compare Wheeler, 6–7.

52. Connors, 200.

53. Editorial, *Roanoke Times,* 1 November 1970, sec. A, p. 6.

54. Nunn, 118. Democrats, however, were not enthusiastic.

55. Wheeler, 3.

56. Sturm, *Michigan*, 251–52.

57. Meller, 129.

58. Ibid., 114.

59. Cornwell, 79.

60. McKay, 216.

61. Connors, 89–91.

62. Sturm, *Thirty Years*, 115. The proposed New Mexico Constitution is discussed in "Student Symposium—The New Mexico Constitutional Convention 1969," *Natural Resources Journal* 9 (1969): 422–29.

63. McKay, 221.

64. Cornwell, 80; Sturm, *Thirty Years*, 98.

65. In the one suburban area in Virginia whose local government was hostile, Chesterfield County, the referendum just barely passed.

66. Sturm, *Thirty Years*, 98 (Rhode Island), 115 (New Mexico); Robert W. Meriwether, "The Proposed Arkansas Constitution of 1970," *Nebraska Law Review* 50 (1971): 600, 620.

67. Wheeler, 141, 194.

68. Ibid., 214.

69. Meller, 128; Sturm, *Thirty Years*, 96–97.

70. Sturm, *Thirty Years*, 92; Thone, "A Constitutional Convention," 596, 601–02

71. In contrast to Maryland and Arkansas, where planning the campaign for ratification only began after the convention "which delayed the Maryland campaign and gave the opposition the uncontested field for too long a time." Wheeler, 214. See Nunn, 116.

72. Nunn, 174. See also Meriwether, "The Proposed Arkansas Constitution," 600, 621. Other accounts of Arkansas' ill-fated constitutional revision include Walter H. Nunn, "The Commission Route to Constitutional Reform: The Arkansas Experience," *Arkansas Law Review* 22 (1968): 317–39; Robert Al Leflar, "Constitutional Revision in Arkansas," *Arkansas Law Review* 24 (1970): 155–61.

73. Nunn, 156–58. For example, one "objection" was that the new constitution did not specify the meeting place of the legislature. Ibid., 157.

74. Ibid., 159–60.

75. Ibid., 158–59.

76. Wheeler, 202.

77. Ibid., 198–200.

78. Ibid., 201.

79. Ibid., 207.

80. Ibid., 192, 214.

81. Nunn, 145–47.

82. Meller, 131. At the 1969 special session of Virginia's General Assembly, a proposal to put the question of voting at age eighteen on the ballot came close to being adopted. But after some college students picketed the State Capitol on an unrelated matter, Vote-18 failed in the Senate by a vote of nineteen to twenty.

83. Wheeler, 201.

84. Ibid., 207–08.

85. Nunn, 140.

86. Wolfe, 54. See generally Sturm, *Thirty Years*, 103–04.

87. Wheeler, 193.

88. McKay, 221.

89. Ibid., 213.

90. Editorial, *New York Times*, 27 September 1967, p. 42.

91. Sturm, *Thirty Years*, 103.

92. *Virginia Statistical Abstract* (Charlottesville, VA: University of Virginia Center for Public Service, 2000).

93. V. O. Key, *Southern Politics* (New York: Alfred A. Knopf, 1949), 19.

94. See Michael D. Shear, "Incumbents Face Foes Who Stress Core Republicanism," Washington Post, June 5, 2002.

95. Federalist No. 10.

96. John T. Whelan, "Virginia: A New Look for the 'Political Museum Piece,'" in Ronald J. Hrebenar and Clive S. Thomas, eds., *Interest Group Politics in Southern States* (Tuscaloosa: University of Alabama Press, 1992), 92.

97. For an interesting account of how an array of special interests undermined an attempt at constitutional revision, see Gerald Benjamin, "The Mandatory Constitutional Convention Question Referendum: The New York Experience in National Context," 65 *Albany Law Review* 1017 (2002): 1042.

98. Larry Sabato, *Virginia Votes, 1975–78* (Charlottesville, Va.: University of Virginia Institute of Government, 1979), 71.

99. Larry J. Sabato, *Virginia Votes: 2001 Gubernatorial Elections in Virginia: The Return of Two Party Competition* (Charlottesville, Va.: Center for Governmental Studies, 2001), table 26.

100. R. H. Melton, "Fundraiser by Warner Breaks Record," *Washington Post*, June 18, 2003.

101. Michelle Boorstein, "Race Points Up GOP Divisions," *Washington Post*, June 5, 2003.

102. Bob Gibson, "Bell Takes Lead in Fund Raising," *Daily Progress* (Charlottesville), June 5, 2003. The Virginia Public Access Project reported that a total of $14,786,406 was spent by candidates in the general election for members of the House of Delegates in 2001. See VAPA's database at www.vapa.org.

103. R. H. Melton, "Campaign Costs Soar, Prompting Va. Power PACs," *Washington Post*, June 2, 2003.

104. Ibid.

105. Ibid.

106. Elizabeth Garrett and Elisabeth Gerber, "Money in the Initiative and Referendum Process: Evidence of Its Effects and Prospects for Reform," in M. Dane Waters, ed., *The Battle Over Citizen Lawmaking* (Durham, N.C.: Carolina Academic Press, 2000), 73.

107. Ibid., 79.

108. A successful venture capital businessman, Mark Warner was elected as Governor of Virginia in 2001. A former Secretary of the Navy, John Warner was elected in 1996 to his fourth term in the U.S. Senate. In addition to leadership roles as a member of Congress, Tom Davis was elected in 1998 as chairman of the National Republican Congressional Committee.

109. Larry J. Sabato, "The 2002 Elections, Virginia: Eye of the Hurricane" (unpublished), 9.

110. Ibid.

111. R. H. Melton, "N. Va. Rejects Rise in Sales Tax," *Washington Post*, November 6, 2002. In Northern Virginia, the sales tax proposal was defeated by 55 percent to 45 percent. See Commonwealth of Virginia, "November 5th, 2002 General Election," sbe.vipnet.org/nov2002/c_13_UUU.htm. In Hampton Roads, the referendum was defeated by a nearly 2-to-1 margin. Louis Hansen, "Voters Turn Transit Plan into Road Kill," *Virginian-Pilot* (Norfolk), November 6, 2002.

112. Louis Hansen and Debbie Messina, "Referendum Defeated by 2-to-1 Margin," *Virginian-Pilot* (Norfolk), November 6, 2002.

113. R. H. Melton, "Voters' Real Message Was a Call for Smart Solutions," *Washington Post*, November 14, 2002.

114. Nearly 73 percent of those who voted favored the bond issue for higher education, and nearly 69 percent voted "yes" for bonds for state parks. See sbe.state.va.us/web_docs/election/results/2002/nov/. Proponents, calling themselves Foundation 2002, included the political elite of both parties, as well as business and education leaders. See Jeff E. Schapiro, "Bond-Issue Vote Critical to Colleges," *Richmond Times-Dispatch*, October 27, 2002.

115. The proposed amendment was approved by almost 73 percent of those voting. See website cited in note 114, *supra*.

116. Of 45 proposed constitutional amendments placed on the ballot since 1970, thirty-seven have been approved, and eight defeated. State Board of Elections, "Official Election Results: Proposed Amendments to the Constitution of Virginia" (revised June 17, 2003).

117. James L. Bugg, Jr., "Mills E. Godwin, Jr.," in Edward Younger, ed., *The Governors of Virginia: 1860–1978* (Charlottesville, VA: University of Virginia, 1982), 373.

118. Ibid. 377. On Godwin's career, see M. Carl Andrews, *No Higher Honor: The Story of Mills E. Godwin, Jr.* (Richmond, Va.: Dietz Press, 1970).

119. See J. Y. Smith, "Ex-Va. Governor, University Head Colgate W. Darden, Jr., 84, Dies," *Washington Post,* June 10, 1981.

120. In World War I, Darden volunteered for the French Ambulance Corps. and received the Croix de Guerre for valor. He later served as a U.S. Marine Corps pilot, nearly losing his life in a crash. See Stuart I. Rochester and Jonathan J. Wolfe, "Colgate W. Darden, Jr.," in Younger, *Governors of Virginia,* 291–93.

121. Sandra Day O'Connor, "A Tribute to Justice Lewis F. Powell, Jr.," 101 *Harvard Law Review* 395 (1987).

122. John C. Jeffries, Jr., *Justice Lewis F. Powell, Jr.* (New York: Charles Scribner's Sons," 1994), xi.

123. Richard H. Fallon, Jr., "A Tribute to Justice Lewis F. Powell, Jr.," 101 *Harvard Law Review* 399, 401 (1987).

124. See A. E. Dick Howard, "Mr. Justice Powell and the Emerging Nixon Majority," 70 *Michigan Law Review* 445 (1972). For a superb account of the life and jurisprudence of Powell, see Jeffries, *Justice Lewis F. Powell, Jr.*

125. See A. E. Dick Howard, "Hardy Cross Dillard: Life Upon the Wicked Stage," 56 *Virginia Law Review* 10 (1970): 11.

126. George Clemon Freeman, Jr., "Hardy Cross Dillard, 1902–1982," 69 *Virginia Law Review* 809 (1983): 810.

127. Warren Fiske, "President Bestows Freedom Accolade on Civil Rights Lawyer Oliver W. Hill," *Virginian-Pilot* (Norfolk), August 12, 1999.

128. J. Harvie Wilkinson, III, "Linwood Holton," in Younger, *Governors of Virginia,* 407.

Part II

Putting Constitutional Reform on the Agenda

4

Constitutional Reform in Alabama

A Long Time in Coming

H. Bailey Thomson

On January 31, 2003, Alabama's new Republican governor, Bob Riley, convened a diverse group of citizens in Montgomery to begin deliberating changes he proposed for the state's 1901 Constitution. Thus he fulfilled his promise that constitutional reform would be the first item on his agenda to make Alabama more competitive for jobs and its government more efficient. In creating by executive order the Alabama Citizens' Constitution Commission, he gave the group ninety days to draft five changes he wanted to propose during the 2003 legislative session: providing "limited" home rule for counties on a local option basis, lessening reliance on designating revenues for particular purposes, strengthening the governor's veto power, recompiling the 1901 Constitution to remove amended language, and requiring a three-fifths majority of the legislature to impose new statewide taxes. Riley said he would ask the commission members to look at other areas of the 1901 Constitution as reform moved forward.

Riley argued, as have many other Alabamians, that the 1901 Constitution's restrictions and antiquated provisions hinder efforts to reform government and improve the economy. As a result, Alabama fares poorly in comparisons with neighboring states. In particular, Riley has pointed to North Carolina's economic success to show the connection between progressive government and concrete results. By contrast, one would be hard pressed to find a politician from another state who held up Alabama as an inspiration. The U.S. Census Bureau reported, for example, that Alabama lost 12,200 people in 2001–02. Yet the state is the geographical heart of a booming region. Why are people going elsewhere? Analysts and business leaders attributed the trend to declining prospects for good jobs.

As one exclaimed in exasperation, "It's disheartening that we're not growing as fast as Mississippi."[1]

This article explores how constitutional reform has emerged since 2000 as a centerpiece for political, economic, and social change in a state that typically addresses its most serious issues only after the federal courts require a response. Repeated failures to revise or replace the 1901 Constitution, beginning within less than a generation of its ratification, illustrate the difficulty of achieving broad reforms, particularly when issues of race cloud discussions about substantive progress. Meanwhile, the legislature and local governments have resorted to, as of early 2003, 743 amendments to patch the Constitution and evade its restrictive language. Thus Alabama's Constitution has ballooned to nearly 350,000 words, making it by far the nation's longest. One wag noted the document is about the length of *Moby Dick*, give or take a few whaling chapters.[2]

Since 1914, advocates for constitutional reform have arisen mainly from among the state's business progressives, with the exception of Governor James E. Folsom, Sr., whose two administrations in the post–World War II years revived populist themes that had lain dormant since the 1890s. What separates present attempts from previous ones is that for the first time advocates managed to create a dialogue at the grassroots level, mainly through the founding of Alabama Citizens for Constitutional Reform. The nonprofit organization and the movement it has helped inspire have enjoyed extraordinary coverage and support from the state's newspapers, in contrast to the press's lukewarm interest in previous reform efforts. This article examines the present movement's birth and tactics—a subject that the author approaches from first-hand experience as an advocate and cofounder of ACCR. Further, it looks at prospects for reform under the new gubernatorial administration. But first, let us briefly review the history of the 1901 Constitution and the earlier efforts to revise or replace its provisions.

ORIGIN OF THE 1901 CONSTITUTION

Alabama has had six constitutions, all written by conventions. Historians have praised the first document, which accompanied the state into the Union, for providing universal manhood suffrage for whites and embodying the aspirations of Jacksonian democracy. The next three constitutions reflected the state's experiences in leaving the Union and its forcible reintegration during Reconstruction. The 1875 Constitution, in turn, represented the return of conservative Democrats to power with the strong support of white yeoman farmers, who favored minimal government and low taxes. The new document limited the state's taxing authority, reduced the number of state offices, cut public salaries, and prevented local governments from lending credit to or subsidizing private corporations. The 1875 Constitution even forbade the state from engaging in internal improvements—a reaction to development schemes during Reconstruction that had more than quadrupled the state's debt. (With good reason, Governor Joseph E. Johnston, elected in 1896, called the 1875 document a "constitution of prohibition.")[3]

African Americans continued to vote after the 1875 Constitution signaled the return of conservative rule, but the removal of federal soldiers from the state made them easy targets for intimidation. In the Black Belt region, where many of the state's plantations lay, local whites actually came to value African Americans as voters—but only in a fictitious sense. Having regained control of the election machinery and having largely forced independent-minded blacks from politics, these whites developed ballot fraud into an art form. Their purpose no longer was to seize power from blacks, who made up about three-fourths of the plantation region's population; they already had accomplished that goal. Instead, conservative Democrats wielded the Black Belt's heavily black voting rolls as a club against other parts of the state, particularly those counties where the populations were mostly white and where agriculture was dependent on small farms. As one observer explained to Booker T. Washington, the famous black educator at Tuskegee, "[The black man] not only does not vote where his vote is regarded as dangerous, but upon the contrary, his vote is usually *'counted'* wherever it is needed, upon the side of [D]emocratic candidates. They would rather count the Negro *in* as a democrat than count him *out* as a [R]epublican."[4]

Fraudulent voting became particularly critical for the plantation interests when agrarian unrest swept Alabama, as it did in many other southern and western states, in the late 1880s. Caught between falling prices and rising costs, small farmers demanded the government's help to stabilize incomes and battle what they perceived to be greedy corporations, especially railroads. The movement split the Democrats into warring factions and eventually inspired the formation of the Populist Party. The agrarians' champion, Reuben Kolb, twice sought the governorship during the emotional and sometimes violent campaigns of 1892 and

1894. At one point, three different parties competed: the conservative Democrats, the Populists, and the Republicans.[5]

Faced with this threat to their power, conservative Democrats began toying with disfranchisement. Particularly worrisome to them was the agrarians' appeal across racial lines for class solidarity between white and black farmers. Conservatives in the Black Belt even considered surrendering their fictitious black majorities in return for stripping African Americans elsewhere from the voting rolls. Moreover, they reasoned that voting restrictions such as literacy and property requirements eventually would snare most poor whites as well, thereby devastating the agrarians' electoral base. A legislative act passed in 1893 made voting more difficult, especially for poorly educated citizens, and thereby diminished the agrarians' resistance. Finally, in 1901 the conservatives rolled up sufficient majorities in the plantation districts to carry an election calling for a constitutional convention in Montgomery. They brazenly hoisted the banner of white supremacy to cover a political agenda that went far beyond race.[6] Advocates of this strategy were emboldened in 1898 when the U.S. Supreme Court allowed Mississippi's disfranchisement plan to stand on the dubious notion that the state had not targeted blacks per se when it imposed literacy tests and the payment of poll taxes on citizens who wanted to vote.[7]

The convention's 155 delegates, while elected, came mostly from well-to-do circles of planters, lawyers, and businessmen. No African Americans served in that body and certainly no women. There were some dissident voices, men who were concerned about the worsening plight of small farmers and workers. And there were even a few Republicans who challenged the notion that a single party—a party for white men only—should rule the state.[8] Leaders of the convention, however, offered no concessions nor did they hide their determination to establish white supremacy. "There is a difference . . . between the uneducated white man and the ignorant negro," declared John B. Knox, a railroad lawyer, in his presidential address to the delegates. "There is in the white man an inherited capacity for government, which is wholly wanting in the negro."[9]

As the proceedings of the convention indicate, the framers meant to establish rule not just for whites but for only the right kind of white people. While quickly eliminating blacks' participation at the polls, the nation's most restrictive voting rules eventually would disfranchise an even larger number of poor whites. Suffrage provisions, for example, went beyond literacy and property holding to require that voters pay $1.50

annually in poll taxes. The tax was accumulative until the age of forty-five—a feature that put the cost of voting at $36, well beyond the means of many small farmers. The new rules also disqualified, under section 182, anyone from voting who had been convicted of a crime from a long list of offenses, which included vagrancy, a charge often used to keep blacks and poor whites in line, and miscegenation.[10] The convention's bosses did provide for a two-year grace period from complying with all of these new rules, ostensibly so that Confederate veterans and their sons might register before the door closed.

Although some delegates considered themselves to be progressives, even justifying their votes for disfranchisement on the argument that they were purifying democracy by removing unfit voters, the convention did not challenge the existing order of things. Representing mainly a coalition of planters and industrialists, its leaders wanted to preserve a weak state government and a docile and uneducated workforce. Thus the new document kept much of the anti-Reconstruction provisions of the 1875 Constitution, carrying forward, for example, its prohibition against the state's building roads, bridges, and docks, or making other internal improvements. Also preserved was the prohibition against local governments' entering into economic partnerships with corporations. Moreover, the proposed new constitution actually lowered taxes from the parsimonious levels permitted by the 1875 document. Real reforms, meanwhile, went begging. For example, the convention refused to provide better regulation of railroads. It also failed to correct the abusive system of leasing the state's convicts to private companies—a sore that would fester on the state's conscience until 1928.[11]

When the convention sent its handiwork to the voters for their ratification, opposition formed across racial lines. Even as the convention was under way, black leaders such as Booker T. Washington had petitioned delegates to treat their race fairly. Washington did not openly agitate against ratification. Instead he argued that restrictions, if applied fairly to both races, would make votes of educated, property-owning blacks more valuable—rather than be tossed aside with others in fraud. As his leading biographer has noted, Washington was no great democrat.[12] Washington later would work behind the scenes, however, to have the new constitution's disfranchising provisions thrown out by the federal courts. Other blacks adopted this strategy as well, although they were vociferous in their criticism of the document. On September 25, 1901, more than 100 African Americans, united behind the leadership of A. N. Johnson, editor of the Mobile Press, met in Birmingham and called on poor whites to vote against the proposed constitution, since the latter group would also suffer disfranchisement under its suffrage article. The black protesters vowed to boycott the election and put their hopes in the U.S. Supreme Court.[13] White opponents of the proposed constitution, meanwhile, were far less likely to call for united action. "I am not speaking for the Negro in this campaign," retorted former Governor Johnston. "I am speaking for the white man, who can vote now because the old constitution said so, but next year only the Lord and three registrars will know what he can do."[14]

The 1901 Constitution's champions proved to be better organized and enjoyed the support of leading daily newspapers, who equated the proposed constitution with white supremacy and honest government. Proponents also had one last trump card to play. As totals came in on November 11, 1901, from the plantation districts, results showed the Democrats had outdone themselves in a final act of deceit. The "yes" vote was more than 95 percent in six Black Belt counties where African Americans accounted for 75 percent of the population. Elsewhere, the proposed constitution lost, 76,263 to 72,389, in what was probably a more accurate reflection of the majority's will.[15] Despite the certainty of fraud, Governor William D. Jelks certified the new constitution on November 21, 1901.[16]

EARLIER REFORM EFFORTS

The state's new charter achieved its framers' goal of eliminating any electoral threat to the privileged classes. By 1908, only 2 percent of black males could vote in Alabama. Less noticed was an even greater numerical decline over time of participation among whites, so that by 1940 only about a third of the state's adults were even registered to vote.[17] The Constitution also ensured a minimal role for government in keeping with the 1875 predecessor's many restrictions. Soon, however, governors began to chafe from the straightjacket on their power to address challenges of the twentieth century. The first to complain publicly was Emmet O'Neal, whose father had been governor before him. The younger O'Neal had served in the 1901 convention. He had argued for home rule to provide more autonomy to local governments, but the majority preferred to centralize power within the legislature, where it could be more easily manipulated and controlled by conservative business and planter interests.

O'Neal was elected governor in 1910 on the pledge to run the state like a good business, thereby reducing fraud and waste. Yet once in office, he recoiled from how few options the 1901 Constitution allowed for responsive government. In particular, he deplored how the state lacked money for schools. "The first and most important step to improve the educational conditions in Alabama would be the convening of a constitutional Convention to revise our present antiquated fundamental law," O'Neal said in a speech to University of Alabama alumni in 1914.[18] He summarized his arguments in his annual report to the legislature in 1915, declaring that the defects of the present document "are so numerous and radical, and so intermingled in the different sections" that only remodeling the entire Constitution could suffice.[19]

In the early 1920s, Governor Thomas E. Kilby, a progressive from the emerging industrial city of Anniston, likewise condemned the Constitution's restrictive nature. To make government work more efficiently, he advocated naming a commission to recommend ways that a convention might rewrite the 1901 Constitution. Yet like O'Neal, Kilby left for others the great task of drafting what amounted to a new business plan for the state. Similar calls for reform came from two other sources before World War II. First, the Brookings Institution, in a report it prepared in 1932 at the request of Governor B. M. Miller, observed that no significant improvements in government could occur without rewriting many of the restrictive provisions of the 1901 Constitution. Later in that decade, a group of citizens who called themselves the Alabama Policy Committee began studying the Constitution and issuing papers about its defects. In 1938, the group called for a new constitution and then recommended a model document of its own. The efforts, however, produced no reforms.[20]

The most ardent champion for a new constitution proved to be not a business progressive but rather a spiritual heir of populism. Governor James E. Folsom had grown up listening to his father and uncle, an avowed populist, talk about politics. Voters in Coffee County, where they lived in the southeastern corner of the state, had been sympathetic to the agrarian revolt in the 1890s and opposed to the 1901 Constitution. As an adult, Folsom moved to Cullman County in northern Alabama to run his family's insurance business. There he found a similar political history. Thus Folsom's successful candidacy for governor in 1946 managed to span two distinct regions of the state and help unite them under a neopopulist platform.[21]

"Big Jim," who stood six feet and eight inches tall, campaigned with a string band called the Strawberry Pickers. They would warm up the crowds in school auditoriums or courthouse squares. Then Folsom would take the microphone and, holding up a corn shuck mop, promise to clean out Montgomery. He liked to talk about letting a "cool, green breeze" blow through the Capitol. In his rustic plain speech, he articulated what many people wanted, as attention shifted to peacetime and hopes for prosperity. He promised to build new roads and provide better schools. Old people would have small pensions, and teachers would earn adequate pay. Above all, Folsom maintained that citizens should rule and not the plantation owners and industrialists who traditionally ran things in Montgomery.

Folsom shocked the political establishment, first by making the run-off election and then by defeating Lieutenant Governor Handy Ellis by 55,000 votes. Unlike many Southern politicians, Folsom did not appeal to racial prejudice, nor did he blame "outside agitators" for the state's poor image and its low rankings on services such as public education. Rather, he tried to explain to people that Alabama had inflicted much of the backwardness on itself through its failure to embrace the nation's democratic ideals.[22] True to his promise, Folsom brought constitutional reform to center stage. Unlike O'Neal and Kilby, he was prepared to commit political capital to this issue. Indeed, he declared in his inaugural address on January 20, 1947, "I am not afraid of too much democracy. I am afraid of what happens to people when they have too little democracy."[23]

A few weeks later, Folsom called the legislature into special session to demand it approve a constitutional convention. Only through rewriting the state's fundamental charter, he argued, could citizens hope to achieve fair representation in place of the rotten borough system that had prevailed since 1901. Folsom complicated his efforts, however, by also asking the Senate to confirm three new trustees for the state's land-grant college at Auburn. He intended to remove the powerful Agricultural Extension Service from political participation, an ambition that its leaders and their allies in the Alabama Farm Bureau were determined to thwart. They worked through friendly senators to inflict a humiliating defeat on Folsom.[24]

Nevertheless, Folsom repeatedly called lawmakers into special sessions to consider constitutional reform. His first objective remained reapportionment of the legislature to break the stranglehold that the planter-industrialist coalition had enjoyed since 1901. In particular, Folsom wanted more representation for what he called the "piney woods and hill country," areas that in the 1890s had revolted against rule by conservative Democrats. The legislature's refusal to reapportion itself according to population punished the former populist strongholds, while punitive voting rules continued to disfranchise most African Americans and many poor whites. Folsom made some of his best arguments in a radio address on April 3, 1949: The main purpose of the 1901 Constitution, he told his listeners, was to deny the ballot to Alabama's black citizens. But the document's many voting restrictions, especially a punitive poll tax, had disfranchised poor whites as well. Thus the 1901 Constitution was profoundly racist and antidemocratic and contrary to the values that Americans had just fought to protect in World War II. Second, Folsom decried how the 1901 Constitution made no provision for allowing local people to govern themselves. Instead, legislators passed local laws for counties, often swapping favors among themselves to promote pet legislation. Indeed, the Constitution so distrusted government at all levels that it impeded progress and the creation of good jobs. Finally, the Constitution enshrined an unfair tax system that afforded certain groups special privileges, while denying the state adequate revenues. This practice violated the principle that each should pay according to his means. The governor concluded his remarks by stating, "I believe that the progress we have made in the past 50 years will be many times surpassed during the half century ahead if we do not remain hide-bound by old-fashioned laws. And certainly the greatest single need toward that progress is a new constitution."[25]

Folsom could not succeed himself in office, but the four years that intervened between his first and second terms left him more determined to finish what he had started in 1947. Reelected without a run-off in 1954, he once again pushed for the long-awaited constitutional convention. Some legislators indicated they might go along if a convention could be limited to certain topics. They feared that the immensely popular Folsom might pressure the convention into allowing a governor to succeed himself. More indicative of the times, however, was their concern that a convention might weaken white supremacy.[26] Indeed, legislators from the Black Belt made no effort to hide the intent of the present voting laws. In opposing a bill to abolish the $1.50 poll tax, Representative W. L. Martin of Greene County retorted that such action might "destroy the fundamental principles behind the constitution." Noting that blacks outnumbered whites six to one is his county, he warned colleagues they might be sitting next to an African-American lawmaker if the poll tax were repealed.[27] The Alabama Supreme Court heightened such fears when it ruled that section 284 of the Constitution allowed for no restrictions on a convention.[28]

Folsom called the legislature to another special session on January 3, 1956, and again he asked for a convention.[29] The issue of school desegregation, however, quickly overtook his reform agenda. On January 19, the legislature passed, with just four dissenting votes, a resolution declaring the U.S. Supreme Court's 1954 decision *Brown v. Board of Education* to be "null, void and of no effect." Folsom reacted with disdain, calling a press conference to scold the legislators for ignoring constitutional reform and for being obsessed with the race issue.[30] His political strength, however, which had been so evident the year before, quickly began to dissipate in relation to his continued moderation on race.

Emotions boiled over on February 3 when Autherine J. Lucy, an African American, began attending classes at the University of Alabama. A riot ensued in Tuscaloosa, and on February 6 the Board of Trustees suspended its first black student, ostensibly for her own safety. Folsom's failure to act decisively during this crisis, coupled with many white Alabamians' anger over his lack of enthusiasm for resisting civil rights, caused him to suffer a humiliating loss the following May, when Alabama voters overwhelmingly rejected his bid for a place on the Democratic National Committee. His crusades over, Folsom limped through the rest of his term in an alcoholic daze.[31]

Constitutional reform would be revived a decade later by a lawyer from Decatur named Albert Brewer. He had served in the legislature during the second Folsom administration and went on to be speaker of the House. In 1966 he won election as lieutenant governor. Though forced to operate within the state's rigid segregationist system, Brewer wanted a new constitution. Like Folsom, he chafed at the planter-industrial coalition's control of the state's politics, to the detriment of his native Morgan County on the Tennessee River. Brewer got his chance when Governor Lurleen Wallace, a surrogate in office for her pugnacious husband, George, died of cancer on May 7, 1968. Upon succeeding her, Brewer began pursuing a progressive agenda, which included a new constitution.

He advocated a constitutional commission and in 1969 asked the Legislature to adopt a suitable plan for proceeding. After considerable wrangling within that body over how to appoint a commission—including one suggestion that all 140 legislators should serve—a conference committee finally produced an acceptable method. It called for a commission of twenty-one members, with the governor appointing fourteen of them. In signing the new legislation, Brewer put the full support of his young administration behind what would be the most ambitious effort since 1901 to draft a new constitution. He appointed Conrad Fowler, a respected probate judge from Shelby County, as chairman of the group and advised commissioners that they should concentrate on those areas of the old document that most needed reform. The group assembled a staff of experts and began deliberating.[32]

As the new commission worked, Alabama's politics continued to boil over racial integration—and over George Wallace's ambitions. Wallace told Brewer that he would not oppose the latter's election to a full term, but the former governor reneged because he needed access to high rollers who would contribute to his next presidential campaign in return for lucrative state contracts. Once in the race, Wallace returned to the segregation issue, which had propelled him to office in 1962, and he excoriated national politicians, federal bureaucrats, and others whom he accused of taking away control of local schools. Most of the daily newspapers, however, threw their support behind Brewer, and the first primary ended with Wallace trailing. Shocked at what appeared to be a repudiation of his politics, Wallace and his supporters resorted in the second primary to a bagful of dirty tricks so outrageous that even the nation's press took notice. So that no one missed the point, Wallace's campaign newspaper warned that blacks were about to seize control of the state. The appeal to old prejudices worked, thereby ending Brewer's promising career as a reformer.[33]

Though orphaned and hardly a priority of the legislature, the Brewer commission pressed on with its work. It presented its final report on May 1, 1973, along with its proposed revision of the 1901 Constitution. The changes it recommended for the legislature to consider recognized seven basic principles for reformers to follow. One called for removing "undue and unnecessary restrictions on the power of the Legislature." Annual sessions were viewed as one step toward this goal. Another principle advocated vesting more authority in the governor, in recognition of greatly increased responsibilities. Likewise, the state's court system needed modernization. One particularly significant feature was a proposed new article that would grant home rule to local governments, even to the point of allowing counties to operate under charters ratified by their electors. If adopted, this model for home rule would have tracked efforts in other southern states to provide for local democracy on issues such as growth management, environmental protection, and exercise of police powers.[34]

Wallace and the legislature took little notice of the commission's recommendations, with a couple of notable exceptions. Legislators did approve and offer to voters in 1973 an amendment to rewrite the 1901 Constitution's judicial article. With the electorate's approval of what became amendment 328, Alabama replaced its chaotic and often ridiculed judicial system with one that quickly earned praise.[35] The leadership of Chief Justice Howell Heflin, who went on to become a U.S. senator, demonstrated that any reform, regardless of how well-intentioned, required a strong champion to overcome entrenched opposition.[36] Two years later, voters approved amendment 339, which provided for annual sessions of the legislature. Reformers hailed this action for providing legislators with more flexibility to address the state's problems.[37]

Throughout these discussions, reformers had assumed that the legislature could revise the 1901 Constitution or even draft a new document to replace it, subject to voters' ratification. Indeed, they considered such a proposal from Governor Fob James, who succeeded Wallace in 1979. The Senate approved a proposed constitution he offered, but the House refused to go along. In 1983, the legislature under the leadership of Lieutenant Governor Bill Baxley, who presided over the Senate, recompiled the 1901 Constitution and offered some improvements. The proposed document already was ready for submission to voters when a last-minute challenge, led by Rick Manley, a senator from the Black Belt region, persuaded the Alabama Supreme Court to declare Baxley's method to be unconstitutional. The court's majority narrowly interpreted section 286 of the Alabama Constitution to mean that only a convention could draft a new document. The legislature could not simply offer what amounted to a new document under the guise of amending the Constitution. Instead, the legislature had to proceed with revision on a piecemeal basis, although presumably it could offer more than one article at a time to voters.[38]

THE CURRENT REFORM MOVEMENT

The Need for Reform

The case for replacing the 1901 Constitution remains overwhelming, even as the history of reform provides a sad story of frustration. The document suffers from at least three serious defects:

First, the Constitution places such severe restrictions on government that it often fails to meet the demands of a modern society. Stark evidence of this deficiency can be found in studies published in 1999 and 2001 by *Governing* magazine, in collaboration with the Maxwell School of Syracuse University. These studies ranked state governments' performance in various areas. In both studies, Alabama placed last.[39]

Second, the Constitution is profoundly distrustful of democracy, especially when exercised at the local level. In fact, Alabama is the only southeastern state that denies its counties the authority to plan for growth. Neighboring states allow counties to pass their own laws, provided they are consistent with statewide policy. By contrast, about half of the Alabama legislature's agenda is devoted to issues of local interest, while lawmakers often ignore larger statewide questions.[40] Local governments often have little choice but to seek a change in fundamental law to achieve some needed action at home, such as pest control or even the removal of dead farm animals. Every critic of the Constitution has his favorite amendment to evoke a risible response to the document's statutory nature, but local governments depend on such changes for authorization to do their essential work.

Finally, the 1901 Constitution enshrines an unfair and ineffective tax system. Indeed, a study published in the February 2003 issue of *Governing* ranked the system among the nation's bottom three for its unfairness.[41] Because two of the major tax sources—property and income—are shielded by the Constitution and thereby difficult to change, governments and school boards in Alabama must rely to a dangerous degree on regressive and fickle sales taxes. Therein lie the seeds of the financial crisis that Riley, the new governor, inherited. On the eve of their regular session, lawmakers learned they would need $500 million more than their experts had forecast to maintain present levels of spending and meet rising costs for pension and health care for public employees.[42]

Compounding the state's present financial difficulties is the practice of designating, either by constitutional or statutory law, how nearly 90 percent of state dollars must be spent. By comparison, Mississippi earmarks less than 30 percent of its public dollars, and North Carolina only 15 percent. The United States average is about 22 percent.[43] As a consequence of Alabama's extreme reliance on earmarking, the legislature may not shift dollars from the $4.2 billion education fund to the much smaller general fund to relieve, say, crowding in prisons. The Constitution earmarks revenues from the income tax for teachers' salaries, and the powerful Alabama

Education Association ferociously guards this source. Besides, Alabama's public school system requires, by conservative estimates, at least an additional $1 billion to achieve the goals that its board desires.

A modern constitution, by contrast, would establish broad principles under which government would operate, while not imposing restrictions to impede good lawmaking. Certainly, it would recognize that local problems need to be solved at home and not in Montgomery. While protecting citizens' rights, it would organize government into efficient branches. To provide for revenues, the constitution would need only to authorize certain types of taxation. By contrast, the present document is a virtual tax code in itself, specifying provisions right down to assessment rates for motor vehicles.[44] Finally, a modern constitution would speak to citizens' aspirations for their democracy. The U.S. Constitution is the model for the world because it embodies and articulates the belief that free people can govern themselves in a republic. That achievement contrasts with the Alabama's Constitution's shameful attempt to roll back democracy and freeze into place conditions that discouraged people from becoming educated, productive citizens.

The Process of Reform

Such arguments received renewed attention in 1994, when the *Mobile Register* published a special report on the Alabama Constitution titled "Sin of the Fathers."[45] Motivation for this considerable investment of staff energy came from earlier investigations into persistent problems that bedeviled the state, particularly in the areas of inadequate educational funding and inefficient government at both state and local levels. The report, published in a tabloid format, provided in-depth explanation on how the document exacerbated these and other problems. An accompanying series of editorials, which called for a constitutional convention, became a finalist for the Pulitzer Prize. The newspaper's work inspired a conference in Montgomery in December 1995, attended by scholars, business leaders, politicians, and journalists. After hearing speeches from political leaders and papers by scholars and legal experts, the participants held a mock convention in the Alabama House's chamber. Later, the event's sponsors published the conference's proceedings.[46] They also sponsored a statewide town meeting, televised by Alabama Public Television and moderated by David Mathews, president and chief executive officer of the Kettering Foundation. Panelists in various cities aired their views, pro and con, on the merits of constitutional reform.

Unfortunately for the reformers, however, the election of Fob James to his second term as Alabama's governor—this time as a Republican instead of a Democrat—put on hold any hopes for leadership on this issue. James not only had lost interest in rewriting the 1901 Constitution by this time but even showed hostility toward reform in general. For example, he expressed pride that Alabama had the nation's lowest taxes per capita. However, scholars such as Wayne Flynt, a distinguished history professor at Auburn University, noted the correlation between low taxes among Mississippi, Alabama, Louisiana, and Arkansas and with the low standings in certain key measures of quality of life, such as children living in hunger, births to teenagers, low per-capita incomes, and high school dropouts.[47] Meanwhile, the Constitution continued to swell with new amendments, most of them addressing local matters.

Lieutenant Governor Don Siegelman trounced James from office in 1998, but the Democrat did not immediately embrace reform either. His failure to win voters' approval for a state lottery left him chastened to the point that he announced in early 2000 that he would not tilt at windmills such as constitutional and tax reform. Siegelman's ill-chosen words immediately inspired the *Birmingham News* to dub him "Don Quixote" and to ridicule his timidity in face of growing problems at the state level.[48] When Siegelman finally did support reform a year later, many citizens remained skeptical of his sincerity. The *Mobile Register*'s cartoonist characterized his new enthusiasm as that of a convert on his political deathbed.[49]

Leadership for constitutional reform, meanwhile, surfaced among the citizenry when the West Alabama Chamber of Commerce in Tuscaloosa held a rally on April 7, 2000, to put the issue on the state's agenda. Former Governor Brewer and William Winter, a former reform-minded governor of Mississippi, were among the speakers, along with historian Wayne Flynt at Auburn, whose research and writing had pricked the state's conscience for years. Well attended and covered by the press, the rally brought back memories of old-style politics with its string music, food, and impassioned speeches. More important, the event marked the beginning of a statewide organization that would devote its energies to achieving the reformers' goals. The rally's participants confirmed Dr. Thomas E. Corts, president of Samford University in Birmingham, as the new chairman, while designating a dozen citizens to guide the new organization's formation.[50]

Alabama Citizens for Constitutional Reform (ACCR), the new reform group, could count on something new: Support was growing among business leaders for fundamental improvements in how Alabama governs itself. The old legislative coalition of Birmingham-area industrialists and large landowners from the Black Belt had disintegrated by the early 1960s, as urban interests diverged significantly from the old status quo on issues such as reapportionment and public services.[51] Moreover, urban business leaders came to recognize that they needed a well-educated workforce more than they needed a miserly tax system and weak government. By the 1990s a new generation of business leaders had emerged, inspired by examples such as William Smith, an heir and executive at Royal Cup Coffee who organized and led the state's most prominent educational reform group, A Plus. The Public Affairs Research Council, a small think tank in Birmingham, provided citizens and lawmakers with independent analysis of the state's problems through regular publication of reports on issues such as taxation and education.

ACCR's organizers recruited a diverse group of leaders and civic activists for its board. Operating at first from the author's spare bedroom, the non-profit group gradually built membership and began issuing newsletters and holding public events. In January 2001, it opened a small office in Montgomery and hired a young consultant named Bill Smith, who had experience in managing Republican political campaigns. He helped refine ACCR's message and create a legislative agenda for 2001.

Crafting a legislative strategy was essential because the Legislature must initiate and approve any constitutional changes. By a three-fifths vote of each legislative chamber, it may submit proposed constitutional amendments to voters, as provided in section 284. Section 286 authorizes a majority of all members in each legislative chamber to call a constitutional convention. The legislature decides how delegates will be selected and how the convention will organize itself. Once adopted, the proposal for a convention must be submitted to the electorate for approval.

Leadership in the House of Representatives had tried on several occasions prior to 2001 to revise the 1901 Constitution on an article-by-article basis, beginning with the more outrageously antiquated provisions, but had succeeded only after federal legislative or court action already had nullified the original language. Thus in 1996 Amendment 579 replaced the lengthy article VIII, which contained the infamous restrictions on voting. Four years later, voters ratified Amendment 667, which removed the prohibition on interracial marriages found in section 102. But progress stalled after those revisions. Representative Jack Venable of Tallassee, chairman of the House's Rules Committee, proposed in 2002 to amend six more articles. His target was outdated language, such as found in article XIII, which authorizes state banks to circulate bills as money and to redeem them in gold or silver, and article II, which inaccurately describes the state's boundaries. Opponents, however, read dark conspiracies into his proposed changes. The House approved the amendments, but the Senate either refused to act or added provisions that Venable would not accept.[52]

Despite such vocal protests against even a cleanup of constitutional language, public opinion polls consistently showed strong support for revision among citizens at large. The great majority of respondents who supported reform favored the convention method. For example, ACCR employed Washington pollster Jan van Lohuizen to conduct a scientific survey of six hundred registered voters from March 3 through 6, 2002. He found that two-thirds of the respondents were aware of reform efforts. Of that group, 58 percent favored writing a new constitution, while only 12 percent trusted the legislature to do the job.[53]

In hopes of encouraging the legislature to push reform higher on its agenda while addressing the fears that many lawmakers expressed about holding a convention, ACCR in 2001 supported an alternative approach proposed by Representative Ken Guin, chairman of the House Elections Committee. He proposed an amendment that would permit the legislature to submit a new constitution for voters' approval. In effect, this amendment would nullify the Alabama Supreme Court's 1983 *Manley* decision,[54] which limited legislative reform to no more than a few articles at a time. Guin was unable to generate sufficient interest among his House colleagues to pass the proposal, although he did manage to bring the issue to the floor for debate. The majority of members clearly were not ready yet to take responsibility for drafting a new constitution themselves, nor were they disposed to delegate that authority to a citizens convention.[55]

Still, reform continued to gain attention, as ACCR built a bipartisan base that managed to transcend the bitterness between Democrats, who retained a comfortable majority in both houses, and Republicans, who continued to smart over how the majority party in 1999 had prevented their colleague, Steve Windom, from exercising the traditional powers of lieutenant governor as presiding officer of the Senate. ACCR gained statewide attention in April 2001 when Siegelman publicly endorsed its mission at a rally in Montgomery. Later that year, he summoned the spirit of Jim Folsom in calling for a convention to write a new constitution. He said schoolchildren would be the main beneficiaries once a new document lifted restrictions on how communities taxed themselves for education. At the time, the state's educational system was in the throes of "proration"—a reduction in spending that the 1901 Constitution mandates when revenues fall short of the budget's expectation. Siegelman vowed that schools would not suffer such a fate again under his watch if he could help it—a stance that drew praise from editorialists.[56]

ACCR continued to hold rallies and forums around the state through its strategy of educating and motivating voters. Donations from public-minded corporations, along with dues and contributions from about 1,500 members, allowed the organization to hire a small staff. This emphasis on organization sharply distinguished the present movement from previous efforts. Although five governors and a lieutenant governor had advocated constitutional reform and on three occasions their efforts had even inspired proposed new documents, no citizens group had operated independently to build grassroots support for change. Indeed, this growing bipartisan movement belied the scoffing of some legislators and special interests that no one cared about a new constitution.

The movement also triggered intense reaction from groups claiming to represent conservative Christians. Opponents began to crank up web sites and issue press releases, warning that a new constitution could lead to higher taxes, antireligious actions, or worse. It seemed that the more outlandish and conspiratorial their responses, the more likely these opponents were to appear alongside the reformers on talk shows and televised town meetings.

Although the state's newspapers covered opposition groups, sometimes providing them with more attention than their numbers might warrant, reporters and editorial writers began conducting their own investigations of the constitutional issues. In the process, their remarkably thorough work helped make the complex history and issues of constitutional reform accessible to newspaper readers, while moving the subject higher on the public agenda. In this aspect of public attention, the present experience differed remarkably from previous efforts to achieve reform. In the early 1970s, for example, the state's newspapers showed little interest in the work of Brewer's commission, in part because it dragged on for more than three years, often with little enthusiasm among some of its members. A generation earlier when Folsom had repeatedly brought the legislature into special sessions to call a convention, the dailies had focused more on his political and personal failures rather than on their obligation to explain the issues behind constitutional reform. By contrast, Alabama's newspapers began in 2000 publishing carefully researched reports and issuing thunderous editorials for change. This massive body of journalistic work amplified ACCR's message to an extraordinary volume, while providing independent evidence in support of reform.[57] Meanwhile, the attention lavished on constitutional reform helped inspire renewed scholarly interest in the subject. The *Alabama Law Review*, for example, devoted an entire issue in the fall of 2001 to constitutional reform.[58]

Among the principles that ACCR had promulgated in 2001 was a strong preference for a convention of citizen delegates to draft a new constitution. (The board, however, did not rule out pursuing revision through an article-by-article basis, preferring to emphasize the larger goal of reform over any particular methods.) With the help of Professor Howard Walthall and former Governor Brewer at the Cumberland Law School at Samford University, ACCR's staff and legislative specialists translated this preference into a resolution calling for a convention. Sympathetic lawmakers introduced the resolution in the 2002 regular session.[59]

The legislation offered the following provisions:

- During the next general election, voters would decide whether to call a constitutional convention.
- If they said yes, then seven months later, they would elect 105 delegates from the newly apportioned House districts. These districts would ensure a fair representation of minority voters.
- Delegates would convene the following August to organize and elect a president. Afterward, they could adjourn to wherever they saw fit to conduct their business. They would be fairly compensated for up to 120 days. They would also have the support of the legislative staff to conduct their work.
- The convention would present its document to the voters for ratification no sooner than 90 days after the work was finished. This interim would assure voters ample time to get copies of the proposed constitution and study it.
- If voters approved, the new constitution would take effect the following January 1.

In offering its plan for calling a convention, ACCR meant to provide the legislature with a blueprint rather than insist that the legislation be accepted or rejected in its original form. In retrospect, the failure to consult with more legislators beforehand, particularly members of the black caucus, left opponents with an excuse to dismiss the legislation without giving it full consideration. While Siegelman publicly endorsed ACCR's legislation and substituted it for a convention plan he had announced earlier, the governor's office proved to be of little help in securing legislative support. Nevertheless, ACCR's plan did survive its first committee hearing, a raucous affair in which opponents of every persuasion testified along with advocates for change. But the bill failed on a voice vote on the House floor.[60] To add insult to that inglorious end, legislators awarded their "Black Shroud" to one of the bill's sponsors, in recognition that the proposal was dead on arrival.

ACCR did see the passage without opposition of its proposed amendment to clarify confusion over interpretations of section 286 and guarantee that voters would have final say on any new constitution. This proposal sought to quell fears, fanned by opponents of reform, that a convention might run wild and saddle citizens with unpopular provisions and higher taxes. In the general election of November 4, 2002, the measure, now Amendment 714, passed with an approval rate of 81 percent—by far the largest margin of that election.

The arguments offered by opponents to ACCR's carefully drawn plan for a convention deserve some comments here, even as Riley has chosen to pursue reform through amendments to the present document.

First, legislators expressed fear that special interests would dominate a convention. ACCR's response was that its proposed legislation imposed some of the tightest restrictions possible under present law on political contributions and gifts. For example, a supporter could contribute only $100, either in money or services, to a candidate for delegate. A candidate could accept no gift, not even a cup of coffee. By contrast, Alabama law imposes no limit on how much an individual or a political action committee may donate to someone running for the legislature. Legislators even refused to end the practice of political action committees' transferring money back and forth to one another, thereby obscuring the sources of political contributions. Equally insidious is that a lobbyist may spend up to $250 per day on each legislator—plying him or her with meals, trips, and other gifts—without having to report the expenditure to the state Ethics Commission.

Second, some African-American legislators argued that minorities would not be sufficiently represented in a convention, particularly if the elections were nonpartisan. ACCR's plan called for electing 105 delegates on a non-partisan basis from newly drawn House districts because their boundaries already had passed muster with the federal courts as fairly representing Alabama's racial composition. In ACCR's view, electing delegates on this basis would virtually guarantee a strong minority presence in a convention, just as the districts assure such representation in the legislature. Under the plan, the remaining delegates would be the twelve lawmakers whom the legislature elects every four years to serve on a council that conducts business between sessions. Without being large enough to dominate the proceedings, this group would bring to the convention valuable experience in the practical aspects of government. Four of the elected council members in 2002 were African Americans. Such arguments, however, failed to quell the objections, although many black legislators assured ACCR's leadership that they favored constitutional reform.[61]

Finally, certain legislative leaders insisted, mostly in private conversations, that drafting a constitution was too complicated to entrust with citizens elected as convention delegates. Their concerns, however, did not explain why the same voters, who appeared to be quite competent when electing legislators, could not be trusted to select delegates for a convention. This attitude on the part of lawmakers was in stark contrast to sentiments expressed in public opinion polls and letters to the editor that voters actually trusted citizen delegates far more than legislators to draft a new constitution. ACCR's plan actually prohibited legislators and other statewide elected officials from running as a delegate on the grounds that responsibility for writing job descriptions for such elected officials was best left to the employers themselves: the citizens.

Whatever their reasons for opposing a convention, legislators sidestepped the central issue: Who deserves the final say in Alabama? Article I, section II of the Alabama Constitution vests all political power in the people. They have an "inalienable and indefeasible right to change their form of government in such manner as they may deem expedient." But for now, at least, it appears that the people will have to exercise this right indirectly through the Legislature, which shows no inclination to surrender any of its considerable prerogatives to a convention of elected delegates.

With the 2002 legislative session over, politics focused on the primaries and general elections of 2002. Siegelman announced that he would campaign for a constitutional convention and launched a series of town meetings around the state to discuss this issue and others. As the campaign progressed, however, Siegelman said less about constitutional reform and focused instead on condemning large companies for escaping taxation through loopholes in a new state corporate tax law—a law that Siegelman earlier had blessed. With this tactic, he resorted to a populist theme of condemning big business for the state's inadequate revenues, ignoring that middle-class homeowners were among the major beneficiaries of the regressive tax structure. Congressman Bob Riley, meanwhile, won the Republican primary and offered himself as a progressive alternative to Siegelman. Riley targeted financial scandals that the *Mobile Register* and other newspapers had uncovered within the Siegelman administration as evidence that Alabama needed new leadership. Moreover, he announced that he would run government in keeping with sound business practices and that he would immediately begin addressing chronic problems in the tax system and the 1901 Constitution. Riley rejected a constitutional convention as the best means for achieving reform, preferring instead to appoint blue-ribbon commissions to recommend changes.

Already, ACCR had anticipated the need to move beyond principles and provide a blueprint for substantive changes to the Constitution. Former Governor Brewer suggested at the executive committee's meeting in December 2001 that ACCR revive the idea of asking a diverse group of citizens to recommend reforms. ACCR's board accepted the challenge and then raised money through its members and private donors to support the work. The board appointed twenty-two commission members largely from outside its organization, drawing on dozens of nominations from around the state. In a highly publicized press conference in Montgomery, ACCR's chairman, Thomas Corts, introduced Secretary of State Jim Bennett, a long-time advocate for reform, as the commission's new chairman. The author agreed to serve as the group's volunteer educational director, and Professor Walthall at the Cumberland Law School became its volunteer technical director. They assembled two dozen technical advisers who agreed to draft papers on various issues and present their findings at the commission's statewide hearings. This group of experts included political scientists and legal scholars, as well as retired justices of the Alabama Supreme Court.

The commission held its organizational meeting on July 15, 2002, at Huntsville's Constitutional Village—the site of a convention that wrote Alabama's 1819 Constitution. Several hundred citizens turned out to view the proceedings, and more than forty people spoke to the commission members on whether Alabama needed a new constitution. Most agreed that it did. Similar events occurred later in 2002 in Birmingham, Mobile, and the Auburn/Opelika area.

The commission divided into five committees to make recommendations in the areas of local democracy, taxation and indebtedness, economic development, education, and government organization. The committees met independently and, in many cases, conducted their own research to supplement that provided by the experts. Each committee chairman, in turn, participated in drafting the commission's final report and submitted it to Chairman Corts and the ACCR board on January 16, 2003—just four days before Riley took his oath of office. Newspapers quickly publicized the report and their editorial boards weighed in with thoughtful editorials, generally endorsing the commission's conclusions.[62] (In the summer of 2003, Cumberland published the academic papers and the commission's report in its law review.)

The timing of this work proved to be propitious indeed. Once in office, Riley kept his campaign promise and announced the appointment of his own commission to undertake selected revisions of the 1901 Constitution. He also journeyed to Huntsville to connect symbolically with the state's 1819 constitutional convention, which produced a model document for its time. With his administration's first executive order, Riley announced that Secretary Bennett would chair his commission, just as he had led the ACCR group. The vice chairman would be Lenora Pate, an energetic lawyer and activist from Birmingham. Thirty-three other citizens with diverse backgrounds and political views filled the commission's ranks. The group's assignment was to propose amendments that would (1) bring limited home rule to Alabama's counties, (2) strengthen the governor's veto powers, (3) eliminate earmarking of revenues, (4) recompile the 1901 Constitution into a more user-friendly document, and (5) impose a three-fifths majority vote in the Legislature for any tax increases.[63] The author of this article served as cochairman of the home rule committee.

The Governor's call to action on the first three items closely tracked the ACCR commission's recommendations. The last two items, however, concerned many reformers. They feared that recompilation might become an excuse for making few if any substantive changes. Simply removing dead language and organizing local amendments in some coherent fashion would leave the status quo untouched. Moreover, the

Public Affairs Research Council and the legislature's research staff already have offered similar recompilations as a convenience to lawmakers and citizens. Opponents of the three-fifths rule, meanwhile, deplored the prospect of erecting yet another constitutional barrier to achieving tax fairness. Supporters of the measure countered that it was necessary to guard against runaway taxation once tax reform removed other constitutional barriers. Despite such reservations, the commission voted on March 14 to approve the work of its five committees and send the recommendations to the Governor.[64]

Earlier, Riley had indicated he would ask another blue-ribbon group to address tax reform. His action had precedent, although not one to inspire much confidence. Twice in the early 1990s, similar blue-ribbon commissions returned sensible suggestions for broadening the state's tax base and lessening its dependence on regressive taxation, but the legislature refused to act.[65] In 1991 the *Birmingham News* won a Pulitzer Prize for editorials that championed tax reform. Yet as a speaker noted at the 2003 meeting of the Public Affairs Research Council, children who entered kindergarten that year never enjoyed the benefit of adequate tax revenues to support their education.[66]

True to his intentions, Riley immersed himself in proposing to the Legislature a package of tax reforms that would not only provide an additional $675 million to fund existing programs but also provide for long-term revenue growth. In the process, he proposed to address the notoriously regressive nature of the present tax system, especially its reliance on sales taxes. A deeply religious man, Riley drew inspiration for his actions from an evangelical law professor's indictment of Alabama's tax system. Susan Pace Hamill, in her thoroughly documented and theologically couched arguments, condemned the system for violating Judeo-Christian teachings by oppressing the poor for the benefit of the wealthy. In her commentaries for newspapers and frequent speeches, Hamill asserted that constitutional reform and tax reform are inseparable and must be pursued vigorously to redeem the state from its sinful practices.[67]

Riley drew support from a group of top corporate executives who amassed a war chest of several million dollars to take this fight first to the legislature and then to the voters. Their leader was one of the state's most astute lobbyists, William O'Connor, who left a lucrative position as head of the Business Council of Alabama to organize the campaign. A gifted speaker with a broader social agenda than typically has been the case for BCA's executives, O'Connor envisioned tax reform coming together with constitutional and education reforms in an all-out effort to catapult Alabama into regional leadership.[68]

Indeed, the work of the tax reformers intersected in key areas with that of Riley's constitutional commission. For example, local governments and school boards are prohibited by Amendment 373 from raising ad valorem taxes without first securing the legislature's permission and then holding a referendum to seek voters' approval. Repeatedly, Riley emphasized the high priority he placed on decentralizing government in Alabama so that elected county officials could decide local matters such as taxation without first seeking either a legislative act or a constitutional amendment. Riley qualified his endorsement of local home rule by insisting that voters have the right to approve any local tax increase. Still, he pitted himself on this issue against many legislators, particularly in rural areas, who did not want to surrender their virtually dictatorial powers over their counties.

Despite the common interests among reformers, the Riley administration's energies became absorbed in negotiating a complex package of statutory bills and proposed constitutional amendments to overhaul the tax system. What emerged was the most ambitious plan in the state's history to provide adequate funding for education, law enforcement, and other key services, while significantly alleviating the tax system's regressive burden. In the process, the five proposals for constitutional reform drifted without significant attention from the governor's office. When the legislative session ended, the governor had a $1.2 billion tax package ready to present voters for their approval, but only one of his commission's proposed constitutional reforms survived. The legislature approved an amendment that would allow it to recompile the present constitution into a more concise document.

Meanwhile, Riley created one of the most unusual coalitions the state has seen to promote the constitutional amendments necessary to enact his proposed tax reforms. Many corporate leaders from Birmingham and other cities joined hands with social justice groups and school advocates to make the case for additional revenues. The powerful Alabama Education Association, whom many consider to be the state's number one interest group, threw its influence behind the campaign. These advocates also enjoyed the endorsement of mainstream religious denominations that called for better treatment of the poor through fair taxation. Aligned against this coalition, however, was the Alabama Farmers Federation and its allies within the state's powerful timber industry. These traditional opponents of higher ad valorem taxes cultivated support among certain religious conservatives, such as the state's Christian Coalition group. And to Riley's dismay, many of the state's leading Republicans condemned the tax proposals for being contrary to their party's philosophy. While the governor drew praise from the nation's news media for his courageous actions,[69] his opponents managed to instill enough fear and distrust among the electorate to condemn his tax plan to an ignominious defeat. By a two-to-one majority, voters on September 9, 2003, turned down their governor's package, thereby forcing the legislature in special session to begin considering dramatic cuts in spending for services and agencies that already were among the most poorly funded in the United States. The election confirmed a deep, almost pathological distrust among Alabama's electorate for government at all levels, while putting even more pressure on an antiquated constitutional system to produce at least some temporary fix for long-festering problems.

CONCLUSION

In the introduction to his authoritative *Reference Guide*, William H. Stewart observes, "It is impossible to separate Alabama constitutionalism from issues of race relations. . . . One cannot presume to understand the Constitution without an understanding of the politics of race."[70] What was patent in 1901 remains at least beneath the surface of present discussions about reform. Among the motivations of people who seek to replace or revise Alabama's Constitution, which authorizes much of the state's regressive tax system, is a desire for constructive biracial discussions about the future. As long as fear and resentment divide Alabamians along racial lines, reformers reason, the state will continue to lag behind its neighbors in economic and political development. Overcoming this resilient tradition, however, remains the biggest challenge, in that both whites and blacks express concern over who will write the new laws and for what purposes. It is simply a given in Alabama that voters often prefer to endure the devil they know rather than to risk replacing it with something new, particularly when uncertainty arises over who will benefit. The growth in power and wealth of special interest groups, such as those who represent teachers, big landowners, trial lawyers, and large businesses, exacerbate old populist fears that advantages will accrue to some citizens at the expense of others.

Nevertheless, constitutional reform and the related issue of tax reform made great advancements on the state's political agenda from 2000 to 2003, often to the surprise of jaundiced veterans of Alabama politics. While the fear factor continues to manifest itself in both overt and subtle ways, public discussion has focused more on fundamental issues, such as local democracy and fair taxation, than at any time in recent memory. Despite the defeat of his tax package at the polls, Bob Riley staked his claim to membership among the celebrated fraternity of "New South" governors who helped modernize their states' government and identified strongly with improved education and economic development. With his reforms, he sought to unite the state's citizens, white and black, behind economic progress and fair taxation. He refused to propose a painless solution to the state's problems, such as a lottery, as did his predecessor. Instead, Riley simply asked citizens to join hands across racial lines and work with him to bring Alabama into the twenty-first century. Because the problems Alabama faces are so fundamental and the funding crisis is so severe, there is reason to believe that events of 2003 may prove to be the opening skirmish for a greater battle ahead.[71] If indeed, as some pundits predict, a calamity must befall the state before it will finally rid itself of the albatross it assumed in 1901, then all indicators suggest that the looming budget difficulties of 2004 and beyond may finally motivate the legislature to seek constitutional relief.

Notes

1. *Birmingham News,* January 28, 2003.

2. Sam Hodges, "World's Biggest but Nobody's Proud," *Mobile Register,* December 11, 1994.

3. The standard work on this history remains Malcolm Cook McMillan's *Constitutional Development in Alabama, 1798–1901: A Study in Politics, the Negro, and Sectionalism.* (Chapel Hill: University of North Carolina Press, 1955.) For a discussion of yeoman whites' support of the 1875 document, see Samuel L. Webb, "Jacksonian Democrat in Postbellum Alabama," *Journal of Southern History,* LXII (May, 1996): 54–55.

4. Michael Perman, *Struggle for Mastery: Disfranchisement in the South, 1888–1908* (Chapel Hill: University of North Carolina Press, 2001), 181. Perman quotes Edgard Gardner Murphy, a noted reformer.

5. For a good summary of these events, see Samuel S. Webb, "The Populist Revolt in Alabama: Prelude to Disfranchisement," in *A Century of Controversy: Constitutional Reform in Alabama,* ed. Bailey Thomson (Tuscaloosa: University of Alabama Press, 2002): 1–14.

6. Harvey H. Jackson III, "White Supremacy Triumphant: Democracy Undone," in *A Century of Controversy: Constitutional Reform in Alabama,* ed. Bailey Thomson (Tuscaloosa: University of Alabama Press, 2002): 17–31.

7. *Williams v. Mississippi,* 170 U.S. 213 (1898).

8. For an analysis of how delegates voted and other useful data, see appendices in Sheldon Hackney, *Populism to Progressivism in Alabama* (Princeton: Princeton University Press, 1969), 335–61.

9. *Official Proceedings of the Constitutional Convention of the State of Alabama,* 1901, vol. I, 12.

10. William H. Stewart, *The Alabama State Constitution: A Reference Guide* (Westport, Conn.: Greenwood Press), 106.

11. For a good account of the consequences of such failures, see Douglas A. Blackmon, "From Alabama's Past, Capitalism Teamed with Racism to Create Cruel Partnership," *Wall Street Journal,* July 16, 2001. Blackmon reported that thousands of convicts died from abuse, while proceeds from their labor provided the state with one of its principal sources of revenue.

12. Louis D. Harland, *Booker T. Washington: Making of a Black Leader, 1856–1901* (New York: Oxford University Press, 1972), 299–303.

13. John Sparks, "American Negro Reaction to Disfranchisement, 1901–1904" (Master's Thesis, Samford University, 1973), 77–790.

14. Quoted in McMillan, *Constitutional Development in Alabama,* 343.

15. Ibid., 350–51.

16. United States Constitution and the Alabama Constitution of 1901, Centennial Edition (2001)136–37.

17. Ibid., 352–54.

18. Emmet O'Neal, *Educational Reform and a New Constitution* (Montgomery: Brown Printing Co. 1914), 5–6.

19. *Journal of the House of Representatives* (1915), 1:310–24.

20. William H. Stewart, "Failure of Reform: Attempts to Rewrite the 1901 Constitution," in *A Century of Controversy: Constitutional Reform in Alabama,* ed. Bailey Thomson (Tuscaloosa: University of Alabama Press, 2002): 50–52.

21. Two biographies of Folsom connect his populist roots with his political actions: George E. Sims, *The Little Man's Big Friend: James E. Folsom in Alabama Politics, 1946–1958* (Tuscaloosa: University of Alabama Press, 1985); and Grafton, *Big Mules & Branchheads: James E. Folsom and Political Power in Alabama.* The author also draws on the reminiscences of his uncle, former state Sen. Fuller Kimbrell, who served as Folsom's cocampaign chairman in 1954 and as the finance director for the governor's second administration.

22. Carl Grafton and Anne Permaloff, *Big Mules and Branchheads: James E. Folsom and Political Power in Alabama* (Athens: University of Georgia Press, 1985): 73–75.

23. James E. Folsom, "Inaugural Address; January 20, 1947," in *Speeches of Gov. James E. Folsom, 1947–1950* (Wetumpka Printing Co., n.d.), 5.

24. Sims, *The Little Man's Big Friend*, 53–58.

25. James E. Folsom, "Radio Address on the Need for a Constitutional Convention, April 3, 1949," in *Speeches of Governor James E. Folsom, 1947–1950* (Wetumpka Printing Co., n.d.), 132.

26. *Birmingham News*, April 14, 1954.

27. *Montgomery Advertiser*, May 5, 1955.

28. Opinion of the Justices, 81 So. 2nd 678 (1955); *Birmingham News*, July 12, 1955.

29. *Birmingham News*, January 3, 1956; *Montgomery Advertiser*, January 4, 1956.

30. *Birmingham News*, January 21, 1956; Sims, *The Little Man's Big Friend*, 183–84.

31. Sims, *The Little Man's Big Friend*, 178–88.

32. William H. Stewart, Jr., *The Alabama Constitutional Commission: A Pragmatic Approach to Constitutional Revision* (Tuscaloosa: University of Alabama Press, 1975), 6–12.

33. Anne Permaloff and Carl Grafton, *Political Power in Alabama: The More Things Change . . .* (Athens: University of Georgia Press, 1995), 291–99; interview with Albert Brewer, Montgomery, Alabama, December 12, 2002.

34. *Proposed Constitution of Alabama: Report of the Constitutional Commission, May 1, 1973* (Reprinted by Samford University Press, 2002), iii–ix.

35. Tony A. Freyer and Paul M. Pruitt, Jr., *Reaction and Reform: Transforming the Judiciary Under Alabama's Constitution, 1901–1975*, 53 *Alabama Law Review*, 77–79 (2001).

36. For a discussion of Heflin's tactics in securing this reform, see John Hayman, *A Judge in the Senate: Howell Heflin's Career of Politics and Principle* (Montgomery: New South Books, 2001), 172–86. For background on the Alabama court system at the time of this reform, see G. Alan Tarr and Mary Cornelia Aldis Porter, *State Supreme Courts in State and Nation* (New Haven: Yale University Press, 1988), pp. 69–123.

37. Stewart, The Alabama State Constitution, 173. The original provision in 1901 restricted the Legislature to quadrennial meetings.

38. *State v. Manley*, 441 So. 2d 864 (1983).

39. Results from the studies may be found in the February 2001 issue of *Governing* or on the magazine's web site at http://www.governing.com/gpp/2001/gp1glanc.htm.

40. *Huntsville Times*, June 21, 2000.

41. *Tuscaloosa News*, February 4, 2003; "Tax Laws Make Alabama a Laughingstock Again," editorial, ibid., February 5, 2003. The full report can be found at *Governing*'s web site at http://www.governing.com/gpp/2003/gp3intro.htm.

42. *Birmingham News*, February 28, 2003.

43. "How Alabama Taxes Compare," Report by the Public Affairs Research Council of Alabama, No. 42 (Spring 2001), which is available at http://parca.samford.edu.

44. Alabama Constitution of 1901, Amendment 373 of section 216, provision (a).

45. *Mobile Register*, December 11, 1994.

46. The proceedings may be found on the ACCR web site at http://www.constitutionalreform.org/symposium/symp_papers.html.

47. *Birmingham News*, January 18, 1998.

48. See, for example, "The Constitution, Again Another Chance to Build a New Windmill," editorial, *Birmingham News*, September 25, 2000.

49. *Mobile Register*, March 27, 2001.

50. The author had the pleasure of serving on the chamber's steering committee and later on ACCR's founding group.

51. Permaloff and Grafton, *Political Power in Alabama*, 137–39.

52. For a summary of action, see Bailey Thomson, "Alabama's Politics Can Be Peculiar," *Mobile Register*, April 28, 2002.

53. Memorandum to the author from Bill Smith on behalf of Alabama Citizens for Constitutional Reform, August 20, 2002.

54. See footnote 38 for reference.

55. *Birmingham News*, March 21, 2001.

56. See, for example, "Siegelman's Call: Governor Can Take Action on Constitutional Reform," editorial, *Birmingham News*, October 26, 2001.

57. A perusal of ACCR's web site, which has links to much of this reporting and commentary, reveals the intense interest of the press.

58. *Alabama Law Review*, vol. 53, Fall 2001, Number 1.

59. HJR 152 of the 2002 Regular Session of the Alabama Legislature.

60. *Huntsville Times*, March 24, 2002.

61. The author attended a lively session with the Black Caucus on December 4, 2002, in Tuscaloosa, along with ACCR Chairman Thomas E. Corts, and heard these concerns firsthand, along with expressions of support for the broader mission of reform.

62. *Huntsville Times*, January 17, 2003; *Mobile Register*, January 24, 2003; "A Solid Foundation: Constitution Group's Report Not Perfect, but Great Start," editorial, *Birmingham News*, January 19, 2003; "Document Outlines Road to Reform," editorial, *Tuscaloosa News*, January 22, 2003.

63. *Montgomery Advertiser*, Jan. 23, 2003; *Birmingham News*, January 24, 2003.

64. Alabama Citizens' Constitution Commission, "Report of the Alabama Citizens' Constitution Commission to Governor Bob Riley," March 27, 2003.

65. See "How Alabama's Taxes Compare." For a good overview of the issue, see James W. Williams, Jr., "Alabama's Revenue Crisis: Three Tax Problems," in *A Century of Con-*

troversy: Constitutional Reform in Alabama, ed. Bailey Thomson (Tuscaloosa: University of Alabama Press, 2002): 101–13.

66. Don Logan, "Remedial lesson: State still failing schools," *Birmingham News*, February 2, 2003.

67. Susan Pace Hamill, "An Argument for Tax Reform Based on Judeo-Christian Ethics," *Alabama Law Review*, vol. 54, no. 1 (Fall 2002): 1–112; Shailagh Murray, "Divinity School Article Debates Morality of Alabama Tax-Code," *Wall Street Journal*, February 12, 2003.

68. Interview with William O'Connor, Tuscaloosa, Alabama, November 25, 2002.

69. See, for example, Alan Erenhalt, "Big Mule Renewal," *Governing*, July 2003, at http://www.governing.com/archive/2003/jul/assess.txt. Erenhalt, who has followed Alabama politics closely, concludes that eventually the state's business leaders, often known as the Big Mules, will get what they want: an adequate and fair tax system.

70. Stewart, *The Alabama State Constitution: A Reference Guide*, 5.

71. Riley's respected finance director, Draton Nabers, Jr., reaffirmed the reality of a $675 million deficit for 2004 in an essay titled "State deficit no 'far cry' from projections." See *Birmingham News*, September 21, 2003.

5

The Mandatory Constitutional Convention Question Referendum:

The New York Experience in National Context

Gerald Benjamin

Voters in New York expressed little confidence in government; turnout at the polls was consistently abysmal. Legislative elections rarely offered real choices; incumbents almost never lost. Gridlock was the norm in a state legislature that featured the most persistent divided partisan control in the nation. The state budget had not been passed on time in thirteen years.[1] The state personnel system was sclerotic. A torturous local government web—a "system" in name only—diffused accountability and drove up costs. State and local taxes, especially local property taxes, were among the highest in the nation.[2] The result of all this was a state and local service delivery system that was expensive, inequitable, and often inadequate. Education is the best example. Mean per pupil education spending was very high.[3] Children in the suburbs were well served, or at least had a fighting chance. But most children—especially minority children in urban centers—were simply not being educated.[4]

Yet, when asked in 1997, in the midst of these conditions, to vote on the question "Shall there be a convention to revise the constitution and amend the same?" New Yorkers responded with a resounding "No." The vote was 929,415 in favor of a convention, to 1,579,390 against. Perhaps even more tellingly, a plurality of citizens who came to the polls in that year—1,693,788 of them—simply ignored the question entirely! The

---

This essay was first published in the *Albany Law Review*, vol. 65 (2002), pp. 1017–50.

idea of holding a convention was rejected even though Governor Mario M. Cuomo had earlier endorsed it as the state's best chance for reform; even though the commission he appointed worked for several years to prepare for it; and even though by the time of the vote virtually every daily newspaper in the state had published an editorial in favor of holding a constitutional convention.[5]

The convention question was on the ballot in 1997 because a century-and-a-half earlier (in 1846) a Convention in New York added a constitutional requirement that the question of whether to call a convention be asked every twenty years.[6] The idea for a mandatory convention referendum at regular intervals first appeared in the late eighteenth century in the constitutions of Massachusetts, New Hampshire, and Kentucky.[7] The Empire State is currently one of fourteen in the United States whose constitutions require the periodic submission of such a question.[8] Perhaps because the idea was included in the Model State Constitution, many of these states adopted the provision relatively recently: Alaska (1956), Connecticut (1965), Hawaii (1950), Illinois (1970), Michigan (1963), Missouri (1945), and Montana (1972). Additionally, Rhode Island added the periodic convention-call provision to its constitution in 1973.[9]

One rationale for such provisions is that the sovereign people should have some way of making changes in their governmental structure without having to rely on action by those in statewide and legislative offices, many of whom may be beneficiaries of a flawed status quo. Another is the Jeffersonian view that it is healthy for democracy for each generation to define anew its governing arrangements. Thomas Jefferson wrote in 1816 that "'Each generation [has] . . . a right to choose for itself the form of government it believes most promotive of its own happiness. . . . [A] solemn opportunity of doing this every nineteen or twenty years should be provided by the Constitution.'"[10] A third, more conservative reason for these provisions is that periodic convention votes are a way of actually testing public support for political reform ideas, and of simultaneously channeling political energy and "avoiding agitation."[11] Such referenda are more likely to confirm the status quo than to result in conventions actually being called, this view holds.

New York's failure to authorize a constitutional convention through an automatic convention question referendum is hardly unusual. In a comprehensive review published in 1970, Robert J. Martineau found that there were seventy-two votes resulting from the automatic convention referendum provisions of state constitutions between the founding of the nation and 1969. Twenty of these (27.8%) led to the calling of conventions in five states: Michigan, Missouri, New Hampshire, New York, and Ohio. Yet more than half of these conventions—eleven of the twenty—were in New Hampshire, which until recently provided for no means other than a convention for amending the state constitution.[12]

Since 1970 there have been twenty-five additional referenda resulting from automatic call provisions. (See table 5.1.) Four produced conventions: two in New Hampshire and one each in Hawaii and Rhode Island.

TABLE 5.1
Constitutional Convention Question Referendum Outcomes
in Mandatory Referendum States, 1970–2000

State	*Year*	*Yes*	*No*	*Outcome*
Iowa	1970	204,517	214,663	No
Alaska	1972	29,192	55,389	No
New Hampshire	1972	96,794	73,365	Yes
Ohio	1972	1,291,267	2,142,534	No
Hawaii	1976	199,831	61,264	Yes
New York	1977	1,126,902	1,668,137	No
Iowa	1980	404,249	640,130	No
Alaska	1982	63,816	108,319	No
Missouri	1982	406,446	927,056	No
New Hampshire	1982	115,351	105,207	Yes
Rhode Island	1984	155,337	131,648	Yes
Hawaii	1986	139,236	173,977	No
Connecticut	1986	207,704	379,812	No
Illinois	1988	900,109	2,727,144	No
Maryland	1990	321,412	470,477	No
Oklahoma	1990†			Not held
Iowa	1990	179,762	491,179	No
Montana	1990	53,630	245,009	No
Alaska	1992	84,929	142,735	No
Ohio	1992	1,674,373	2,660,270	No
New Hampshire	1992	210,340	217,575	No
Michigan	1994	777,779	2,008,070	No
Rhode Island	1994	173,693	118,545	No
Hawaii	1996	164,132	123,021	No*
New York	1997	929,415	1,579,390	No
Iowa	2000	299,972	598,318	

*Majority of all those voting at the election required to call a convention.
†No vote. Legislation necessary to meet constitutional mandate never passed

Source: Obtained by the author from state boards of elections.

Thus, the success rate during the past three decades (16%) has been substantially lower than in the past. No conventions have been authorized by voters under an automatic call provision in the fourteen states since the positive outcome in Rhode Island in 1984. A 1996 referendum in Hawaii produced a supportive majority of those voting on the question, but no constitutional convention was held. Litigants who claimed that the required majority had to be of all those who voted at that election were supported in the courts.[13]

Despite the mandate in its state constitution that the question be asked every twenty years, no vote was held in Oklahoma in 1990 on whether to call a convention. Janice C. May reported that "the legislation necessary to place the referendum on the ballot did not clear the legislative process and no vote was taken."[14] Failure to provide for balloting on the question is only one of the ways state legislatures have sought to block conventions by inaction. Another is by failure to authorize the preparatory work to educate the public on the importance and meaning of the convention vote, and then arguing that in the absence of preparation a convention would be too risky.[15] A third is by failure to provide for the election of delegates or for the logistical support necessary to hold a convention.

Because the New York State Constitution prescribes the precise question to be asked of the voters—"Shall there be a convention to revise the constitution or amend the same?"—the agenda of a constitutional convention in New York may not be limited.[16] The situation is similar in eight other mandatory question states.[17] Six mandatory convention states also allow constitutional amendment through an initiative—a more targeted method for bypassing those in power to make change.[18] The availability of such an option may make the convention route to constitutional change even less attractive.

The inability to limit a convention's agenda makes gaining the cooperation of the state legislature—termed "indispensable" by a team of political scientists who comprehensively reviewed the extensive efforts at state constitutional change in the 1960s—extremely problematic.[19] Legislatures began as the dominant governmental institutions in the separation-of-powers systems of the American states. Constitutional change over more than two centuries has, in general, been a story of the diminution of the role and powers of legislatures. It is no surprise, then, as Albert Sturm noted, that legislatures, as the principal "repositories of general policy making authority," are natural enemies of unlimited constitutional conventions.[20]

Timing and Election Cycles

Predictable electoral cycles and fixed decision points are a defining characteristic of American politics. Public officials run for offices with fixed terms, usually two or four years; election day for most national, state, and even local offices is the first Tuesday after the first Monday in November. Longer cycles are defined by term limits—traditionally for statewide elected officials—but, lately in many states, for legislators as well. The convergence or divergence of these cycles affects voter turnout, ballot length, the availability of campaign resources, and a number of other factors that may impact political outcomes in a particular election year. Often, structural arrangements are made to limit or eliminate specific convergences. In thirty-five states with four-year terms for governor, gubernatorial elections are held in even-numbered years that are not presidential election years. In Virginia, New Jersey, Kentucky, Louisiana, and Mississippi gubernatorial elections are held in odd-numbered years.[21] To cite a less-known example of structural arrangements made to limit or eliminate specific convergences, the New York State Constitution provides that city-elected officials be chosen in odd-numbered years, and that all their terms expire in odd-numbered years.[22] Peter Galie writes that this was intended by Progressives in 1894 as a "home rule" provision that "separated state and national elections from municipal elections so only municipal issues would determine the outcome."[23] Of course, it also sheltered elections for state offices from the turnout that might be stimulated in New York City and other big cities by convergent mayoral elections.

The mandatory constitutional question provision adds another long cycle to fourteen states' political systems. There are clear effects when this cycle converges with the cycle for other elections. For example, a comparison of the numbers voting in Iowa, Alaska, and New Hampshire in presidential and nonpresidential even-numbered years—three states whose cycles result in periodic referenda in both—confirms the commonsense expectation that convergence with relatively high-turnout elections result in higher numbers of citizens voting on the mandatory constitution question. (See table 5.1.)

As the prime players, incumbents in state elective offices are keenly aware of the potential that a constitutional convention could change the fundamentals of state politics and government. These office holders are, therefore, among the most attentive to the prospect of holding a convention. But additionally, the long cycle created by the mandatory question is most likely to command their attention when it places the vote on the convention question in their own reelection context. When reelection and convention question cycles converge on the same election day, candidacies for reelection may be affected by the question's presence on the ballot. Moreover, when such a convergence occurs, the incumbent is more likely to be required to pay attention while campaigning to the question of constitutional change, and therefore to take a position on the need for a convention. This is important because a key technique used by opponents of conventions in mandatory referendum states is "passive aggression." That is, by failing to prepare for and otherwise ignoring the prospect of a convention, incumbents seek to deny it visibility and to make calling it seem more risky.

The state constitution may pay specific attention to the convergence of election cycles in considering when to ask the mandatory convention question. For example, the Connecticut Constitution provides that the mandatory question appear on the ballot in an even-numbered year, assuring its convergence with a presidential or gubernatorial election and all state legislative races.[24] The New York Constitution does not do this. In fact, New York's mandatory convention question was the only one offered in the last three decades that was voted on in an odd-numbered year. (See table 5.1.) No statewide-elected officials or candidates for state legislature were on the ballot when New Yorkers were asked to vote on whether or not to hold a convention in 1997, and there was no presidential election to stimulate voter turnout. Conditions therefore were optimal for incumbents to minimize their attention to the convention question, if they chose to do so. In the highly disciplined majority parties in both of New York's legislative houses, passive aggression to the idea of a convention was a clear strategy. With few exceptions, the only overt legislative advocates for calling a convention were in the partisan minorities of each house—Democrats in the Senate, Republicans in the Assembly—the victims of a bipartisan gerrymander that had continuously denied them (and their predecessors) power for decades.

It is true that the predictability of the time of the question's appearance on the ballot does offer an opportunity for potential advocates of constitutional reform. It is best for such advocates if they happen to be a candidate for governor or an incumbent governor. In New York, Governor Mario Cuomo was such an advocate. Cuomo was a third-term incumbent likely to seek reelection. A former professor of law, the governor had previously asked the legislature to place a convention question on the ballot to address his reform agenda for state government.[25] Knowing that there certainly would be a convention referendum vote in November 1997, he enlisted the help of the State University of New York's Rockefeller Institute in planning for a convention, after a researcher there published an essay on the potential of a convention for resolving persistent problems of governance in New York.[26] In the Spring of 1993, Governor Cuomo appointed a Constitutional Revision Commission to prepare the groundwork and give visibility to the issue.[27]

But the lack of convergence between the electoral cycles made the timing problematic. The mandatory provision in New York brought the convention question to the voters three years after Cuomo's bid for a fourth term, and a year before the end of that term, detaching it from the focal point of statewide politics. Cuomo apparently acted in the year prior to his likely third reelection bid in 1994 to dramatize the potential for reform through a convention. But an event almost five years in the future—light years in political time, as the Commission's first chairman Peter Goldmark described it—had little hope of gaining serious attention in the election. In fact, in 1994, Cuomo himself became the key issue. Opponents appealed for votes for George Pataki, Cuomo's Republican opponent, simply on the basis that Pataki was not Cuomo. The governor's advocacy of a convention during the campaign, when discussed at all, was dismissed by adversaries as an effort to shift responsibility for the state's problems during his tenure to the legislature.[28]

Pataki had built his political career in the legislature. As a minority party Assemblyman he had advocated serious structural changes in state government, but he was noncommittal on the convention question as a gubernatorial candidate—the vote was far off, there was no real pressure to take a position, and its advocacy would not be popular with the Republican majority in the State Senate. When Cuomo was defeated, the main advocate for a convention was lost to the state's political system. Also, and less obviously, the convention idea remained identified with him at a time when a newly elected Republican government was seeking to define itself in stark contrast to the outgoing governor and his record. Pataki promised in his campaign to reduce the number of state departments and agencies. When he received the Constitution Commission's report it gained the distinction of becoming the first state agency to become defunct during his governorship.[30]

It is instructive to contrast the situation in New York in 1997 with that in 1965. Standards and methods for districting the New York State Assembly and Senate—favoring upstate Republicans—were entrenched in the state constitution of 1894 and were a persistent issue in state politics thereafter. Applying the one-man/one-vote principle in *WMCA, Inc. v. Lomenzo*, the U.S. Supreme Court in June 1964 found the apportionment of the state legislature unconstitutional. A complex swirl of litigation and political maneuvering followed. Democrats captured control of both legislative houses in 1964 (the Johnson landslide year), and in 1965 passed a bill, the Travia-Zaretzki Bill, calling for a constitutional convention to address the reapportionment question. Somewhat surprisingly, Governor Nelson Rockefeller—a Republican—signed the bill.[31] Thus, the convention question was put on the ballot in 1965. A gubernatorial election was scheduled for the next year. Rockefeller, seeking his third term, was at the nadir of his popularity. In modern New York politics, Democrats from outside the New York City metropolitan area are not nominated for governor. Howard Samuels, a wealthy upstate Democratic businessman with gubernatorial aspirations, saw that a campaign in support of a convention was an opportunity to establish his political reputation and break through this geographic barrier. Using his own money, he organized a Citizens Committee for a Constitutional Convention and led the effort for a "yes" vote to the constitutional question.[32] The campaign was successful and a convention was called. Samuels's political bona fides were established. In the end, however, he was not nominated for governor, and Rockefeller once again prevailed in the general election.

This story holds two points. First, a convention was called because of an immediate compelling political need in the legislature. A national-level decision had upset the political status quo in the state. Notwithstanding its disabilities from a legislator point of view, a convention was a potential remedy for a life-or-death political problem. It was a state, not national, process, and thus more subject to influence from the state legislature than from the federal courts. A convention also provided an opportunity for Democrats—in a rare moment of legislative dominance—to undo a Republican advantage in the state legislature that had been in place for the entire twentieth century. In addition, the electoral cycles were nearing convergence. With a gubernatorial election in the offing, a statewide campaign for reform through constitutional change provided an attractive opportunity for an ambitious politician to establish himself.

Commission and Staff

In 1993, Governor Cuomo appointed an eighteen-person Constitutional Revision Commission made up of New Yorkers of some prominence and balanced in all the usual ways: partisanship, race, ethnicity, gender, geography, organizational base, ideology, and profession.[33] The chair was Peter C. Goldmark, Jr., then the head of the Rockefeller Foundation. Goldmark had been State Budget Director under Governor Hugh Carey, and later served as the executive director of the Port Authority of New York and New Jersey. As State Budget Director, he worked with Governor Carey to successfully bring the state through its fiscal crisis in the mid-1970s.

Commissioners were not selected merely because they had a commitment to the constitution convention idea. Some, like former Republican Governor Malcolm Wilson, were thoroughly familiar with the state constitution, deeply experienced in state government, and convinced that a convention was needed. Others, like former hostage Terry Anderson, knew little about state government or the state constitution, and learned about the convention's potential simultaneously with receiving inquiries about their possible interest in being appointed. Notwithstanding its balanced membership and the assurances the governor gave Goldmark that his inquiries could go freely wherever they took him, the commission was very much seen as Cuomo's. The legislature took no role in the appointment process, another example of its strategy of passive aggression.[34] The loyalty of Republicans appointed by a Democratic governor—even former Governor Wilson—were somewhat suspect in GOP party councils.

In this context, with a modest budget from the governor's discretionary funds and no legislative appropriation, Goldmark's tasks were to build a staff, knit the group together, bring all commissioners to a reasonable level of information on the issues, lead the commission in developing an agenda, and bring the convention question to the public. The three key staffers he chose had experience serving the Commission that had successfully developed the new charter that New York City adopted in 1989.[35] Early meetings were devoted to creating a working relationship among the commissioners, launching a research program, and establishing a network of relationships with interested constituencies throughout the state.

HISTORY'S LEGACY

Experience has shown that voters may call a constitutional convention only to find that nothing then happens or that action is long delayed. This is why several states have provisions in their constitutions that take the matter out of the hands of the legislature and make a positive result on the mandatory constitution convention question self-executing. As one authority on state constitutional change has written: "In view of the difficulty encountered in many states in obtaining legislative action looking toward a referendum on the question of constitutional revision, the self-executing character of the provisions of this article is . . . extremely important."[36]

The self-executing provision of the New York constitution was added in 1894.[37] It came on the heels of an eight-year delay in assembling the convention called by New Yorkers voting on the mandatory convention question in 1886.[38] Roiled by partisan differences, the governor and legislature could not agree on how delegates would be selected. Seeking to avoid a repeat of this experience, the 1894 convention adopted a provision that requires the election, at the next following general election, of three delegates from each state Senate district and fifteen at-large delegates. It specifies when and where the convention will meet, requires that delegates be paid at the same rate as Assembly members, and indicates how vacancies will be filled. It even establishes in some detail the procedures and decision rules for the convention.[39]

One generation's solutions are another's problems. The partisan and good government concerns raised by these self-executing provisions—as the 1997 referendum vote approached—caused the Constitutional Revision Commission to give them priority attention.[40] As a result of New York's bipartisan legislative gerrymander, Senate districts are designed by Republicans to favor Republicans.[41] This was not a problem for Republicans, but most Commissioners were, of course, Democrats, as were many good-government advocates. Another worry was the use of Senate districts as multimember districts, and the required election of some delegates at-large, statewide. At-large elections and multimember districts had come to be "red flags" under the Federal Voting Rights Act. Commission members would not support processes that were or appeared to be racially discriminatory. Moreover, even if these procedures passed muster or could be made to, the mere consideration of potential Federal Voting Rights Act problems raised by the electoral process prescribed in the state constitution almost guaranteed that—if they were used and a convention was authorized—litigation in federal court would follow.[42] An additional concern—at least of reformers who were not party stalwarts—was that (though not constitutionally mandated) delegate election would be partisan and conducted under the existing New York state election and campaign finance laws, advantaging the major parties and persons already holding elective office.

Here, more recent history came into play—the history of delegate selection for New York's 1967 Constitutional Convention.[43] Elections were partisan. Legislative leaders dominated the Convention, which was organized on a partisan basis and functioned substantially in accord with legislative rules. Sitting legislators and others in the government industry were heavily represented at the convention. And, especially offensive to some, during the year that the convention met, the constitutional provision for delegate compensation "required" the legislators who were also delegates, and others on public payrolls, to collect two salaries and the attendant pension benefits.

Some of these problems were amenable to statutory remedies. Others could not be fixed except by constitutional amendment.[44] Both methods required legislative action. Even with its early start, time was short for the Commission to develop and propose changes. Within its first year it succeeded, and its changes were published in an interim report. The legislature, however, did not "own" the Commission. Its leaders did not want a convention. If they simply failed to act to fix what reformers saw was a flawed process (in part because it might have benefited legislators personally by allowing them to "double dip" as delegates) a further barrier to organizing support and gathering votes for a convention would be raised. There was thus no hope that these bills or amendments would be passed. It was a classic catch-22.

The history of the 1967 convention was important in another way, as well. The new constitution it proposed failed at the polls. This allowed those opposed to calling a convention in 1997 to label the 1967 experience as an expensive failure, a "waste of money." Considering the politics surrounding the submission of that document to the people, this was a gross oversimplification. Moreover, the recent history of the state included an example of a very successful convention, and one that arose as a result of the automatic call—the convention of 1938.[45] But the story of the last war was most compelling. Some veterans were still around, and not all spoke well of the experience. History, thus, was one more weapon to use against approval of the convention call in 1997.

THE COMMISSION REPORT

The Commission did its work. Meetings, which were open to the public, were regularly held. Research was commissioned and published. Contacts were established with media outlets and interested groups throughout the state. A periodic newsletter was developed and distributed. Educational materials were prepared for schools. Hearings and editorial board meetings were held throughout the state. Commissioners and staff made radio and television appearances and spoke before interested groups.

Nevertheless, no center of political support for a convention outside the commission developed. With process concerns unaddressed, few established groups responded to "good government" appeals for a convention. There were some expressions of support from Chambers of Commerce and newspaper editorial boards; but the League of Women Voters, the New York Public Interest Research Group (NYPIRG), and Common Cause all held back.[46] The prospect of important structural changes in state government—term limitation, initiative and referendum, judicial reform, reform of election administration, the creation of a legislative districting commission—neither garnered endorsement of the Commission nor catalyzed the organization of a substantial mainstream supportive constituency in the state. Among organized interests, the prospect of an open-ended convention was feared more for what it might undo than valued for what it might do. Protecting concrete particular interests was a far more compelling priority than creating an opportunity for speculative gains for a general interest. Neither environmentalists concerned about the loss of "forever wild" protection for the Adirondack and Catskill preserves, nor civil service unions worried about the "merit and fitness" and pension protection provisions in the state constitution were calmed by the argument that no convention elected in New York would change these.[47]

The problem for the chairman and staff was to find a direction for the Constitutional Revision Commission that would produce a consensus or near-consensus in the group when efforts at outreach, public hearings, and editorial board meetings had generated little public attention, and in a political environment in which traditional reform groups, labor unions, environmentalists and minority groups—most of these elements of the core Democratic constituency in New York—were either skeptical or openly hostile. It was clear almost from the first that agreement among the commissioners on the need for a constitutional convention would be impossible to obtain.[48] Even key commission staffers differed on this basic question. Yet, in light of political and governmental conditions in the state, and the commitment of several commissioners to the idea that fundamental change was needed, the approach taken by the commission headed by Nelson Rockefeller in 1957 was not attractive. That group had been strongly divided along partisan lines. It presented its work in the form of information for the voters about the pros and cons surrounding the issues a convention might address, but made no recommendation for an "up" or "down" vote on the referendum question.[49]

Peter Goldmark's solution in 1994 was to shift the focus from the convention itself and place it on "policy areas of persistent crisis in which perceived failure feeds the view of New Yorkers that government in the state is either simply not working or working to their detriment."[50] In its deliberations the Commission narrowed these to four: "fiscal integrity, state [and] local relations, education, and public safety." These were, it said, "core areas . . . infused with significant constitutional dimensions in New York. They are fundamental functions of government that are largely within the capacity of states and localities to affect in basic ways. And they are widely regarded by the public as needing basic reform."[51] The Commission proposed the creation of four Action Panels designed to break the political/policy logjam in all of these issue areas. The panels would create integrated packages of legislation and constitutional amendments by the close of the 1996 legislative session. In creating these panels, the Commission also asked that the governor and legislature "clearly commit themselves to take definitive action on these final proposals by a date certain."[52]

This approach was modeled after policy processes devised at the federal level to transcend "ordinary politics" and used for reforming social security, closing military bases, and arriving at trade agreements under the General Agreement on Tariffs and Trade (GATT). This gave the governor and legislature one last chance, and made the endorsement of a constitutional convention conditional. "A large majority of the members of this Commission recommends a 'yes' vote on the constitutional convention question in 1997," the report concluded, "if the state fails to achieve far-reaching reform between now and that vote."[53] Commission members who were advocates of a convention had little expectation that the Action Panel plan would be adopted in Albany. They accepted this conditional endorsement as the strongest outcome they could get in support of a convention. Meanwhile, many of those who continued to have some reservations were brought into the majority, while retaining some political "wiggle room."

Former Governor Malcolm Wilson placed himself on record as unconditionally in support of a constitutional convention. Stanley Hill of District Council 37 (a major New York City public employee union) filed a dissent, citing his disagreement with the priorities of the report and his confidence in the "existing legislative structure." A supplementary statement was filed by Commissioner Peggy Cooper Davis, Professor of Law at the New York University School of Law, in which she was joined by Margaret Fung of the Asian-American Legal Defense and Education Fund. Professor Davis argued that the action-forcing mechanism proposed by the commission was not suitable to its purported purposes; that a convention would be an inappropriate response to the failure of the action-forcing mechanism to bring reform in the four core areas of concern; and that a convention called without prior reform of the delegate-selection process would be "especially unfortunate."[54]

Ms. Fung added a special concern about calling a convention at a time when political conservatism was ascendant in New York. In her statement she wrote, "The November 1994 elections have produced a starkly different political reality." She was referring, of course, to Mario Cuomo's defeat by George Pataki in the gubernatorial election and the Republican sweep into control of Congress. Ms. Fung continued, "The new Republican Governor has promised drastic changes in the role of state government, and the success or failure of these proposals for reform will become apparent to New Yorkers over the next few years. With a newly elected Congress whose majority seems intent on shunting federal responsibilities back to the states, the governor and the legislature will have a chance to demonstrate whether their vision of government works."[55]

THE CAMPAIGN

During the summer of 1997 it seemed likely that New Yorkers would call a constitutional convention. All the problems of state government nonperformance in Albany persisted. A massive fight over the repeal of rent control in New York City forcefully reminded citizens downstate of the degree to which they were governed from Albany, and revived the constitutional "home rule" issue in the city's mayoral election.[56] A Quinnipiac College poll completed in July 1997 showed that most registered voters in New York (61%) were still unaware that the convention referendum was in the offing, but also revealed that a majority thought a convention was a good idea.[57] Polls persisted in showing majorities for a convention throughout the fall. There was especially strong popular support for two major structural changes in state government that a convention might bring: term limits, and initiative and referendum.[58] But there was no center of organized advocacy for a convention, nor was there any serious financing for a pro-convention campaign. The Commission no longer existed, and even if it did it would have been constrained by state law from spending public money for advocacy rather than the providing of information.

A number of other prominent political figures from across the political spectrum joined former Governor Cuomo in support of a convention. One was Tom Golisano, a Rochester area businessman who had spent $6.6 million in seeking the governorship on the Independence Party ticket in 1994. Another was Governor George Pataki, who declared himself in favor of a convention on October 7, 1997, about four weeks before the scheduled vote. Still another was liberal Democratic Assemblyman Richard Brodsky of Westchester, who defied the leadership in his house to take this stand. Many upstate Republican Assembly members were convention advocates; and, in western New York, Democratic State Senator Richard Dolinger was also very active.[59]

Advocates argued that government in New York was in crisis and that, though the convention process was not perfect, it was the only way around the entrenched legislature to fix the system. The convention was, in this author's words: "a chance, not a guarantee. . . . We cannot be sure that holding a constitutional convention will give our state a more democratic, accountable political system or a more effective government. We can be sure, however, that we have insufficient democracy, unaccountability and ineffectiveness now. And judging from experience, we can also be sure that without a convention we will not have improvement."[60]

Proponents also pointed out that calling a convention required three votes: authorization of the convention, election of the delegates, and ratification of the convention's proposals. If citizens took the first step, they would also have to take the second to make change. If they did not like the results of the convention's work, however, they could simply reject it at the polls. A loose network of speakers crossed the state making these arguments in debates organized by civic groups, in the media, and before editorial boards. But on substantive matters convention proponents had no common message. These were truly strange bedfellows. Cuomo denounced Pataki's late endorsement of a convention as opportunistic.

Pataki—the anti-Cuomo—could not imagine appearing with his predecessor in public to support the convention idea. An attempt by advocates to form a bipartisan group of "198 New Yorkers for a New Constitution" never got off the ground.[61] Brodsky sought to craft a progressive agenda, including children's rights, privacy rights, and a code of corporate responsibility. Pataki had no interest in these—he talked of term limits as well as initiative and referendum. Golisano also favored term limits. But Cuomo had no use for this idea, and supported only an indirect initiative process. The former governor wanted a thorough overhaul of the state constitution and urged trust in what the democratic process of a convention would bring.[62]

Meanwhile, with the exception of the Business Council and Chambers of Commerce, virtually every organized interest in the state opposed the convention. "Politicians and lobbying groups . . . have either pointedly chosen not to take a stand or, with startling unanimity, have come out against the idea of a convention," wrote Betsy Kolbert in the New York Times.[63] Organized labor, civil rights groups, environmental organizations, abortion rights advocates, and the trial lawyers association joined to create "Citizens Against a Constitutional Convention." The Conservative Party, Change New York (a smaller government/antitax advocacy organization), the League of Women Voters, and the Association for the Bar of the City of New York were also opposed.

The reasons for opposition varied, tracking those earlier heard by the Constitution Revision Commission. Conservatives stressed high costs, the likelihood of domination of the process by sitting politicians, and the further likelihood of few results. Though the legislative majorities persisted in their passive aggressive strategy, the State Senate did float a $50 million cost estimate for a potential convention—exaggerated, according to the Governor—to lend substance to this argument. Liberals feared what they saw as a rigged electoral process prescribed in the constitution, the possible loss of rights protections, or the introduction into the constitution of new restrictions—for example on abortion rights. Unions worried about pension protection. Environmentalists were concerned about the "forever wild" provisions. Whatever their motivation, all these erstwhile adversaries could unite on one thing: that a constitutional convention was a bad idea.

Lacking organization, convention advocates did little fundraising. They pinned their hopes on finding one rich "angel" to finance their side. Former Governor Cuomo did not come forward with the surplus that remained from his last failed campaign. Ron Lauder was only interested if the convention would surely support term limits, a change he had successfully championed via referendum for inclusion in the New York City Charter.[64] Of course, no such guarantee could be given. Tom Golisano appeared for a while to be a potential second coming of Howard Samuels: a rich upstater with gubernatorial ambitions, who might seek to rise to further statewide prominence as a reformer through a self-financed campaign for a convention. Golisano met with Cuomo and others and listened, but in the end he provided only $300,000—spent almost entirely on media in western New York—for the pro-convention effort. Opponents, however, did have a potential source of political manpower and money—organized labor. With polls showing that a convention was likely to be called as election day approached, phone banks were manned and purse strings untied. Counting on a low turnout, the Citizens Against a Constitutional Convention deployed $750,000 for a media blitz in the last few days before the election.[65] Their television advertisement pictured two fat, balding, white men partying, while a voice-over delivered this message: "The same old insiders, the bigwigs and billionaires, want to rewrite New York's Constitution. Is that a good idea? And they expect New York taxpayers to pay $50 million for their constitutional convention. Fifty million tax dollars? Your taxes, their party. It's time to tell the bigwigs and the billionaires that the party is over. On Tuesday, November 4, send them a message. Vote no on their constitutional convention."[66]

"The progressive opponents of the convention have adopted the most antigovernment rhetoric of the right," reacted Gene Russianoff, a highly respected leader of NYPIRG, a reform organization that had remained neutral on the question.[67] Russianoff may have been right, but the tactic worked. Extensive editorial support throughout the state and positive late poll results notwithstanding, the tide was turned.

The turnout was low. (See table 5.4.) The interest in a convention identified in earlier polls failed to overcome the lack of information also indicated in those polls. There was too little organization among advocates of the convention idea, and potentially supportive voters were not mobilized. Of the four referendum questions on the ballot in 1997, the convention question ranked third in voter participation, and received the fewest "yes" votes. (See table 5.2.) A proposal to borrow $2.4 billion for school construction, championed by Assembly Speaker Sheldon Silver, drew significant support in New York City and attracted the greatest number of voters. The convention went down to defeat in every county in the

TABLE 5.2
New York State Constitution Question Referendum Votes in the Twentieth Century

Year	*Yes*	*No*	*Blank*	*Question Total*	*Election Total*	*Registered*	*Blank % of Total*	*Vote % of Registered*
1914*	153,322	151,963	5,153	305,285	310,438	N/A		
1936	1,413,604	1,190,275	2,986,214	2,603,879	5,590,093	6,218,334	46.6	89.9
1957	1,242,568	1,368,063	2,608,204	2,610,631	5,218,835	6,450,009	50.0	80.9
1977	1,126,902	1,668,137	1,936,054	2,795,039	4,731,093	7,856,241	59.1	60.2
1997	929,415	1,579,390	1,693,788	2,508,805	4,202,593	10,550,560	59.7	39.8

*This is the result of a special election held on April 7, 1914.

TABLE 5.3
Voting Participation on Proposition Questions in New York, 1997

	Vote		
Question	*Yes*	*No*	*Total*
Constitutional Convention	929,415	1,579,390	2,508,805
Monetary Jurisdiction of Courts	1,074,603	1,359,910	2,434,513
Civil Service Veteran's Bonus	1,663,611	883,312	2,546,923
$2.4 Billion School Bond	1,265,150	1,430,830	2,695,980

Source: New York State Board of Elections, www.elections.state,ny.us/elections/1997/.

state. (See table 5.3.) Results were closest in Sullivan County in the Catskills, and in Monroe County, including the City of Rochester. In Monroe County there was extensive public television programming on the question, where Tom Golisano financed a supportive media campaign.

The 4,202,593 voters who came to the polls on election day comprised 39.8 percent of the 10,550,560 New Yorkers who were registered. Of those who entered voting booths across the state, a total of 2,508,805 citizens were recorded on the convention question. Turnout plummeted and drop-off from the top of the ballot had decreased over the decades. As a result, the size of the electorate voting on the question remained remarkably stable for much of the twentieth century. The 1997 vote marked the first time in the century that a majority of those voting on the question in New York City did not favor a convention.[68] In fact, only 14 percent of voters in New York City favored a convention, compared to 26.1 percent of voters outside of the City. As earlier noted, the mandatory convention question was defeated by a vote of 1,579,390 to 929,415. The majority comprised 15 percent of those registered to vote in the state; 37.5 percent of those voting in the election; and 62.9 percent of those recorded on the question.[69]

Lessons Learned

State legislators traditionally dislike constitutional conventions, especially those that are unlimited. It is their powers and prerogatives that are likely to be at stake when these are held. Legislatures can refuse to call conventions themselves and—as in New York in 1997—resist their being called

TABLE 5.4
New York State, November 4, 1997, General Election Referendum Question Vote:
"Shall there be a convention to revise the constitution and amend the same?"

County	*Yes*	*No*	*Blank, Void*	*Total*
Albany	26,148	48,654	21,293	96,095
Allegany	2,491	6,195	3,022	11,708
Broome	13,186	25,446	8,351	46,983
Cattaraugus	4,446	13,271	7,478	25,195
Cayuga	3,597	10,620	5,807	20,024
Chautauqua	9,900	19,199	13,054	42,153
Chemung	5,597	7,492	5,156	18,245
Chenango	2,902	6,580	2,901	12,383
Clinton	6,987	10,226	7,775	24,988
Columbia	5,013	9,815	4,820	19,648
Cortland	3,295	6,893	4,270	14,458
Delaware	3,246	6,635	3,429	13,310
Dutchess	17,504	27,018	12,769	57,291
Erie	82,458	131,759	84,343	298,560
Essex	4,252	5,876	5,734	15,862
Franklin	2,968	5,970	5,477	14,415
Fulton	3,306	8,026	3,709	15,041
Genesee	4,496	7,047	2,673	14,216
Greene	3,660	7,598	4,137	15,395
Hamilton	857	1,884	1,071	3,812
Herkimer	4,091	7,666	4,946	16,703
Jefferson	6,550	9,612	5,566	21,728
Lewis	1,622	3,635	2,442	7,699
Livingston	7,017	8,640	3,876	19,533
Madison	4,020	8,637	5,601	18,258
Monroe	72,874	73,172	29,899	175,945
Montgomery	3,589	7,242	3,628	14,459
Nassau	61,275	135,894	126,341	323,510
Niagara	16,143	29,143	15,694	60,980
Oneida	16,876	25,978	24,364	67,218
Onondaga	30,566	55,890	30,401	116,857
Ontario	9,918	12,406	4,876	27,200
Orange	22,353	28,162	23,106	73,621
Orleans	2,958	4,676	2,116	9,750
Oswego	6,446	15,546	10,670	32,662
Otsego	4,718	8,572	5,972	19,262
Putnam	5,203	10,786	8,901	24,890
Rensselaer	14,466	27,397	13,496	55,359
Rockland	14,986	34,120	26,209	75,315
St. Lawrence	5,427	11,204	9,603	26,234
Saratoga	14,994	27,608	8,405	51,007

(continued on next page)

TABLE 5.4 *(continued)*

County	*Yes*	*No*	*Blank, Void*	*Total*
Schenectady	13,127	23,815	9,694	46,636
Schoharie	2,678	5,551	2,390	10,619
Schuyler	1,271	2,718	1,903	5,892
Seneca	2,269	4,562	2,927	9,758
Steuben	5,905	9,679	6,089	21,673
Suffolk	67,266	135,129	68,840	271,235
Sullivan	6,989	7,006	8,076	22,071
Tioga	3,145	5,589	1,370	10,104
Tompkins	6,821	9,295	3,707	19,823
Ulster	16,515	23,043	14,593	54,151
Warren	5,727	9,063	4,357	19,147
Washington	4,481	8,038	3,949	16,468
Wayne	7,655	10,372	2,651	20,678
Westchester	50,620	90,917	88,180	229,717
Wyoming	2,590	5,915	2,867	11,372
Yates	1,739	2,981	1,210	5,930
Total Outside NYC	731,199	1,265,863	796,184	2,793,246
Bronx	26,210	39,317	135,859	201,386
Kings	44,425	72,724	277,966	395,115
New York	63,298	81,170	194,225	338,693
Queens	51,381	89,150	227,202	367,733
Richmond	12,902	31,166	62,352	106,420
Total NYC	198,216	313,527	897,604	1,409,347
STATEWIDE TOTAL	929,415	1,579,390	1,693,788	4,202,593

Source: New York State Board of Elections, www.elections.state.ny.us/elections/1997.

as a result of mandatory referendum questions (in the fourteen states where this option exists). In 1997, legislative resistance worked in New York. More generally, we know that few constitutional conventions have been called by the mandatory referendum route.

But legislators cannot always keep the door barred, because in eighteen states, constitutions may be changed through the initiative and referendum process. The use of the constitutional initiative in recent years has produced structural changes in state government of enormous consequence. Term limitation is one example. Tax limitation is another. These results have not been favored by most state legislators and governors. And the incremental process through which they were achieved did not consider the range of consequences for the systems into which they were introduced. Especially with regard to term limitation, these are only beginning to be understood.

The use of the constitutional initiative to accomplish feats that legislators dislike gives them reasons to reconsider their hostility to constitutional conventions. Conventions might be a way to restore the status quo ante, or at least to modify changes achieved through direct democracy. Legislatively initiated conventions to undo highly visible changes achieved through the use of the constitutional initiative would surely be denounced as antidemocratic. Calling them would thus be most difficult politically. But what about the use of the more deliberative process for constitutional change when it arises automatically, reflective of Thomas Jefferson's prescription for periodic redesign of democratic institutions to meet the demands of contemporary conditions?

This suggests that legislators in many states—those that have the constitutional initiative but do not have a mandatory convention question—have a stake in introducing constitutional changes to adopt a mandatory question provision. New York, of course, does not have initiative and referendum. Its legislature has proven itself dead-set against conventions called without its support. Nevertheless, the 1997 experience with the mandatory constitutional convention question in New York, when viewed in comparative context, does offer some general lessons about the utility of this kind of provision for achieving constitutional change, and the politics that surround it.

A Dozen Lessons for State Constitutional Reformers

1. The mandatory convention question offers a crucial periodic opportunity to reconsider and debate the fundamentals of state and local government. The rejection of an opportunity to hold a convention, if a considered choice, may be an important expression of support for the existing system. Under current political conditions in the United States, however, this opportunity is rarely seized.
2. Conventions are not likely to be called as a result of a mandatory convention question. Experience in New York and comparative analysis show that this process is a very uncertain route to constitutional change.

3. The fixed cycle for the mandatory question makes incidental any convergence between the timing of the convention question and the timing of a felt need in the polity for constitutional change.
4. Specifying the convention question in the constitution in a way that requires that any convention have an unlimited agenda is a major barrier to a convention being called.
5. Care should be taken to avoid self-executing provisions, like those in the New York Constitution, that strengthen arguments against holding a convention.
6. To maximize turnout, political visibility, and the harnessing of the convention question to political ambitions of existing or potential statewide leaders, it is best if the mandatory question is asked in a year in which there are major statewide and state legislative elections on the ballot.
7. Governors are likely to be champions of conventions. Governors or gubernatorial candidates are uniquely situated to mobilize people and resources for statewide, good government reform efforts.
8. If conditions in a state appear to need serious reform, citizens are not presumptively afraid of state constitutional conventions. But they will hear from opponents, so citizens' willingness to consider a convention must be reinforced with compelling, understandable commonsensical advocacy.
9. Official commissions are important in preparing for a convention, but they are not enough. A reasonably financed organizational structure outside the government is essential to generate the political support that will be needed to call a convention.
10. Organized business interests are those most likely to respond positively to economy, efficiency and effectiveness arguments for structural change in government through constitutional conventions.
11. Legislative leaders and legislators will almost always be against a convention. To gain their support, especially if a convention is unlimited, there must be the prospect of some powerful potential political gain for them as individuals or the legislature as an institution (e.g., the removal of term limitation).
12. Particular interests with established legislative relationships and a stake in the constitutional status quo are likely to align with the legislature and against change.

NOTES

1. See Joel Stashenko, "If New York Voters Oblige on Election Day," *Associated Press Pol. Serv.*, October 17, 1997, available at 1997 WL 2555925; Gus Bliven, "For the 13th Time, the State Budget is Late," *Syracuse Post Standard*, April 2, 1997 (Editorial), at A8, available at 1997 WL 5730231.

2. See Kevin Collison, "Reform Urged in Bid to Avoid State Constitutional Convention," *Buffalo News*, February 26, 1995 at A13, available at 1995 WL 5446979.

3. See Documents, *Rutgers Law Journal*, vol. 2 (1995), p. 1390. In fact, in 1992 New York spent $8,429 per pupil, the third highest in the nation.

4. Researchers for the Constitutional Revision Commission reported that out of approximately 4,000 New York state schools, there were about 1,000 schools, primarily in city neighborhoods, whose students "cannot meet minimum standards on measures of basic skills." Ibid.

5. See Janice C. May, "State Constitutions and Constitutional Revision, 1990–91," in *The Book of the States*, 1992–93, vol. 29 (Lexington, Ky.; Council of State Governments, 1992), p. 4 (noting that Governor Cuomo expressed "strong support" for a constitutional convention). Terry Andersen, a commission member, wrote in "N.Y. Citizens Will Have to Reform State," *Newsday, March 28, 1995* (available at 1995 WL 5103773) that though the New York State Temporary Commission on Constitutional Revision had concluded that immediate constitutional reform was the best cure for New York's troubled state government and there were many editorials in favor of a constitutional convention, policy makers were silent "without public interest"; Highlights of the Commission's Reports may be found in the *New York Times*, February 25, 1995 (available at LEXIS, News Library).

6. New York Constitution of 1846, article XIII, section 2.

7. See John Dinan, "'The Earth Belongs Always to the Living Generation': The Development of State Constitutional Amendment and Revision Procedures," *Review of Politics*, vol. 62 (2000), p. 662.

8. The states and the lengths of their automatic submission cycles are: Hawaii (nine years); Alaska, Iowa, New Hampshire, and Rhode Island (ten years); Michigan (sixteen years); and Connecticut, Illinois, Maryland, Missouri, Montana, New York, Ohio, and Oklahoma (twenty years). See May (1992), p. 4, note 7.

9. See National Municipal League, *Model State Constitution*, 6th ed. (New York: The League, 1966), art. XII, 12.03(a) and Albert Sturm, "State Constitutions and Constitutional Revision," Council of State Governments, Th*e Book of the States*, vol. 21 (Lexington, Ky: The Council, 1972), p. 20, table 3.

10. John Dinan, "Framing a "People's Government": State Constitution-Making in the Progressive Era," *Rutgers Law Journal* vol. 30 (1999), p. 934. (quoting Letter from Thomas Jefferson to Samuel Kercheval (July 12, 1816), in Adrienne Koch and William Peden eds., *The Life and Selected Writings of Thomas Jefferson* [1944]) p. 575.

11. See Dinan (2000), pp. 662–63 and n. 44 (citing the remarks of Mr. Donaldson made during the Maryland Constitutional Convention of 1850).

12. Robert J. Martineau, "The Mandatory Referendum on Calling a State Constitutional Convention: Enforcing the People's Right to Reform Their Government," *Ohio State Law Journal* vol. 31 (1970), p. 424 and n. 14, pp. 439–46. See also Eugene M. Van Loan III, "Amending the Constitution by Convention," 42, *New Hampshire Bar Journal* vol. 31 (2001), pp. 55, 56, 58 n. 5 (noting that a convention was the sole means of constitutional amendment in New Hampshire until 1964, when an amendment granting the amending power to the legislature was added to the state constitution).

13. In the 1996 election in Hawaii, 163,869 voters cast ballots in favor of holding a convention, while 160,153 voted against holding one. *Bennett v. Yoshina*, 140 F.3d 1218, 1222–23 (9th Cir. 1998). Nevertheless, some 45,245 voters left the question blank on their ballots, meaning that a majority of all votes cast did not favor holding a convention. The court said: "It is perfectly constitutional for a state to demand that a proposition win not only a majority of the votes cast, but a majority of all the votes that could have been cast" (p. 1227).

14. May (1992), p. 4, n. 27.

15. See Martineau (1970), p. 424 (noting that the legislature can defeat a convention completely by failing to pass the legislation necessary to implement a convention).

16. N.Y. Constitution, article XIX, 2.

17. The eight other mandated question states are Alaska, Connecticut, Hawaii, Iowa, Missouri, Montana, Rhode Island, New Hampshire, and Ohio. May (1992), p. 25. Additionally, the Montana Constitution specifies an "unlimited convention" in its sections on calling a convention, though not in the section addressing the automatic call. Montana Constitution, article XIV, 1–3.

18. The six states also allowing constitutional amendment through an initiative are Illinois, Michigan, Missouri, Montana, Ohio, and Oklahoma. See Council of State Governments, *Book of the States, 2000–2001*, vol. 33 (Lexington, Ky.: Council of State Governments, 2000), p. 7, table 1.3. In four of these states, the mandatory language is specified, or a limited convention seems precluded by language in the state constitution. See, for example, Illinois Constitution, article XX, 2a ("The State Board of Elections . . . shall . . . certify to the several county clerks any proposal to amend the constitution."); Michigan Constitution, article XII, 1.XII(2) (permitting amendments to "be proposed . . . by petition of the registered electors of [Michigan]"); Montana Constitution, article XIV, 1 (mandating an "unlimited convention"); Oklahoma Constitution, article XXIV, 3 (supplying the right to amend the Constitution by "initiative petition").

19. Albert L. Sturm, *Thirty Years of State Constitution-Making: 1938–1968* (New York: National Municipal League, 1970), p. 3.

20. Sturm (1970), p. 85.

21. See Council of State Governments (2000), pp. 171–72, table 5.7. New Hampshire and Vermont also hold gubernatorial elections in even-numbered years that are not presidential election years, but governors in those states serve two-year terms.

22. N.Y. Constitution, art. XIII, 8.

23. Peter J. Galie, *The New York State Constitution: A Reference Guide* (Westport, Conn.: Greenwood Press, 1991), p. 240.

24. Connecticut Constitution, art. XIII, 2; see also Wesley W. Horton, *The Connecticut State Constitution: A Reference Guide* (Westport, Conn.: Greenwood Press, 1993), p. 163.

25. See Mario M. Cuomo, "The Critics are Wrong, New York Needs a Constitutional Convention" (Letter to the Editor) *Albany Times Union*, April 25, 1994, p. A6.

26. Gerald Benjamin, "Change the Rules, Change the Game," *Empire State Report* (October 1991), p. 37.

27. Executive Order No. 172, *N.Y. Comp. Codes R. & Regs.*, title 9, 4.172 (1993).

28. See Kevin Sack, "In Quest for Perot Constituents, Cuomo Attacks, Pataki Parries," *New York Times*, September 25, 1994, p. A1.

29. See Executive Order No. 30, *N.Y. Comp. Codes R. & Regs.* title 9, 5.30 (1996).

30. N.Y. Constitution of 1894, art. III, 2–5. See also *WMCA, Inc. v. Lomenzo*, 377 U.S. 633 (1964).

31. Henrik N. Dullea, *Charter Revision in the Empire State: The Politics of New York's 1967 Constitutional Convention* (Albany: Rockefeller Institute Press, 1997), pp. 49–57. See also Calvin B. T. Lee, *One Man, One Vote: WMCA and the Struggle for Equal Representation* (New York: Scribner, 1967), pp. 133–45.

32. Dullea (1997), pp. 67–71 (stating that the goals of the committee were to show bipartisan support for a constitutional convention, to demonstrate that the question was not an upstate versus downstate battle, and to provide editorial writers with necessary information for their support).

33. Gerald Benjamin and Henrik N. Dullea (eds.), *Decision 1997: Constitutional Change in New York* (Albany: Rockefeller Institute Press, p. 1997), pxvi; see also Temporary State Commission on Constitutional Revision, *Effective Government Now for the New Century: A Report to the People, the Governor, and the Legislators of New York* (Albany: The Commission, 1995). The Commission members were Peter C. Goldmark, Jr., Terry Anderson, Amalia V. Betanzos, Jill M. Considine, Peggy Cooper Davis, Henrik N. Dullea, Shirley W. Eberly, Margaret Fung, Stanley W. Hill, Mary Ann Brigantti-Hughes, James L. Larocca, Nathan Leventhal, Murray Light, Richard P. Nathan, Keith C. St. John, David Sive, Peter G. Ten Eyck, II, and Malcolm Wilson.

34. Neither the legislature nor the governor appointed a commission to prepare for the mandatory convention vote in 1977. The state had just overcome a serious fiscal crisis, and since there was a general feeling that a convention on the heels of this effort would not be well timed, no convention was authorized by the voters. In 1957, the Republican legislature agreed to join with Averill Harriman, the Democratic Governor, in appointing a commission, but only after it retained control of two-thirds of the appointments and the chairmanship. See Dullea (1997), pp. 31–38. Again, a call for a constitutional convention was defeated by the voters. Nelson Rockefeller's work as chair of this effort provided a base for his gubernatorial run in 1958, and his commission staff provided the core for his staff as governor.

35. His staff based in Albany included Gerald Benjamin, who had been working on this issue at the Rockefeller Institute, as Research Director. His staff based in New York

City included Eric Lane as Counsel to the Commission, and Pauline Toole as Communications Director. Other staffers were Melissa Cusa and Michael L. Owens. Teri Potente, assistant to Peter Goldmark at the Rockefeller Foundation, also played an important role.

36. W. Brooke Graves, "Constitutional Revision," in National Municipal League, Committee on State Government. *Model State Constitution with Explanatory Articles*, 5th ed. (New York, The League, 1948), p. 51.

37. N.Y. Constitution of 1894, art. XIV, 2. The modern version of the self-executing provision appears in N.Y. Constitution, art. XIX, 2.

38. See Peter J. Galie and Christopher Bopst, "The Constitutional Commission in New York: A Worthy Tradition," *Albany Law Review*, vol. 64 (2001), p. 1294.

39. N.Y. Constitution of 1894, art. XIV, 2. Similar provisions appear in N.Y. Constitution, art. XIX, 2. See Burton C. Agata, "Amending and Revising the New York State Constitution," in Benjamin and Dullea (eds.) (1997), pp. 331 and 339.

40. Temporary N.Y. State Commission on Constitutional Revision, *Interim Report: The Delegate Selection Process* (Albany: The Commission, 1994), pp. 1–4.

41. David I. Wells, "Legislative Districting and the New York State Constitution," Benjamin and Dullea (eds.), pp. 105, 110–12.

42. See *Delegate Selection Process* (1994), pp. 5–7, quoting Lani Guinier, "The Triumph of Tokenism: The Voting Rights Act and the Theory of Black Electoral Success," *Michigan Law Review* vol. 89 (1991), p. 1094.

43. See generally Dullea (1997).

44. For example, the dual compensation problem could be fixed either by constitutional amendment or by statute. *Delegate Selection Process* (1994), pp. 22–24.

45. Agata (1997) described the 1938 Convention, having passed "[fifty-eight] proposals, submitted to the people in nine parts," as "substantially successful," pp. 340–41.

46. See Editorial, "Call a Constitutional Convention," *New York Times*, October 28, 1997, at A22; Elsa Brenner, "A New Constitution: Yes or No?," *New York Times*, November 2, 1997, p. 16; Sarah Metzgar, "State Convention Issue Makes for Odd Bedfellows," *Times Union* (Albany), September 21, 1997, p. A1; "Major Media Campaign Airs Statewide as N.Y. State Constitutional Convention Vote Nears," *PR Newswire*, October 24, 1997, available at LEXIS, News Library, PR Newswire File. Galie and Bopst (2001), noted that though such groups as the League of Women Voters, Civil Service Employees Association (C.S.E.A.), American Federation of Labor–Congress of Industrial Organizations (A.F.L.-C.I.O.), and the National Organization of Women (N.O.W.) were opposed to a convention, they recognized "the need for constitutional reform," p. 1286.

47. The New York State Constitution explicitly provides that state land "shall be forever kept as wild forest lands." N.Y. Constitution, art. XIV, 1. The state constitution also protects citizens working under service appointments and citizens who are members of retirement plans. N.Y. Constitution, art. V, 6–7. The fear of losing or altering these protections by way of a constitutional convention was a major area of concern; see James Dao, "Unions Oppose Constitutional Assembly," *New York Times*, November 1, 1997, p. B5.

48. The Commission's Interim Report (*Delegate Selection Process* [1994], p. 37) indicates that commissioners disagreed over the delegate selection process, and that two commissioners regarded altering this process as "an essential precondition" before calling a constitutional convention. Three commissioners ultimately dissented from the Commission's call for a convention. *Effective Government Now for the New Century* (1995), pp. 29—32.

49. See Dullea (1997), p. 34.

50. *Effective Government Now for the New Century* (1995), p. 11.

51. Ibid., p. 12.

52. Ibid.

53. Ibid., p. 22.

54. Ibid., pp. 29–30.

55. Ibid., p. 31.

56. See Clyde Haberman, "Rent Accord: Just Another Albany Deal," *New York Times*, June 17, 1997, p. B1.

57. See "Voters Favor Convention on State Constitution," *New York Times*, July 24, 1997, p. B4. The poll was conducted between July 14 and July 20, 1997, by telephone, with a sample size of 1,008 respondents. Of those polled, 53 percent favored a convention, 17 percent thought it was a bad idea, and 30 percent were undecided.

58 . See Richard Perez-Pena, "Scorn for Albany Unites Forces Urging a New Constitution," *New York Times*, October 26, 1997, p. 36.

59. Descriptions of the politics surrounding the convention question here and following are drawn from the personal involvement of the author and news accounts. See Richard Perez-Pena," Constitution is Stealth Issue of 1997, Attracting Strong Feelings, " *New York Times*, September 27, 1997, p. B4; Tom Precious, "Coalition Aims to Block State Constitutional Revision," *Buffalo News*, September 16, 1997, p. A6; James Dao, "Pataki and D'Amato Back Constitutional Convention," *New York Times*, October 8, 1997, p. B5; Metzgar (September 21, 1997); and Tom Precious, "Unions Rally Members to Defeat Convention, Little Publicity and Strong Union Turnout Could Defeat the Proposal," *Syracuse Post-Standard*, October 29, 1997, p. A7.

60. Gerald Benjamin, "The Affirmative Case: Vote 'Yes' for a Constitutional Convention," *City Law*, vol. 3 (1997), pp. 49, 51.

61. One hundred and ninety-eight was the number of delegates that would be elected to a convention if it were held.

62. See news articles cited at fn. 62; Richard Perez-Pena, "Voters Refuse to Take Chances on Bond Act and Convention," *New York Times*, November 6, 1997, p. B3; and "Cuomo, Challengers State Positions in Gubernatorial Campaign," *Buffalo News*, November 2, 1994, p. C3 (Election Guide).

63. Elizabeth Kolbert, "Divisive Idea Calls Cuomo Out of Shell, " *New York Times*, October 9, 1997, p. B2.

64. See "Deep Six These Six," *New York Daily News*, November 3, 1997, p. 32 (Editorial).

65. See Richard Perez-Pena, "Voters Reject Constitutional Convention," *New York Times*, November 5, 1997, p. B1.

66. Ibid.

67. Dao (November 1, 1997).

68. See Gerald Benjamin, "Constitutional Revision in New York State: Retrospect and Prospect," in N.Y. State Bicentennial Commission, *Essays on the Genesis of the Empire State* (Albany: The Commission, 1979), p. 39, table II.

69. Source for voting data is: New York State Board of Elections, www.elections.state.ny.us/elections/1997.

6

Direct Democracy and Constitutional Reform

Campaign Finance Initiatives in Colorado

Anne G. Campbell

This chapter examines the political dynamics behind Colorado's campaign finance reform initiatives in 1994, 1996, and 2002 as a way to understanding why, when, and how direct democracy is employed to enact constitutional change. Many have expressed concern about the initiative process, by which citizens and groups of citizens are empowered to propose statutes or constitutional amendments directly to a popular vote. That concern is particularly intense when it comes to amending states' constitutions by citizen-initiated ballot measures, instead of by legislative referenda that are subsequently put to a popular vote. In addition, critics of constitutional initiatives decry their use to ensconce public policy reforms in a document that they believe should only contain fundamental, "organic" law. Colorado's campaign finance reform efforts provide a valuable case to study the use of direct democracy to propose constitutional change, with three separate attempts to achieve reform via both statutory and constitutional initiatives over the past ten years.

In order to investigate constitutional change via the initiative process, this chapter considers direct democracy using a framework that examines how the proponents of campaign finance reform in Colorado used the initiative process to achieve their policy goals. After a brief examination of the broader history of the mechanisms of constitutional change in Colorado,

---

The views expressed are those of the author and do not necessarily reflect the official policy of the Air Force, the Department of Defense, or the U.S. government.

I proceed with an examination of why these proponents of reform escalated their issue directly to the electorate via the initiative, what determined the timing of their measures, and the considerations involved in drafting their ballot measures. This case illustrates how the initiative process serves as an alternative policy-making agenda for those whose attempts to promote change through the institutions of republican government are thwarted by entrenched interests. It also demonstrates that the initiative process is most conducive to proposals for change that reflect the views of the voting public, and that they are apt to be the result of significant deliberation and compromise. Finally, the Colorado case demonstrates how initiative proponents may resort to proposing their measures as constitutional amendments as a defensive mechanism against government officials who have proven to be particularly hostile to their policy proposals.

MECHANISMS FOR CONSTITUTIONAL CHANGE IN COLORADO

The Colorado Constitution dates from 1876, the year Colorado became a state. Although the Constitution retains most of the institutional framework adopted in 1876, it has been amended dozens of times, doubling in length over the past 126 years.[1] The frequent amendment of the Constitution coincides with the expectations of the delegates who drafted it, who noted they had "provided liberally for the amending of the Constitution, thus giving to the people frequent opportunities of changing the organic law when experience and public policy may require it."[2] Article XIX authorizes the General Assembly to propose a constitutional convention by a two-thirds vote of each house, to be held if a majority of citizens voting at the next general election endorses the proposed convention. It also authorizes the General Assembly to propose amendments by a two-thirds vote of each house, which would take effect if ratified by a majority of those voting at the next general election.

In 1910 Colorado amended its constitution in order to introduce a third method of constitutional change, the initiative, empowering the people to propose statutes and constitutional amendments directly. If supporters collect the requisite signatures in support, then their citizen-initiated measures appear on the ballot at the next general election. Coloradans have employed this power extensively, initiating eighty-five measures from 1964–2002, including "many of the most controversial issues

TABLE 6.1
Constitutional and Statutory Ballot Measures in Colorado, 1964–2002

	Constitutional Amendments	*Statutes*	*Total*
Citizens' Initiatives	61 (23)	24 (8)	85 (31)
Legislative Referenda	62 (49)	14 (7)	76 (56)
Total	123 (72)	38 (15)	161 (87)

Note: Numbers based on the Colorado General Assembly, "A History of Statewide Ballot Issues Since 1964," last updated 5/12/2003, available at the Legislative Council Staff's online research publications: www.state.co.us/gov_dir/leg_dir/lcssstaff/research/Ballot_Hist_table_top.htm.

Figures in parentheses indicate the number of measures that passed. The number of statutes includes two legislative "Question" referenda seeking government authority to assume new debt.

on the ballot."[3] Initiative proponents have overwhelmingly favored addressing these controversial issues through amendments rather than statutes—since 1964, sixty-one of the eighty-five ballot initiatives in Colorado have been proposed as constitutional amendments.[4] Altogether, 32 percent of amendments to the Colorado Constitution during the past thirty-eight years have been made via the initiative process.

From the outset the initiative was controversial in Colorado. The proposal to adopt the initiative divided the state along partisan lines, with Democrats favoring its adoption and Republicans opposing it.[5] Proponents viewed the initiative—like the referendum, the recall, and other electoral reforms—as necessary to counter the perceived corruption of the institutions of representative democracy. Legislatures, courts, and political parties were widely perceived as having been "captured" by wealthy special interests and as unresponsive to the people and the public interest. The initiative thus sought to ensure that the people were heard even when powerful interests prevented their concerns from being addressed in the legislature.

The initiative remains controversial in Colorado (and elsewhere) today. Opponents of the initiative, which include many members of the Colorado General Assembly, insist that the initiative process circumvents the legislature, curtails the opportunity for debate and deliberation that might result in better-refined policy proposals, and ties the legislature's hands on issues. Proponents agree that initiatives seek to circumvent the legislature and tie its hands—indeed, these are seen as virtues—but they argue that their measures involve more debate and deliberation, and more concern for the public good, than do many laws enacted by the legislature. This last claim is particularly important when constitutional initiatives are at issue, because adequate debate and deliberation are crucial when instituting major constitutional reforms.

The Policy Agenda and Constitutional Initiatives

Three considerations—conflict escalation, timing, and issue framing—are crucial for understanding how constitutional initiatives become part of the policy agenda. Conflict escalation refers to how political actors encourage "bystanders" (in this case, the electorate) to weigh in on an issue in order to effect policy change.[6] Typically, policy entrepreneurs play a key role in drawing the public's attention to an issue, thereby forcing elected officials to act or at least publicly address the issue. However, because the scope and duration of public attention and concern tend to be limited, politicians may seek to avoid politically disadvantageous issues that are opposed by active and well-organized interest groups by waiting out the "issue attention cycle" of the public and the media.[7] By circumventing these policy subsystems, direct democracy seeks to create an alternative policy agenda.

Timing is likewise crucial in promoting significant constitutional reform. Objective changes in the environment, ranging from natural disasters to economic downturns, may serve as "triggering events" and create "windows of opportunity" for pursuing reform.[8] This can be done by enlisting the support of strategic politicians seeking issues that "strike a chord" with the public and enhance their political fortunes. However, some reforms do not appeal to those politicians, either because taking a position might alienate key constituencies and powerful groups or because the reforms threaten the self-interest of politicians. In such circumstances, direct democracy provides an alternative path for responding to these windows of opportunity.

Issue framing is also important. Policy entrepreneurs who seek to push issues onto the legislative agenda must frame them so that they are "fresh, clear-cut, easily synopsized, affecting as large a portion of the news audience as possible, and packaged with reforms that seem able to resolve the problems."[9] Legislators tend to shun policy initiatives that are not likely to generate much public interest or are likely to generate significant opposition from influential groups. Direct democracy changes issue framing in two respects. First, issues that cannot be framed to attract legislators may nonetheless find their way onto the ballot, because their supporters are focused on policy change, not reelection. Second, whereas legislators have broad discretion in designing the policies that they will support to deal with the issues before them, the initiative process allows supporters to control not only the issues addressed but also the proposed policy solutions.

These observations reveal that the political dynamics of direct democracy differ considerably from the political dynamics within representative bodies. As our discussion of campaign finance reform in Colorado will show, the initiative process provides an alternative path for fundamental reform when state legislators are at odds with popular sentiments. The proponents' rationale for using the initiative process to escalate conflict, as well as in deciding when to promote their policy changes as initiatives, was determined by events in the legislative and executive branches, but public opinion was also critical to the timing of their initiatives. In terms of issue framing, the initiative proponents sought to draft their initiatives to appeal to the general voting public in both form and substance, and they resorted to constitutional measures as a defense against future tampering by state legislators.

Campaign Finance and Constitutional Reform in Colorado

In 2002 Colorado voters addressed ten measures on the statewide ballot, including four constitutional amendments. Among these was a constitutional initiative (Amendment 27) on campaign finance reform that was approved by 66 percent of voters. The lopsided vote for the amendment could have been predicted, for a very similar initiative sponsored by the same groups had been adopted by voters had been adopted by voters in 1996. Why, then, was the issue on the ballot once again?

Conflict Escalation: Campaign Finance Reform in Colorado, 1974 to 1996

In fact, campaign finance reform has appeared periodically on the state's legislative agenda since the early 1970s and on Colorado's statewide initiative agenda since the early 1990s. The General Assembly first enacted campaign finance legislation in 1974, in the wake of Watergate. The Colorado chapter of Common Cause, formed just a few years before, lobbied in support of this legislation and continued to press in ensuing years for additional legislation to strengthen the 1974 law. In 1992 efforts at wholesale reform failed, when the governor vetoed a bill that had passed the General Assembly (House Bill 92-1316) and Common Cause failed to qualify its proposed initiative for the ballot. After the governor vetoed another reform effort in 1993 (HB 93-1159) despite significant bi-partisan support in the legislature,[10] the Colorado chapters of Common Cause and the League of Women Voters teamed with several other groups in 1994 to qualify an initiative for the ballot, but it failed with only 46 percent of the vote. These groups enjoyed better success two years later when their statutory initiative passed by an overwhelming margin (66 percent of voters supported the measure), superseding less stringent requirements adopted by the legislature earlier in 1996.

According to the proponents of the 1994 and 1996 campaign finance initiatives in Colorado, they turned to direct democracy precisely because they did not foresee achieving meaningful reform through regular legislative channels. According to Richard Bainter of Common Cause of Colorado:

> We generally try to go through the legislature first. We just think that's good public policy. That's what the legislature is there for, and actually the initiative is . . . our opinion of it is that it's kind of a "safety valve." It's there for times when the legislature won't act.[11]

Pat Johnson of the League of Women Voters of Colorado concurred, noting that although one legislator introduced legislation in 1996 similar to their initiative, it "never got out of committee, so there was no full debate, no full consideration. And we gave them their chance, and what they wanted to do was make it all go away . . . and this is what they get!"[12] The problem, as she saw it, lay not with which party controlled the legislature, but with legislators' self-interest and the opposition of the powerful groups such as the Colorado Education Association that contributes heavily to legislative campaigns: "They're all against us, because you're talking to a leadership that controls the money and dishes it out." According to Common Cause's Bainter, the only reason the General Assembly enacted a campaign finance law in 1996 was the threat of an initiative—"It would never have happened if we had not been out there with a ballot initiative.

It was on the people's agenda or it wouldn't have been on their agenda." He noted that the supporters of finance reform went ahead with the initiative because they viewed the legislature's bill as very weak: "If they had passed something stronger, we probably would have stopped, or been tempted to."

Conflict Escalation: Campaign Finance Reform in Colorado, 1997–2002

For the initiative's proponents, the adoption of Amendment 15 in 1996 seemed to have resolved the issue of campaign finance reform. However, as often happens with initiatives, those who lost at the ballot box turned to the courts and the legislature. A 2000 decision by the Tenth Circuit Court of Appeals invalidated Amendment 15's definitions of what constituted independent expenditures, political committees, and political messages, as well as the limits imposed on independent expenditures.[13] The appeals court ruled that other district court decisions, that ruled Amendment 15's dollar limits on contributions to be unconstitutionally low, were made moot by the General Assembly's passage of new, higher limits in 2000.[14]

The General Assembly originally solicited the support of Amendment 15's proponents to help draft the legislation to "fill in the gaps" for contribution limits thrown out by the district court, however, the end result of the legislation was characterized by the *Denver Post* as "gutting" Amendment 15, and its proponents agreed. League of Women Voter's Pat Johnson saw the legislature's bill as a reflection of the fact that "the legislature in general doesn't like campaign finance reform."[15] The current Director of Colorado Common Cause, Peter Maysmith, was also part of the Amendment 15 effort in 1996. He said the legislators:

> blew open some of these loopholes in political giving to the political parties, which we saw exploited in a *big* way this [2002] election. Big time. We worked with them initially and ultimately opposed them strenuously, and lost. That's why we went back to the voters.[16]

Maysmith also recounted that although he thought Speaker George deserved credit for bringing them into the process:

> Ultimately our concerns were ignored. Which, that's his prerogative as Speaker of the House, and the legislature's prerogative. I would argue it's at their peril because the way we did this. You can't ignore us. We didn't act like this was a secret. Every time we talked to somebody we said, "Look, if you ignore us, we're going to go back—we're not just going to run and hide in a corner—we're going to go back to the initiative. And I'm telling you, if I'm a betting guy, I would bet that the citizens are going to once again support campaign finance reform."

After the legislature "gutted" the statutory campaign finance reforms in 2000, the two groups did turn directly to the voters—for a third time. The General Assembly's actions "triggered" the 2002 constitutional initiative that passed, once again, with 66 percent of the vote.

The initiative allows groups disadvantaged by the status quo to appeal their case to the public—to escalate the conflict over the heads of the legislature. Perhaps what is most notable, given the potential for policy change provided by this form of direct democracy, is the *rarity* of its use. While state legislatures regularly pass hundreds of laws each year, and fail to pass hundreds more, only several dozen initiatives appear on the ballot in most years. Something more than legislative action or inaction must determine when people turn to the initiative process for statutory and constitutional reform.

The Timing of Campaign Finance Reform Initiatives

The issue of campaign finance had been on the Colorado legislative agenda and on the agenda of Colorado Common Cause periodically since the early 1970s. What drove Common Cause and the League of Women Voters of Colorado to sponsor initiatives in 1994, 1996, and 2002, in particular? In this case, there were three determinants of the timing of the initiatives beyond the legislature's actions/inaction. First, the groups were convinced that there was a significant problem that necessitated immediate reforms. Second, the initiative proponents believed that their proposed measures would receive the backing of the voters. Third, the groups believed they had sufficient resources to run a campaign. For a "window of opportunity" to exist, all conditions had to be met at the same time.

Both Common Cause and the League had long been convinced there was a pressing need to reform campaign finance law. Shortly after Amendment 15 passed in 1996, Patricia Johnson discussed how recent elections had spurred their initiative, because of the high cost of campaigns for state office. Similarly, when asked why Colorado Common Cause had sponsored Amendment 27 in 2002, Peter Maysmith noted:

> Well, it was basically as soon as we could get back to the ballot. We feel like we have a major problem in Colorado the way our campaigns are financed, and I think the 2002 election was Example 1A of that. . . . If you look at state senate races, there were a number of state senate races that blew past a half a million dollars. Half a million dollars! These guys meet for four months out of the year, they make $30,000. Sure, is it an important post? Yes. Half a million dollars? That's out of control. And if you charted it out, it was doing nothing but growing exponentially. So it isn't like it would have reverted back again in '04. No, it would have just kept right on climbing. We felt that we had to act. Time was a-wasting. The need was pressing.

The initiative proponents and the public interest groups they represented were convinced that there was a major policy problem that necessitated prompt action.

Second, as public interest groups, Common Cause and the League of Women Voters have one advantage when it comes to using the initiative process; they seek policies that will benefit the public, not special interests. However, that is no guarantee that voters will agree with their views of what is good policy, as the campaign finance proponents learned when Coloradans voted down Amendment 15 in 1994. It is clear that the proponents were very much concerned with public opinion when they decided to go the route of direct democracy. Discussing the League's first attempt to pursue reform through initiatives in 1994 and 1996, Patricia Johnson indicated that the coalition relied on polling data, news coverage of the campaign finance issue, and their own sense of Coloradans' views.

> I thought the temper of the public was getting stronger and stronger, as revelation after revelation turned up. After '95 we could see the rumblings getting louder and louder. . . . I just read the papers all the time and watched the decibel level grow. I

> mean people are shouting! When the *Wall Street Journal* writes articles—but I mean, really, I just smelled it. I just knew it *had* to be '96.[17]

In 2002, *Denver Post* polls showed Amendment 27 as having a decline in support shortly before the election—from 63 percent in July and 65 percent in early October, to 52 percent in late October,[18] prior to its passage in November with 66 percent of the vote. However, Ms. Johnson explained she had not been very concerned about the late October poll because the percentages of likely voters who knew they were *against* Amendment 27 remained at 20 percent. Peter Maysmith also remained optimistic about the initiative's chances at the polls because:

> there's such frustration and disenchantment with our politics. I think people are fed up. That's obvious, I think, because if you just talk to your friends and neighbors and go to a coffee shop, and live in this world—people are fed up with politicians and campaigns. And then, of course, if you look at the number of people that aren't voting, if you want a more statistical analysis of where people are, the numbers are lousy. They're down and they're trending down.

The groups opposed to initiatives also have a keen interest in public opinion. While opponents of the 1994 measure, primarily wealthy special interests such as the Tobacco Institute and the Colorado Education Association, spent over $875,000 to oppose Amendment 15 and one other initiative,[19] they barely managed to defeat the measure. Johnson commented regarding both the 1996 and 2002 initiatives that she believed that the lack of significant organized opposition was due to the fact that the groups interested in opposing campaign finance reform did not like the odds of winning, even if they spent another million dollars: "I think money just dried up. People just looked at the polls."

The financial statements of the opposing issue committees in 2002 support Johnson's assessments. In 2002, one group raised less than $60,000 from a few individuals to oppose Amendment 27 along with three other ballot amendments.[20] Another opposition committee collected $12,500 from the Colorado Education Association, Colorado Firefighters, and the Colorado Realtors Political Action Committee, but after commissioning $10,000 of polls, it reported nothing more in the way of contributions or expenditures.[21] The issue committee "Protect Freedom 2002" did not raise or spend any funds for its declared goal to "muzzle voter Amendment 27."[22]

While the proponents believed that public opinion naturally favored their proposals, they also recognized that while campaign finance reform might be *their* priority, and a priority of the members of the groups working on the campaigns, it was not necessarily a priority of most citizens. Johnson conceded in 1997 that "people are not thinking about it; it's not in the forefront of most minds." Maysmith, her 2002 cosponsor from Common Cause, agreed:

> I think it's certainly safe to say that this is not the issue that people get out of bed each morning and think about as they're making coffee and getting the kids off to school. I understand that. But I do think that people, when you pose the question and start talking to them about campaign finance reform, absolutely believe and understand that this is a real critical element or component of how we elect folks, who then of course govern and make decisions that impact us all.

While not driven by a public hue and cry for campaign finance reform, the proponents were convinced of the need for reform and that the legislature would not act to achieve it; and they were also convinced that an overwhelming majority of the public also wanted their proposed reforms. However, they also noted one more key factor in deciding to go the initiative route.

The third determinant of the campaign finance proponents' decision to turn to the initiative process concerned having the resources necessary to run the campaign. With lawyers available on staff at Common Cause and others willing to do pro bono work, the resources to draft the initiative and to help fend off any court challenges to the ballot title or on the basis of a violation of the state's "single subject" requirement for initiatives were not a problem. The first real hurdle for the coalition was the petition stage. In 1994 and 1996 they relied primarily on volunteer petition circulators, with an army of COPIRG and League of Women Voters volunteers standing out in front of grocery stores, shopping malls, and post offices.[23] However, noting that it is getting more and more difficult to rely entirely on volunteer petition bearers, in 2002 the proponents relied heavily on paid petitioners to augment their volunteer efforts, spending

$108,000 to paid signature gatherers between April and the August deadline for qualifying for the 2002 ballot—about half of their total contributions that were about $220,000.[24] The coalition did not wage a paid media campaign, relying instead on free news coverage, opinion pieces, editorials, a web site, and mailings. Overall, even relying on full- and part-time workers and volunteers from Voter Revolt, Common Cause, and League of Women Voters (none of which show up as expenses), the proponents spent over $220,000 for the Amendment 27 campaign in 2002.[25] Initiative campaigns are not cheap, even when the "organized" opposition only spends $60,000.

As a practical matter, just about any proposal for constitutional or statutory reform *could* make it to the ballot. Why, then, are there not dozens of initiatives on the ballot in Colorado in any given year instead of the usual six to eight? There are an infinite number of policy proponents, many of whom would have considerable resources. However, considering the natural bias of the initiative process that, by definition, seeks to bring an issue to the attention of the voters, the role of public opinion is undoubtedly the most limiting factor. Most groups would not consider going through the time and expense of qualifying a ballot initiative, because it does not do any good to get onto the ballot unless the voters are going to vote "yes."

Issue Framing

Issue framing is crucial because initiative proponents must be concerned not only with getting an issue onto the ballot, but also with designing and proposing a specific policy solution. In the multistage process that prevails in the halls of republican government, policy entrepreneurs first seek an elective official to sponsor a policy change, or alternatively, they seek to raise public awareness and concern about an issue that will push the problem onto the policy makers' agenda. Initiative sponsors take on both roles; they serve as both policy entrepreneurs and policy makers. They must define the specifics of the policy solution and, in states like Colorado that allow both statutory and constitutional initiatives, they must also determine which of these forms their measure will take.

A common criticism of direct democracy is that it does not allow for deliberation or the give-and-take of representative democracy; critics argue there is no room for compromise, which will inevitably result in extremist groups proposing extremist policies. A further criticism is that initiative proponents frequently resort to constitutional amendments to enact policy changes rather than "fundamental law." I would suggest that although these criticisms are to some extent interrelated, it may be useful to introduce and discuss them separately. The following discussion demonstrates how public opinion, legal precedents, and the legislature's actions factor into the process of determining the content and form of initiatives.

The previous sections on conflict escalation and timing clarified the importance of the views of the voting public to initiative proponents when it comes to deciding to attempt this time-consuming and costly policy-making process. It makes little sense for a policy entrepreneur to use direct democracy to propose policies that the general public would oppose. It makes equally little sense for the sponsors of an initiative to forward a particular policy solution, even if it is the proponents' preferred solution, if that solution would not appeal to the majority of voters. Both of the national organizations of Common Cause and the League of Women Voters support public financing of campaigns as the best policy for reforming the campaign finance system. The sponsors of the 2002 initiative also personally favor public financing of campaigns, however, they never considered proposing it by initiative. Patricia Johnson of the League of Women Voters of Colorado replied the following in 2002 when asked if the coalition would support public financing:

> We talked about that too. And we just could not see that passing—because of the [state's] financial situation. Things were, the corporate scandals were beginning to surface, and we just didn't think it was a good idea, because we wanted it to pass. Public financing is a good idea, both Common Cause and the League support it, and it's working.

Colorado Common Cause Director Peter Maysmith also cited public opinion and the reality of the fiscal situation in the state as the reason the proponents had to compromise on the very essence of their policy proposal. If the decision about the policy to deal with campaign finance issues were up to them, they would have enacted a system with public financing of statewide political campaigns. However, with the initiative process the proponents know that it is *not* up to them; the proposed policy has to be one that the majority of voters will agree to.

In drafting their initiatives, proponent Peter Maysmith noted that Common Cause was guided by the basic principle of enacting reform that would "help to address the issue of corruption and the appearance of corruption in our politics." In addition, both Maysmith and his co-proponent, Patricia Johnson, indicated that they relied on past experience with campaign finance reform in Colorado and other states across the country. The reforms enacted by Amendment 27 in 2002 contained very similar contribution limits to the reforms enacted by Amendment 15 in 1996, because experience demonstrated "that candidates were able to raise healthy amounts of money and ran robust campaigns under contribution limits in 1998" before those limits were eliminated.[26]

Both proponents were extremely well-versed in legal precedents that had been established with respect to campaign finance reform across the country. After having parts of their 1996 initiative struck down by the courts for being unconstitutional infringements of the First Amendment of the U.S. Constitution, the coalition paid considerable attention to the legal advice of the Brennan Center for Justice, from the New York University School of Law (national experts on campaign finance reform law) when they drafted their 2002 initiative. The proponents spent a great deal of time studying cases themselves, such as the U.S. Supreme Court case *Nixon v. Shrink Missouri Government PAC* that upheld contribution limits as a constitutional means of preventing corruption and the appearance of corruption in political campaigns, and upheld contribution limits that were lower than the 1996 Amendment 15 limits that the district court had thrown out and that the legislature subsequently raised.[27] Just as it does not make any sense to qualify an initiative on the ballot only to have the public shoot it down, it does not make any sense to seek public approval of a policy change only to have it reversed by the courts. Compromise and deliberation were, therefore, an essential part of drafting the campaign finance initiatives.

The decision to sponsor their campaign finance initiative as a constitutional amendment was a major strategic decision for Colorado Common Cause and the League of Women Voters. Common Cause Director Richard Bainter explained why the coalition's first initiative in 1994 was proposed as an amendment:

> We would prefer to do statutory initiatives, again [for] policy reasons and not putting a lot of detail in the constitution. We did a constitutional amendment in '94. Our ballot initiative in '94 was

> constitutional primarily because Doug Bruce had a campaign reform-related initiative on the ballot which was constitutional, and we had to go head to head with that. So that if they both were to pass, ours would be implemented. . . . That's what tipped the scales towards constitutional amendment in '94, but then in '96, without Doug Bruce, there we went the statutory route.[28]

Even then, Mr. Bainter said it was never an easy decision to propose an initiative as a statute.

> I think with any of the issues where people go through the process of putting something on the ballot, I think most of those folks have already tried the legislative route and it hasn't worked. So then you *know* that the legislature is going to be somewhat hostile to what you've done, and it's a hard thing to do, to go through all that work and do it as a statute and know that the legislature is going to—or at least has the ability to make drastic changes to what you've just done. Which is why most initiatives are constitutional in Colorado.

Patricia Johnson noted the coalition's determination to propose a statutory initiative in their 1996 attempt; they wanted to avoid the controversy and negative publicity generated by opposition committees' advertisements and the news media that helped defeat their constitutional amendment for campaign finance reform in 1994. In 1997, Ms. Johnson said they were willing to accept "a little risk" that the legislature would significantly change the statutes enacted by the voters. However, Richard Bainter's comments on the potential for hostile legislative action proved to be prophetic.

When the General Assembly "gutted" the campaign finance reform enacted by their statutory initiative in 1996, Common Cause and the League of Women Voters decided they had no choice but to propose a constitutional amendment for their third initiative in 2002. Once again they were criticized for that decision, even while their critics sympathized with their rationale. The editorial board of the newspaper with the largest circulation in the state, the *Denver Post* said:

> It's constitutional. If passed, the amendment would be part of the state constitution and impossible to fine tune without going

> back to the ballot. Amendment proponents, however, can't really be blamed for making it a constitutional amendment. In 1996, when a similar proposal was statutory, the legislature gutted it. If 27 had been statutory, some of these fatal flaws could have been fixed. But as a constitutional amendment, we just can't support it.[29]

Even after their experiences with the statutory Amendment 15, the coalition did not make that decision to propose a constitutional amendment without a great deal of deliberation. Johnson noted that they looked at whether they could:

> just take the essence of it and just make a very short amendment, [but] then you have the problem of getting the legislature to implement it. There's no way that you could get the thing implemented except by putting it all in [the constitution].

Without some protection from wholesale legislative revision of initiated statutes, Common Cause's Maysmith said they just could not risk another statutory initiative:

> No. We've been there. We've done that. I mean it's a *lot* of work! A lot of volunteer work, staff work, board work. It's a lot of financial resources to mount a ballot initiative. We can't just do that every 4 years—2, 4, 6 years—and just wait for them to gut it.

The proponents of campaign finance reform initiatives in Colorado and the organizations they represented were on principle opposed to using the initiative process to propose policy changes by constitutional amendment. However, the initiative proponents were simply unable to trust the legislature.

There was a great deal of deliberation and compromise regarding both the substance and the form of the three campaign finance reform initiatives. The proponents did not propose what they thought would be the *best* policy, public financing of campaigns. Instead they proposed what they considered to be *better* policy based on experience in Colorado and other states, because that is what they thought the voters would approve. In addition to considerations of what was practicable, they engaged in lengthy consultations with constitutional experts to ensure their initiative would pass constitutional muster when the inevitable court challenges came. Finally, after experience demonstrated that the state legislature was willing to significantly alter their first statutory initiative, Colorado Common Cause and the League of Women Voters Colorado reluctantly resorted to a constitutional amendment in 2002, even though they knew that would give opponents to their measure a significant point for criticism, as it had in their unsuccessful 1994 campaign.

Constitutional Reform Via Direct Democracy

Every state requires that its legislature's proposed constitutional amendments be submitted to the citizenry via legislative referendum for approval or rejection.[30] Clearly, there is a consensus that significant alterations in the form and institutions of democratic government should be decided directly by the people, rather than by their elected representatives. The primary controversy involved in citizens' initiatives to achieve constitutional reform is not, therefore, that the people are voting on constitutional issues, but that the people are circumventing the legislature by determining the *content* of the constitutional amendments. Such amendments, say critics, will not benefit from the deliberation and compromise inherent in measures proposed by state legislatures. Furthermore, the critics continue, citizen-initiated amendments "clutter" state constitutions with public policy prescriptions that do not belong in a document dedicated to "fundamental" law.

During the past forty years, initiative proponents in Colorado have greatly favored the use of constitutional amendments (72 percent) over statutory initiatives (28 percent). This essay has examined the case of campaign finance reform in Colorado as a means of understanding the dynamics behind the use of citizen-initiated constitutional amendments to enact reform. It is a particularly instructive case because the proponents of the three campaign finance measures have attempted both constitutional and statutory initiatives to achieve the same policy reforms on three separate occasions. The examination of the process by which these advocates of reform decided to attempt the initiative process in 1994, 1996, and 2002, as well as the process by which they determined to propose constitutional versus statutory initiatives and the content of those initiatives, provides some valuable insights regarding constitutional reform via direct democracy.

First and foremost, it is clear that the initiative process is used precisely because it *does* circumvent the legislature. In particular, the proponents of campaign finance reform turned to direct democracy because they judged that the majority of voters wanted reforms that the majority of legislators opposed; the bias of the initiative process is such that it favors the introduction of measures that are almost certain to have public support. However, the expense of the initiative process is such that it is primarily used as a last resort. Colorado Common Cause and the League of Women Voters of Colorado turned to the initiative process to enact campaign finance reform only after several years attempting to work with the General Assembly. The legislature's gutting of the successful 1996 statutory initiative, and the subsequent public approval of a similar constitutional initiative in 2002, would seem to indicate that the initiatives' proponents were correct in their assessment that the majority of legislators were biased against reforms that adversely affected themselves. The initiative can be a preferred mechanism for constitutional reform for those issues on which legislators have an inherent conflict of interest.

Second, the record of these three initiatives demonstrates that the initiative proponents regard deliberation and compromise as essential to their success. Because the proponents believed that their optimal solution (public financing of campaigns) would not be approved by the voters, they compromised and proposed an initiative that they believed would improve the political process *and* would pass on election day. Furthermore, in drafting their initiative they considered practical experience with campaign finance rules in Colorado and other states, and they were very deliberate in seeking legal advice and considering legal precedents from all relevant cases on campaign finance reform. It only makes sense to go to the expense of using the initiative process if your measure will likely pass *and* if, once passed, it will stand up to the legal challenges that will inevitably follow.

Finally, experience with campaign finance reform in Colorado demonstrates the logic that is likely at work in the decisions of the overwhelming majority of initiative proponents to pursue constitutional rather than statutory initiatives. Once their 1996 statutory initiative had passed with an overwhelming 66 percent "yes" vote, Common Cause and the League of Women Voters thought that they had achieved their reforms. However, the legislature's willingness to rewrite and delete many of the major provisions enacted into law by the initiative convinced these two groups that they had no choice but to go the route of a constitutional amendment on their next initiative—even though they, themselves, objected in principal to incorporating campaign finance reform in the constitution. When the state legislature is strongly opposed to proposed reforms, the constitutional initiative may very well be the only viable mechanism for reform.

Recent history of campaign finance reform in Colorado reveals how the initiative process, and constitutional initiatives in particular, can be used to fulfill the role for which they were created almost one hundred years ago. Constitutional initiatives can be very effective tools to make government more responsive to the people, by allowing the people to circumvent the institutions of representative government when elected officials are opposed to the views and the interests of the people they are designed to serve.

Notes

1. Thomas E. Cronin and Robert D. Loevy, *Colorado Politics and Government* (Lincoln, Nebraska: University of Nebraska Press, 1993), 53; Robert S. Lorch, *Colorado's Government: Structure, Politics, Administration, and Policy*, 6th ed. (Niwot, Colo.: University Press of Colorado, 1997), 22.

2. Timothy O'Connor, Secretary of State, *Proceedings of the Constitutional Convention Held in Denver, December 20, 1875 to Frame a Constitution for the State of Colorado* (Denver, Colorado; Smith-Brooks Press, 1907), 731.

3. Colorado General Assembly, "A History of Statewide Ballot Issues Since 1964," available at www.state.co.us/gov_dir/leg_dir/lcssstaff/research/Ballot_Hist_table_top.htm and Colorado General Assembly's Legislative Council Staff, *Issue Brief #02–03*, updated by this author to include the 2002 elections.

4. Colorado General Assembly, "History."

5. Cronin and Loevy, *Colorado Politics*, 95.

6. E. E. Schattschneider, *The Semi-Sovereign People: a Realist's View of Democracy in America* (New York: Rinehart and Winston, 1960); Roger W. Cobb and Charles D. Elder, *Participation in American Politics: the Dynamics of Agenda-Building* (Boston: Allyn and Bacon, 1983); Frank R. Baumgartner and Bryan D. Jones, *Agendas and Instability in American Politics* (Chicago: University of Chicago Press, 1993).

7. Cobb and Elder, *Participation in American Politics*; Anthony Downs, "Up and Down with Ecology—The 'Issue-attention Cycle,'" *Public Interest* 28 (1972): 38; Edward G. Carmines and James A. Stimson, *Issue Evolution: Race and the Transformation of American Politics* (Princeton, N.J.: Princeton University Press, 1989); Maxwell McCombs and Jian-Hua Zhu, "Capacity, Diversity, and Volatility of the Public Agenda: Trends from 1954 to 1994," *Public Opinion Quarterly* 59 (1995): 495.

8. Baumgartner and Jones (1993); Thomas A. Birkland, *After Disaster: Agenda Setting, Public Policy, and Focusing Events* (Washington, D.C.: Georgetown University Press, 1997); Carmines and Stimson, *Issue Evolution*; John W. Kingdon, *Agendas, Alternatives, and Public Policies* (New York: HarperCollins Publishers, 1984).

9. Timothy E. Cook, *Making Laws and Making News* (Washington, D.C.: The Brookings Institute, 1989), 121. Also see, Barbara Sinclair, *The Transformation of the U.S. Senate* (Baltimore: Johns Hopkins University Press, 1989).

10. "Romer vetoes bill to reform campaign laws," *Denver Post*, 12 June 1993, sec B.

11. Richard Bainter, Director of Colorado Common Cause, telephone interview by author, tape recording, 2 June 1997.

12. Patricia Johnson, former President of League of Women Voters of Colorado, interview by author, tape recording, Boulder, Colo., 24 April 1997.

13. *Citizens for Responsible Government State Political Action Committee v. Davidson*, 236 F.3d 1174 (10th Cir. 2000).

14. Colorado General Assembly, House Bill 00-1194.

15. Patricia Johnson, interview by author, tape recording, Boulder, Colo., 15 November 2002.

16. Peter Maysmith, Director of Colorado Common Cause, telephone interview by author, tape recording, November 21, 2002.

17. Johnson, 1997 interview.

18. "Mail-in vote, caucus proposals lose ground in latest poll results," *Denver Post*, 25 October 2002.

19. Based on Colorado Secretary of State's summary records for 1994 ballot initiatives and individual issue committee campaign finance disclosure reports field with the Secretary of State, available on the Secretary of State's *Election Center Data*, official website: www.sos.state.co.us.

20. *Election Center Data* for "Citizens for Honest Elections" in 2002.

21. *Election Center Data* for "First Amendment Committee" in 2002.

22. *Election Center Data* for "Protect Freedom 2002."

23. Patricia Johnson, 1997 interview.

24. *Election Center Data* for "Coloradans for Campaign Reform" in 2002.

25. According to *Election Center Data* for "Coloradans for Campaign Reform," Colorado Common Cause contributed $171,000 (not including personnel costs), Voter Revolt contributed $33,000, and the League of Women Voters of Colorado contributed $3,600 as a group, and several dozen individuals also contributed to the pro-Amendment 27 group.

26. Peter Maysmith, 2002 interview.

27. *Nixon v Shrink Missouri Government PAC*, 528 U.S. 377.

28. Richard Bainter, 1997 interview.

29. "No to 27: too many pitfalls," *Denver Post*, 12 October 2002.

30. Initiative and Referendum Institute, "Comparison of Statewide Initiative Processes," p.2, available at www.iandrinstitute.org.

Appendix

Mechanisms for State Constitutional Change

The American states employ four basic methods for constitutional change: the constitutional convention, legislative proposal of amendments, the constitutional commission, and amendment via the constitutional initiative. In most cases, states utilize the constitutional convention when revising their state constitutions—not until 1945, when Georgia did so, was a state constitution written by a constitutional commission.[1] Conventions have also been used to propose amendments, but most amendments are proposed by the state legislature. In some instances, the amendments that legislatures propose originate in constitutional commissions, bodies appointed by the political authorities to study constitutional problems in the state and to propose solutions to those problems. In forty-nine states (Florida is the exception), these commissions recommend amendments to the legislature, which then may adopt the recommendations and transmit them to the people for ratification, modify them and submit the modified proposals for ratification, or ignore the recommendations altogether. Finally, eighteen states permit the people by petition to propose amendments, which become part of the constitution when ratified by the people. These broad categories mask considerable interstate variation in how states structure and regulate constitutional change.

Constitutional Conventions

Constitutional conventions maximize the opportunities for popular participation in constitutional reform. The voters decide whether to hold a convention, they elect the delegates who will propose a new constitution (or amendments), and the constitution (or amendments) take effect only when ratified by popular referendum. Some states—for example, Montana in 1972—have prohibited those holding public office from serving as delegates, to ensure that the convention proceedings not replicate politics as usual. Even in the absence of such restrictions, many convention delegates have never served in the state legislative or executive branches, so conventions provide an opportunity for a new cohort of citizens to become directly involved in the government of the state.

Most state constitutions expressly recognize the power of the people to revise the fundamental law. Several incorporate language drawn from eighteenth-century constitutions, declaring that "all political power is vested in and derived from the people only" and that the people consequently have "an incontestable, unalienable, and indefeasible right" to "reform, alter, or totally change [government] when their protection, safety, prosperity, and happiness require it."[1] However, these provisions offer little guidance about how the people might exercise its power, and so many state constitutions also deal with constitutional conventions in more concrete terms. Some prescribe in detail not only how a convention should be called but also how it will operate. For example, the Delaware Constitution mandates the size of the convention, describes the districts from which delegates will be selected, provides for the filling of vacancies, designates the site at which the convention will meet, and specifies a quorum for convention proceedings.[2] Other state constitutions reserve to the convention the power to determine its own organization, choose its own officers, and determine its rules of procedure.[3] Frequently, however, they direct the legislature to enact laws to carry out the people's will that a convention be held. Thus, the legislature may determine how large the convention will be, how delegates will be elected, how long the convention will meet, and what compensation delegates will receive.[4] Control over these features of the convention can of course have a considerable effect on whether the convention succeeds and on what proposals it puts forth.

Even in states whose constitutions do not expressly deal with constitutional conventions, it is generally acknowledged that the people retain the authority to revise the fundamental law and that the legislature possesses the power to enact laws necessary and proper to enable the people to exercise that authority. Yet the absence of express constitutional language can be important. For example, reasoning from the fact that the Alabama Constitution did not directly authorize limited conventions, the Alabama Supreme Court concluded that the legislature could not restrict the topics that a convention could address or the subjects on which it might propose amendments.[5] This ruling, fueling fears about what an unlimited convention might propose, helped discourage calling a convention in the state.[6]

States vary in the mechanisms they employ to call conventions. All states grant the legislature authority to decide whether a convention call should be placed on the ballot for popular approval, with a two-thirds vote of each house typically required for submission of the question. However, fourteen states—embracing the Jeffersonian notion that no generation can bind future generations on fundamental political matters—also require that the question of whether a convention should be called be placed on the ballot periodically.[7] The effectiveness of this mechanism remains a matter of dispute. In recent years voters have consistently rejected convention calls, and some states have even ignored the constitutional command that the convention question be submitted to the voters.[8] Nevertheless, the prospect of a convention call may induce state officials to address popular concerns, lest they fuel efforts for constitutional reform. In Rhode Island, for example, the legislature in 2003 proposed an amendment to address persistent separation-of-power concerns, one year before the automatic convention call was scheduled to appear on the ballot. Finally, Montana—one of the states that has adopted periodic submission to the voters—has also authorized putting the question of a convention on the ballot via the initiative, although this innovation in the state's 1972 constitution has never been used.[9]

States vary to some extent in the margin they require for ratification of convention proposals. During the nineteenth century several states required that proposals be ratified by a majority of those voting *at the election* rather than of those voting *on the constitutional question*, thus in effect treating the failure to vote on a proposal as equivalent to a "no" vote. Given voter roll-off, this was an almost insuperable barrier to amendment, overcome only by the subterfuge of having parties take positions on proposals and then counting a straight party-line vote as a vote for the proposal. Nowadays, only Minnesota and New Hampshire require a supermajority to ratify convention proposals, and most states permit ratification by a simple majority of those voting on the proposals. Although this might seem to facilitate ratification, convention proposals have enjoyed only mixed success over the last half century.

Proposal of Amendments by the State Legislature

A similar diversity can be found in how states structure constitutional amendment via the state legislature. Forty-nine states require that amendments proposed by the legislature be ratified by the people. In Delaware, the sole exception, an amendment takes effect if it twice receives a two-thirds vote of the membership of each house of the state legislature, with an intervening election at which voters can presumably make known their views.[10] Delaware's mechanism for tapping public sentiment was fairly common in state constitutions until early in the nineteenth century, when it was replaced in most states by ratification by referendum.

For proposing amendments, eighteen states require a simple majority in each house of the state legislature, seven states require a three-fifths vote in each house, and eighteen state follow the federal Constitution in mandating a two-thirds vote in each house.[11] Three states—Connecticut, Hawaii, and New Jersey—permit the legislature to propose amendments either by an extraordinary majority or by a majority vote in two legislative sessions, the second following an intervening election. Four states—Arkansas, Illinois, Kansas, and Kentucky—limit the number of amendments that the legislature can propose at any one time.

For ratifying amendments, forty-four states require a simple majority in a popular referendum, four require a majority of those voting in the election, and New Hampshire requires a two-thirds vote.[12] There seems to be no correlation between the size of the legislative majority necessary to propose an amendment and the popular majority required to ratify it. States that facilitate legislative proposal of amendments by requiring only a simple majority in each house typically do not attempt to check unwise amendments by requiring an extraordinary majority for ratification.

CONSTITUTIONAL COMMISSIONS

Constitutional commissions originated in the United States during the nineteenth century—the first met in New Jersey in 1852—and they became increasingly important in state constitutional reform during the twentieth century.[13] The popularity of this mode of constitutional change derives from two advantages it offers the legislature. First, the commission has resources of time and expertise unavailable to the legislature for considering constitutional problems and for crafting solutions to those problems. Second, legislators have the opportunity to assess the public reaction to commission proposals, and the commission can take the political heat for any unpopular recommendations that it puts forth.

Typically, the selection, size, and composition of a constitutional commission are dealt with by statute or by executive order rather than by the state constitution. The statute or executive order also determines the mandate of the commission—whether it will be a limited commission authorized to address a particular problems or an unlimited commission. Interstate variations among state constitutional commissions have been largely a product of the differing political situations in those states when the commissions were established. However, two states have pioneered distinctive approaches. Utah has by statute created a permanent constitutional commission to study constitutional problems in the state and report its findings and recommendations to the legislature.[14] This innovation has enjoyed considerable success, allowing the commission to identify low-salience constitutional problems and to anticipate future problems, rather than permitting them to reach crisis proportions. Florida in its 1968 constitution authorized the periodic formation of a commission that would recommend constitutional changes directly to the electorate.[15] Florida's innovation resembles somewhat the periodic convention calls found in other states, in that the question of constitutional change is regularly placed before the voters. It also resembles the constitutional initiative (which is also available in Florida) in that it bypasses the legislature altogether in proposing amendments (although legislative leaders do appoint some members of the commission). As Rebecca Mae Salokar's contribution to this volume explains, the Florida commission has enjoyed mixed success in its two efforts at constitutional reform, and thus far no state has emulated Florida's approach.[16] Nevertheless, Florida itself drew on the model of the constitutional commission when in 1988 it created a Taxation and Budget Commission, mandated to meet every ten years, with authority to submit proposals dealing with the state's finances directly to the voters.[17]

Constitutional Initiative

Of the eighteen states with the constitutional initiative, sixteen employ the direct initiative: if proponents collect the required number of signatures on an initiative petition, the initiative amendment is placed on the ballot for popular ratification.[18] Two states—Massachusetts and Mississippi—have the indirect initiative: proposals obtaining a sufficient number of signatures must first be referred to the state legislature and, depending on its action, may only then be submitted to the voters. Some states by statute, others by constitutional provision determine the number of signatures necessary to qualify for the ballot, whether there is a distributional requirement for signatures (e.g., a certain number or percentage in each county in the state), and other crucial procedural issues. Most states require only a simple majority to ratify a constitutional initiative, imposing the same standard used for ratification of amendments proposed by the legislature. However, Mississippi and Nebraska have sought to ensure that constitutional initiatives reflect the popular will by requiring that proposals receive a minimum percentage of the total vote at the election in which they are considered.[19] This combination of the indirect initiative plus difficult ratification requirements has virtually eliminated the initiative as a mechanism for constitutional reform in Mississippi.

NOTES

1. See, for example, Massachusetts Constitution, part I, article VI.

2. Delaware Constitution, article XVI, section 2. The Delaware Constitution's provisions dealing the allocation of delegates likely violate the Federal Constitution, which requires that representation conform to a "one person, one vote" standard. See Randy J. Holland, *The Delaware State Constitution: A Reference Guide* (Westport, Conn.: Greenwood Press, 2002), pp. 232–33.

3. See, for example, Hawaii Constitution, article XVII, section 2.

4. See, for example, Hawaii Constitution, article XVII, section 2.

5. *Opinion of the Justices,* 263 Ala. 141, 81 So. 2d 678 (1955).

6. See Bailey Thomson, ed., *A Century of Controversy: Constitutional Reform in Alabama* (Tuscaloosa: University of Alabama Press, 2002).

7. For a listing, see *The Book of the States, 2001–2002* (Lexington, Ky.: Council of State Governments, 2001), p. 8. On the development of this idea, see John Dinan, "'The Earth Belongs Always to the Living Generation': The Development of State Constitutional Amendment and Revision Procedures," *Review of Politics* 62 (Fall 2000): 645–74.

8. See the contribution of Gerald Benjamin to this volume, "The Mandatory Constitutional Convention Question Referendum: The New York Experience in National Context."

9. Montana Constitution, article XIV, section 3.

10. Delaware Constitution, article XVI, section 1. To facilitate popular consideration of amendments before the legislature, this provision requires that the amendments "be published three months before the next general election in at least three newspapers in each county in which such newspapers shall be published."

11. *Book of the States*, 3, table 1.1.

12. Ibid.

13. See Peter J. Mazzei and Robert F. Williams, "'Traces of Their Labors': The Constitutional Commission, the Legislature, and Their Influence on the New Jersey State Constitution, 1873–1875," *Rutgers Law Journal* 33 (Summer 2002): 1060. See also Robert F. Williams, "Are State Constitutional Conventions Things of the Past? The Increasing Role of the Constitutional Commission in State Constitutional Change," *Hofstra Law and Policy Symposium* 1 (1996): 1–26.

14. This innovation is discussed in Jean Bickmore White, *The Utah State Constitution: A Reference Guide* (Westport, Conn.: Greenwood Press, 1998), pp. 17, 71, 91, 143, 194.

15. Florida Constitution, article XI, section 2.

16. Rebecca Mae Salokar, "Constitutional Revision in Florida: Planning, Politics, Policy and Publicity."

17. Florida Constitution, article XI, section 6.

18. For a listing of states with the constitutional initiative, as well as up-to-date information on its use, see the web site of the Initiative and Referendum Institute: www.iandrinstitute.org.

19. Mississippi Constitution, article XV, section 273, and Nebraska Constitution, article III, section 4.

Contributors

GERALD BENJAMIN is Dean of the College of Liberal Arts and Sciences and SUNY Distinguished Professor of Political Science at the State University of New York at New Paltz. He has published extensively on state and local government, with a particular focus on New York. His most recent book (with Richard Nathan) is *Regionalism and Realism: A Study of Governments in the New York Metropolitan Area* (2002). Professor Benjamin is interested in structural issues in governance, federalism, regionalism, and state constitutional change

BRUCE E. CAIN is Robson Professor of Political Science and director of the Institute of Governmental Studies at the University of California (Berkeley). He is the author of *Congressional Redistricting* (1991), *The Personal Vote* (1987), and *The Reapportionment Puzzle* (1984), and is the editor of several others including *Constitutional Reform in California* (1995).

ANNE G. CAMPBELL was Associate Professor of Political Science at the U.S. Air Force Academy and Lieutenant Colonel, U.S. Air Force. Her wide-ranging research interests have led to publications on the single subject rule for ballot initiatives, arms control negotiations, the proliferation of weapons of mass destruction, and on the effects of electronic commerce on Department of Defense reform.

A.E. DICK HOWARD is White Burkett Miller Professor of Law and Public Affairs and Roy L. and Rosamond Woodruff Morgan Research Professor at the Law School of the University of Virginia. He served as Executive Director of the Virginia Commission on Constitutional Revision (1968–69) and has lectured on comparative constitutionalism worldwide. He is the author or editor of numerous books and articles in law reviews, including *Constitution Making in Eastern Europe* (1993), *Commentaries on the Constitution of Virginia* (1974), and *The Road from Runnymede: Magna Carta and Constitutionalism in America* (1968).

REBECCA MAE SALOKAR is associate professor of political science at Florida International University in Miami. She is the author of *The Solicitor General: The Politics of Law* (1992), as well as of articles in *Justice System Journal* and other scholarly journals, and coeditor of *Women in Law: A Bio-Bibliographical Sourcebook* (1996). Professor Salokar's research focuses on the separation of powers, judicial politics, and constitutional reform.

G. ALAN TARR is director of the Center for State Constitutional Studies and chair of the Department of Political Science at Rutgers University (Camden). He is the author or editor of several books dealing with state constitutionalism, including *Understanding State Constitutions* (1998), *Constitutional Politics in the States* (1996), and *State Supreme Courts in State and Nation* (1988). His research focuses on American state constitutions, subnational constitutions in other federal systems, and American constitutional law.

H. BAILEY THOMSON was professor of journalism at the University of Alabama. His series, Dixie's Broken Heart, which appeared in the Mobile Register October 11 through 17, 1998, won the 1999 American Society of Newspaper Editors' Distinguished Writing Award for editorials. He was the editor and a contributing author of *Century of Controversy: Constitutional Reform in Alabama*, published in 2002 by the University of Alabama Press.

Index

www.ingramcontent.com/pod-product-compliance
Lightning Source LLC
LaVergne TN
LVHW040157080826
844660LV00001B/13

9780791466131